Children's Reading and Spelling

Beyond the First Steps

*Terezinha Nunes and
Peter Bryant*

⟨W⟩WILEY-BLACKWELL

A John Wiley & Sons, Ltd., Publication

Library of Congress Cataloging-in-Publication Data

Nunes, Terezinha.
Children's reading and spelling : beyond the first steps /
Terezinha Nunes and Peter Bryant.
p. cm. — (Understanding children's worlds)
Includes bibliographical references and index.
ISBN 978-0-631-23402-9 (hardcover : alk. paper) — ISBN 978-0-631-23403-6 (pbk. : alk. paper) 1. English language—Orthography and spelling—Study and teaching (Primary) 2. Reading (Early childhood) I. Bryant, Peter, 1937– II. Title.
LB1526.N86 2009
372.63′2044—dc22
2008028291

A catalogue record for this book is available from the British Library.

Set in 10/12.5pt Sabon by Graphicraft Limited, Hong Kong
Printed in Singapore by Utopia Press Pte Ltd

1   2009

Contents

List of Figures

List of Tables

Series Editor's Preface

When children learn to read and to write, new worlds open to them. To parents it is a miracle. To teachers and psychologists it is both wonderful and puzzling. How can children master the reading and spelling of words that they have not seen before? What are the rules that help children in this major task? Do they make inferences about spelling that are based on phonology or on morphology? How important is memorising, and how much word-specific learning goes on? Do children learn form rules (such as "no double letters at the beginning of words" for instance) independently of function rules?

We are very lucky to have this account, based on 20 years of imaginative experiments, analyses and critical thought by Terezhina Nunes and Peter Bryant. They take us through the different views of how oral and written language are connected, and explore the implications of these views for teaching and learning. They present with care the evidence we now have, from their own experiments and those of others. Throughout the book the developmental messages are set out clearly—for instance in the evidence on how children's mastery of functional rules increases with age, and that knowledge about form precedes functional knowledge. The causal patterns are of central interest, for instance in the consideration of correlations between reading and spelling scores over time. Reading scores at 7 to 8 predict spelling scores a year later, rather than vice versa. But over 9 years of age, spelling is a better predictor of reading than vice versa. The research gives us clues about how children learn these rules, and these ideas are then carefully tested with experiments. The lessons from studies of Portuguese, Greek, Spanish and Dutch as well as English are drawn on. The issue of overgeneralisations is considered: the striking and fascinating errors that children make, and the developmental course of these errors over time discussed. The evidence leads Nunes and Bryant to argue convincingly that overgeneralisations result from children forming their own hypotheses about relevant spelling, and that word specific knowledge leads to later morphemic spelling rules.

Does teaching make a difference? The question is particularly pertinent in relation to children's grasp of morphemic spelling rules—the connection between letters and morphemes—which is rarely taught. Instead the learning has been left to "children's own necessarily haphazard inferences". Yet the consistent lesson from the intervention studies that Nunes and Bryant describe is that it is possible to teach children about morphemes and spelling: they learn well, quickly and enjoy it. It is a practical lesson on a centrally important cognitive achievement.

Judy Dunn

Preface and Acknowledgements

About 20 years ago, the two of us started to discuss what else children need to know to be really good readers and writers, after they have taken the initial steps in how the alphabet works. At the time, Julia and Daniel, Terezinha's children, had conquered the basics in reading in Portuguese and English and were making progress in the orthographic stage. We began to be curious about the nature of what they would have to learn about orthography. Was it, we asked, just one great big collection of spellings for all the words, which children have to commit to memory bit by bit, or were there rules for them to learn which would help them to make sense of this mass of spellings? Because they were learning to read and spell in two different languages, we had the great opportunity to make cross-language comparisons from the start.

There were spellings for Portuguese words that could not be predicted from phonology in Portuguese, but could be predicted from its morphology. For example, if a Portuguese word contains the /j/ sound (as in "jelly") and this sound precedes an /e/ or /i/ sound, it can be written either with the letter "j" or the letter "g." Do Brazilian children really need to memorize one list of words spelled with a "j" and another list of words spelled with a "g"? Neither of us is any good at memorizing and we thought that this would be an awful task to ask children to do. So, we started to explore children's spellings in Portuguese and English and started to identify many consistencies in spelling, some of which had till then been treated as unpredictable or irregular spellings.

We found that many English and Portuguese spellings cannot be predicted from the way that the words sound, but are entirely predictable and comprehensible when one takes into account the morphemes that form these words.

Our favourite English example was "magician": the first vowel, represented by an "a," is a schwa vowel and does not sound like /a/ at all;

the letter "c" represents a sound normally represented by "sh," and the last vowel is another schwa vowel, and there is no reason why it should not be spelled as "e" or "u" or "o" from the way it sounds: "ia" is a funny choice, if we think of the way this last vowel sounds. Of course, all the apparent irregularity in the word "magician" goes away when we think of the morphemes that form it, "magic" and "-ian."

Right from the start of this research, we thought that two types of explanation competed for how children learn words whose spelling goes beyond phonology. They could memorize the spellings of all these words (what a task! but why not?) or they might be able to find and learn rules that would make these spellings predictable and comprehensible. We knew of a research move that could help us understand the contribution of memorizing words versus understanding morphemes: to ask children to write pseudowords that contained these non-phonological spellings that could be predicted from morphology. Pseudowords cannot be spelled on the basis of memories of past encounters with them: they are made up, and so their spelling has to be generated by the children. If we told the children: "A spejician has been teaching us about spejic" and asked the children to spell the pseudoword "spejician," we would be able to test whether they made inferences about its spelling based on morphology rather than phonology, and spelled "spejician" with a "c" and then "ian." This is particularly interesting because the stem, "spejic," contains the letter "c" at the end, and there its sound is /k/.

We had the first shot at this in Portuguese (Nunes Carraher, 1985). We considered this a fishing expedition. Up to then, almost all the work we knew with pseudowords had used only stimuli that were entirely predictable from phonology: pseudowords were used to test whether children used grapheme–phoneme correspondences in reading and spelling. The exception in previous research was a paper by George Marsh and his colleagues (Marsh, Friedman, Welch, & Desberg, 1980), who asked children to write pseudowords such as "jation" and "cuscle." Marsh and colleagues were right about something: adolescents and college students could use the "t" in "jation" to represent a sound normally spelled with "sh." But we thought that they were probably wrong about something else: they argued that this was accomplished by the use of analogies based on groups of letters that might have the same sound. This would mean that they would be treating "-tion" as a unit for representing sounds, just as "-ight" is a group of letters with a particular sound. We thought that the solution was in morphology: "inspect" + "ion" are units of meaning, which, when combined, form the word "inspection." Yet their idea was a good one: to dictate pseudowords that cannot be spelled on a grapheme–phoneme correspondence alone.

The studies in Portuguese showed that children and adolescents could indeed spell pseudowords using morphological consistencies: they could predictably choose between the endings "isse" or "ice" in pseudowords. Although these two endings represent the same sounds, they have different functions: "isse" is used as a subjunctive inflection in verbs and "ice" is a derivational suffix used to form abstract nouns. Brazilian students at the end of primary school were more likely to make the right than the wrong choice when spelling pseudowords that were placed in sentences that made it clear whether they were verbs or nouns.

We then collected a sample of English children's stories and analysed the spelling errors that the children made. Mrs Brown, from Windmill Primary School, was an enthusiast for story writing and kindly let us have a large sample. The children's stories were so fascinating that they almost distracted us from the analysis of their spellings. However, two things captured our interest then: their spellings of past tense and their use (either too much or none at all) of apostrophes.

Our story is well known to many after that, and it is the story that we tell in this book. We studied children's spellings of the past tense endings, of consistency in spelling stems, of the use of "ion" and "ian," of the "s" for plurals and the use of apostrophes, among other things. We also studied other types of consistencies in spelling: the orthographic phase is not only about morphemes, but also about conditional spelling rules based on phonology, so we investigated these as well.

Acknowledgements

We worked with a large number of people: researchers, teachers, and children. We are very thankful indeed to all the colleagues who worked in these projects over so many years. So many schools were kind to us, and allowed us to disturb their schedules and helped us in these projects. In our initial studies, we had the help of teachers and children in Wolvercote First School, Botley Primary School, Cassington Primary School, Kennington Primary School, William Tyndale Primary School, Honeywell Infants' and Junior School, Ravenstone Primary School, and Trinity St Mary's Church of England School. Miriam Bindman and Gill Surman worked on the initial project and were excellent collaborators. Our later studies involved a large number of schools also: Bessemer

Grange Primary School, Dulwich Hamlet Primary School, Hargrave Park Primary School, Brecknock Primary School, Honeywell Primary School, Lauriston Primary School, St Joseph Roman Catholic Primary School, St Michael Church of England Primary School, St. Nicholas Primary School in Abingdon, Wheatley Primary Schools in Wheatley, St. Nicholas in Marston; Bayswater Middle School, Larkrise Primary School, Marston Middle School, SS Philip and James Primary School, East Oxford Primary School, Frideswide Middle School, St. Andrews Primary School, Cutteslowe Primary School, St Barnabas Primary School, New Hinksey Primary School, St Aloysius Primary School, and Woodfarm Primary School. We are also grateful to the Army, the RAF and the Royal Navy for allowing us to test large groups of recruits.

Our main collaborators in our projects were Ursula Pretzlik, Deborah Evans, Daniel Bell, Diana Burman, Jenny Olsson, Paul Mitchell, Freyja Birgisdottir, Selly Gardner, Adelina Gardner, Jane Hurry, Julia Carraher, Constanza Moreno, Anne Magnani, Helen Mirelman and Lesley Zuke. We also worked with many research students in the course of this work, among whom were: Athanasios Aidinis, Lily Chan, Kalliopi Chliounaki, Claire Davis, Hélène Deacon, Nenagh Kemp, Annukka Lehtonen, Claire Rankin, João Rosa. Many other people helped us on so many occasions, and we do think of them all with appreciation for their efforts.

The large number of studies that we did over these years, many of which we report here for the first time, would not have been possible without the support of the MRC (Grants nos G9214719 and G9900004), and the ESRC (Grant no. R000237752), the ESRC-Teaching and Learning Research Programme (Grant no. L139251015) and the Leverhulme Emeritus Fellowship awarded to Peter in 2004. The initial studies, carried out in Brazil, had the support of CNPq (the Brazilian National Council for Research). Without their support, it would have been impossible to carry out this sustained research programme on children's reading and spelling. We are hugely grateful for this support.

Finally, there are many colleagues with whom we discussed these ideas over the years. Their genuine interest in the ideas and research reported in this book and the conversations that we had over the years have always made us think more and want to design yet another study. Uta Frith, Michel Fayol, Jesus Alegria, Iris Levin, Lair Levi Buarque, Lucia Browne Rego, Eneida Didier Maciel, Sylvia Defior, Bente Hatgvet, and Márcia da Mota are among the many colleagues with whom we have had long and exciting conversations about orthography. Who would have known that orthography is really such a fascinating matter?

We had two good reasons to do this work over these 20 years: the science of psychology, which we enjoy so much, and the children, who have to learn to read and spell. We hope that this book is a contribution to both.

Terezinha and Peter
Oxford,
February 2008

Chapter 1

Learning to Spell

What is the problem?

Most of children's learning is generative. They learn not just about specific facts or specific actions, but about how to deal with quite new experiences and new situations. Language is one obvious example, and counting is another. We only hear a limited number of sentences when we learn our first language, but a fluent speaker should be able to say anything he or she wants, using sentences never heard before. We learn to count by getting to know a limited number of counting words, but with this knowledge we should be able to count on and on, far beyond the limits of the specific words that we learned.

Learning to read and spell is much the same. What children learn about reading and spelling words should, in the end, make it possible for them to read and spell reasonably well words that they have never seen in written form before. If children memorized the spellings of lists of words and could write those words correctly, and only those, we could conclude that they had learned how to spell words one by one. But this is not what happens, nor what we would want to happen. We want children to be able to spell most words as a result of learning a limited number of words. This book is about how children manage, or in some cases nearly manage, to do so.

The Connection between Language and Literacy

For many years now the idea that literacy is a language-based activity has dominated research on children's reading and writing. For example, an important collection of papers, published in 1972 by Kavanagh and Mattingly, entitled "Language by eye and by ear" summarized the empirical evidence that had been developed up to that time to support the conception of literacy as a language-based activity. The idea shared by the authors of these papers, and by most researchers on reading since then, is that the core cognitive processes in reading and writing are linguistic because what we learn in literacy acquisition is a *written language*. Therefore, analysing literacy learning requires understanding what a written language is and how oral language and written language are connected—that is, understanding "the linguistic connection."

This may seem an easy starting point but there is more than one view of what the relationship between oral and written language is. In fact, this has been a matter of debate for some time; the debate permeates discussions in linguistics, the history of writing, the psychology of literacy and education. In this chapter, we will present two different views of how oral and written language are connected, and explore the teaching and learning implications of these. We will argue that, though these are different views, they are actually quite compatible with each other, and that it is a better approach altogether to develop a theory that integrates the two views.

Two Views of the Relation between Oral and Written Language

The *first* is called the *notational view*. According to Olson (1994), it has been assumed since Aristotle's time that writing is a graphic device for transcribing speech: "written words are the signs of words spoken" (Aristotle, *De interpretatione*). Although scientific revolutions since Aristotle have changed the ways in which we think about the physical world, this classical view of the connection between oral and written language has not been dismissed and continues to receive the explicit or implicit support of linguists (e.g. Bloomfield, 1933; Mattingly, 1972; Saussure, [1916] 1983), historians (e.g. Diringer, 1968; Gelb, 1963; Sampson, 1985), psychologists (e.g. Frith, 1985; Cossu, 1999; Treiman, 1993) and educators (Isaacs, 1930; Montessori, 1918).

Recently, Tolchinsky (2003) detailed this conception by exploring the characteristics of orthographies as notational systems, i.e. as artefacts that enable oral language to be encoded, recorded, transported and reproduced in a systematic way. Adopting definitions proposed by N. Goodman (1976) and Harris (1995), she summarized the features of notational systems in general and showed their value for understanding orthographies. A notational system contains a limited set of elements—letters, in the case of an alphabetic orthography—each with a distinctive form. These elements can be copied and identified in spite of variations in the way that they are copied by different users. The elements are semantically differentiated (i.e. they refer to different elements of what is represented) and can be structured by specific rules (for example, in English orthography we read and write from left to right, top to bottom). Because of these characteristics, notational systems are powerful tools. With a limited set of letters, we can write all the existing words in a language, and even new ones, invented much later than the orthography.

This notational view treats writing as a second-order system—a system of (graphic) signs for (oral) signs. Thus reading and writing are directly related to and entirely dependent on oral language. This conception of the relationship between oral and written language has consequences for theories of how children learn to read and write, and also for how they should be taught. If orthographies are notations for oral languages, children need to learn how this representation works, i.e. what is represented by the orthography and how. Alphabetic orthographies are those in which letters represent phonemes—even if there is no exact correspondence between letters and phonemes. Other ways of representing language through writing are also possible, for example, by using a different unit of analysis of the sounds that make up words: Japanese orthography uses Kana letters to represent syllables rather than phonemes (see Akita & Hatano, 1999, for a more precise description). Within this notational perspective, children must learn how the orthography represents the language that they speak in order for them to learn how to read and write. The notational view of the relationship between oral and written language is easy to understand and we believe that it is implicitly accepted by most people. However, it is not the only view of the connection between oral and written language.

The *second* approach goes beyond the notational view, and treats writing as *written language*—that is, as a system with its own rules to represent meaning, and not only the sounds of oral language. For some linguists (e.g. Siertsema, 1965; Uldall, 1944), a language system goes beyond the way that it is expressed, either in oral or written form. The sounds that we hear in oral language and the letters that we see on the page are only the surface of the language system. The surface representations express meanings that are part of the deep structure of the language.

Because this approach is less familiar to most people than the notational one, it is useful to start from an analogy to the connection between two different oral languages. A sentence in oral language—for example, "The boy chased the dog"—expresses more than each word taken in isolation. The word order indicates that it was the boy that did the chasing—it signals the subject–verb–object (S–V–O) structure of the sentence. The principle of word order is used in English to represent the underlying grammar and it is what allows us to "generate an infinite class of sentences" (Chomsky, 1975, p. 41). This abstract system is the basis for learning any language in spite of the differences that exist between languages, and it is also used to learn a written language.

The approach to writing as a written language starts from the idea that the same sort of deep structure is the basis for written language as well as for oral language. Thus written language can use its own resources to represent the meaning relations that exist in the grammar of the language, even if they are not captured in the same way in oral language. For example, we use "s" to mark the plural of nouns and we use "ed" to mark the past tense of regular verbs but in oral language plural words can have the ending sounds /s/ or /z/ and past regular verbs never sound as "ed" at the end. In principle, someone who understands about plurals and the past tense can learn how these meanings are marked in written language even when they are not phonological notations of spoken language.

When children learn an oral language, they learn to give a phonological form, which is arbitrary, to the semantic and syntactic relations that they wish to express. Similarly, when they learn to write, they learn to give a graphic, arbitrary form to the semantic and syntactic relations that they wish to express. Thus, in this view, an orthography does not represent only the surface form of oral language: there are also connections between the deep structure of the language, which represents grammar and morphology, and the way in which a language is written.

This conception of how oral and written language are related may seem highly academic and without any pragmatic consequences for teaching and learning, but it is not so. If written language is only a different expression of the same language system that can be expressed orally, it should be learned through its connection to the abstract language system, not through its connection to oral language. K. Goodman (1982), for example, argued that in reading instruction "So-called 'linguistic programs' that emphasize phoneme-grapheme correspondences à la Bloomfield and Fries are still emerging, perhaps five or ten years beyond that point where there was any justification at all" (p. 90). He further proposed that

> [A]lphabetic systems don't simply operate on a letter-sound basis. . . .
> Sequences of sounds seem to have relationships to sequences of letters,
> not simply because of the alphabetic principle on which the system was

produced originally, but also because there is a common base underlying both of these. For the user of language, surface oral language and surface written language are related through a common underlying structure. As a language user generates a sentence, his thoughts bring him to a point at which he can apply a set of orthographic rules and write it. (pp. 91–92)

This view of how oral language and written language relate to each other implies that when children begin to read and write they learn a set of rules for expressing and understanding sentences in written form. They learn to produce meaningful sentences in writing, in just the same way as they previously learned to give an oral form to sentences in speech.

The second view of how oral language and written language are related is much less likely than the first to fit people's intuitions, and is more difficult to understand. Yet it is quite easy to find support for it. In written English, as in many other orthographies, we make distinctions in writing which are not marked in the sounds of words.[1] For example, we spell the end sounds /ks/ differently in different words: think of "fox" and "socks," "mix" and "tricks," "tax" and "tracks." If we were simply trying to represent the sounds of oral language, why would we spell these word endings differently? Are these spelling differences illogical and entirely unpredictable? Of course not! These spellings are entirely predictable if we think not only about oral language but also about the connection between oral and written language to an abstract language system that represents grammatical relations. The /ks/ sound at the end of words in English is represented by the letter "x," as in "fox," "mix" and "tax"—except when the word can be decomposed into a stem plus an affix, as in "sock+s," "trick+s" and "track+s."

Linguists, such as Chomsky (1965), have argued that we understand sentences by connecting them to an implicit grammar that represents simpler sentences. He argues that this is what allows us to recognize ambiguities: a sentence that we hear is ambiguous when it can be connected to different underlying simpler sentences. To use one of his examples: the sentence "I had a book stolen" could mean that "I had a book; someone stole it" or "someone stole a book; I asked that person to steal the book." It is easy to make an analogy between analysing an ambiguous sentence by connecting it to different core sentences and analysing a sequence of sounds, such as /ks/ at the end of words, by connecting it to different forms of words: the ending /ks/ can be

---

[1]   In this book, we will use quotation marks when we refer to a word or part of a word and a letter between forward slashes when we refer to sounds.

connected to a plural form, /k/+ "s" or to a singular form, which does not contain the letter "s."

These two views of the relation between oral language and written language have led to diametrically opposed approaches to the teaching of literacy. The first view has emphasized the need to help children become aware of the sounds in their language so that they understand that letters represent sounds. This is sometimes referred to as "attaining an alphabetic conception of written language" (Read, 1971, 1986; Ferreiro & Teberosky, 1983) or "learning the alphabetic principle" (Byrne, 1998). The second view is associated with the idea that children can learn to express language in writing if they are exposed to it (K. Goodman, 1982)—an idea that formed the basis for the "real books" approach to literacy instruction.

Steps towards a Synthesis

In this book, we will pursue a synthesis of these two positions. It is suggested that orthographies are notational systems and, as such, they enable the encoding, recording and reproduction of oral language. However, oral language and written language are not connected only through their surfaces: they are also connected through their relation to an abstract yet specific (e.g. English, French) language system.

The linguist Jean Pierre Jaffré (1997; adopting a modified version of Vachek's, 1973, definitions) explained this view by proposing that writing combines two principles: phonographic and semiographic. The phonographic principle

> is manifested by correspondences between meaningless units of spoken language (phonemes or syllables) and meaningless units of written language (phonograms or syllabograms). The semiographic principle encompasses the units and their functions in the linguistic elements of written language. These units are determined by the morphological structure of the languages in question . . . and by the way in which the written words are assembled. (p. 9)

The semiographic principle is at work, for example, when we spell all regular past verbs with "ed" at the end, irrespectively of whether the endings of the verbs are pronounced as /t/, as in "kissed," /d/ as in "killed," or /id/ as in "wanted." But the semiographic principle is not restricted to the spelling of words as such: it is much more pervasive because it is this principle that we use when we place spaces between words. Words are not phonological units but units defined by meaning and grammar. We say, for example, "I wento school yesterday" but write "went to," placing a space between the verb and the preposition, though we do not pronounce them separately. Words can change phonologically depending on the context in which they are spoken: a child may write "I hat to run" (see Nunes & Bryant, 2006, Figure 1.1, p. 27) not because the child cannot hear the difference between /t/ and /d/ but because the child is transcribing the sounds rather than preserving the identity of the word "had" across different phonological contexts.

Orthographies that rely more on the phonographic principle have been called "transparent," and in these orthographies it is difficult to appreciate the fact that writing and oral language are connected via the deep structure of the language. However, studies of competent adult readers in Italian, a transparent orthography, show that they use both phonographic and semiographic principles in word recognition (we do not review this literature here but the interested reader is referred to the work by Caramazza and his colleagues, in Italian; see Chialant & Caramazza, 1995, for a synthesis). It is much easier to recognize this underlying connection in less transparent orthographies, such as English, where the representation of morphemes often results in spellings that cannot be predicted from the way that the word sounds (such as "fox" and "socks") or might even contradict what would be expected from the sounds. "Magician" is spelled as it is and not as "magishon," though children often do write it that way. The wrong spelling is quite a good representation of the word's sounds, but the correct spelling works at a different level. Even though letter "c" in "magician" no longer represents the sound /k/ as it does in "magic," the first part of the word represents the word's meaning very well. The "-ian" ending is an affix that is called an "agentive": it signifies someone who does something. So, "magic" plus "-ian" is a very good way of representing in writing the meaning "someone who does magic."

The connection between morphemes and spelling, though not immediately obvious, can be easily understood. Once the regularity of the spelling of morphemes is recognized, words that seem highly irregular, like "magician" and "confession," can be seen as regular (magic+ian; confess+ion): regularity in English orthography is based not only on phonology but also on the "visual identity of meaningful parts" (Venezky, 1999)—that is, the use of the same spelling for the same morpheme even when its pronunciation changes.

One should not be tempted to simplify English orthography by thinking that "the visual identity of meaningful parts" is a principle that overrides the representation of sounds. There are many rules that apply when a suffix is added to a base form, which involve changing the visual form in order to preserve the phonological representation. A common rule is doubling letters when we add to a stem a suffix which starts with "e." In English, a vowel that is followed by a consonant, and no "e" after the consonant, is pronounced differently from one that is followed by a consonant plus "e": for example, "hat" and "hate," "hop" and "hope." The pattern Vowel plus Consonant plus "e," which is often called the "split digraph," is well known to teachers and explicitly taught to children in school. When we add a suffix that starts with "e" to a stem, the spelling pattern would be changed into a split digraph, and the vowel would sound differently. In order to preserve its sound, the consonant is doubled at the end of the stem: consider these examples: "tan"–"tanned"; "plan"–"planner"; "clot"–clotted"; "log"–"logged"; "pot"–"potted"; "pin"–"pinned"; "big"–bigger"; "sin"–"sinner"; "cut"–"cutter"; "run"–"runner." This is certainly an added complexity in English orthography, but still reasonably easy to master when we think of written language as representing sounds and also based on a connection to the deep structure of the language.

Subtleties in the Linguistic Connection: Influences across Languages

Borrowing words

Not everything about the linguistic connection in English orthography is so easy. Languages are—and must be—dynamic: new terms can enter into the vocabulary at any time. Some new words might be invented in the language itself, by creating compound words (e.g. spaceship, search-engine) or by composing a new word with morphemes that are already part of the language (e.g. skyscraper). Other novel words can be borrowed from other languages—and then the matter of how they are spelled has to be considered. English orthography honours etymology (Venezky, 1999). This means that the same sounds are often spelled differently in different words because the words come from different languages. Relatively recent borrowing with rare or proscribed consonant and vowel patterns (e.g. "tsunami," "Chianti") might have little effect on English orthography in general. These words could be learned by memory because they are restricted in number. However,

[E]xtensive borrowing over a long period of time—with different reten-tion patterns for spellings and changing spelling-sound relations in the original language—frustrate not only the use of etymology for predicting spelling-sound patterns, but the entire enterprise of orthographic rule making. (Venezky, 1999, p. 8)

So, there is one level of the linguistic connection that does not help much when we want to spell words in English, even if we are aware of the fact that etymology plays a role in English spelling.

Spelling with a borrowed alphabet

It is interesting to pursue the idea of borrowing at this point in the introduction, because of the effect that borrowing the Roman letters has had on English orthography. Latin (and the languages that originated from Latin, such as Italian, Spanish, and Portuguese) and Greek have a small number of vowel sounds, which can therefore be represented with a small number of letters. Borrowing the Roman letters to represent the sounds of the English language creates a problem. If we ignore the issue of variations in pronunciation and think of the kind of English called RP (Received Pronunciation or BBC English), we should be able to distinguish 21 vowel phonemes (O'Connor, 1982, p. 153). It is obvi-ously not possible to represent these 21 sounds by setting them in one-to-one correspondence with 5–7 letter-vowels (A, E, I, O, U, Y and W). So we see that borrowing an alphabet means using it creatively. One way of using it creatively is to invent larger units with more than one letter in order to represent sounds that are different from those repre-sented by a single letter. There is no need to discuss here the variations in pronunciation of vowels across different regions of English speakers —but there is also no reason to argue about the fact that the vowels in "hat" and "hate," for example, are different, and that representing both words with the letters "h," "a," and "t" would be to ignore this difference. Thus English orthography uses the borrowed Roman letters creatively: it uses digraphs—that is, two letters—to represent one vowel phonemes. The importance of some digraphs is immediately seen—such as the split digraphs "a-e," "o-e," "i-e" and "u-e"—but even these are still not sufficient to get 21 vowel sounds represented. Others are still needed, to differentiate, for example, "did" and "deed," and "lock" and "look." But it could be argued that some are not necessary, as they overlap in function with other digraphs—"hope" and "boat" do not have to be distinguished—and the use of extra digraphs for the same function here does make things more difficult for learners.

One of the issues that will concern us in this book is whether children realize quite soon that it does not work to spell vowel sounds on a one-to-one basis by using vowel letters because there are not enough letters to go around for all the sounds. We will analyse their resources for dealing with the shortage of vowel letters before they master conventional spellings.

We now turn to another aspect of English orthography, which has considerable impact on how words are spelled, but is not really about the connection between oral and written language, direct or indirectly, via the surface or the deep structure.

Form and Function in Written Language

In many written languages, including English, some differences in spelling are a matter of form rather than of function. In English, for example, words can end but cannot start with "ss." The pattern "ss" is actually the preferred spelling for one-morpheme words ending in the sound /s/: so "ss" is a common spelling for the /s/ sound but it is illegal at the beginning of words.

Similarly, "ck" is used at the end but not at the beginning of one-morpheme words. The use of "ck" instead of "k" at the end of words can be predicted by a relatively simple rule, which is also positional: "ck" is used after words that have only one vowel letter in the rime before the /k/ (e.g. "brick," "lock," "lack," "truck") and "k" is used after words that have more letters in the rime before the /k/ (e.g. "mink," "book," "leak," "park," "fork").

Another positional rule concerns the use of "ay" and "ai": "ay" is used at the end of stems and can also be used before vowels in the middle of a stem; "ai" is (with very few exceptions) only used in the middle and before consonants (e.g. contrast "may" and "main"; "clay" and "claim").

We think of these positional restrictions in spelling as a matter of "form" only, because they are not obviously related to a linguistic function, either phonological or morphological, even if they tend to apply to morpheme boundaries. This is an intriguing set of spelling patterns, which we hypothesize could be connected to a learning process different from those that apply when form and function go together.

Conclusion

We started out this introduction by posing the problem of reading and spelling as a generative process. It must be generative in order for us to be able to read and spell words that we have never seen before; but the words that we spell cannot be generated in a whimsical way, without any rules, because others should be able to read the words whose spelling we created.

We argued that linguistic processes are at the basis of this generative process in two ways. A prominent linguistic aspect of spelling is that orthographies represent oral language. Thus the letters that we use to represent a new word which we have not learned must guide the readers to how the word should be pronounced. This process is not a simple one-letter-for-one-sound representation; among other reasons for the lack of one-to-one correspondence is the considerable shortage of vowel letters in English. However, English orthography also uses the semiographic principle, in Jaffré's terminology, or the principle that Venezky calls "the visual identity of meaningful parts": if the sounds of a stem change when a suffix is added to it in, for example, pairs such as "magic"–"magician" and "heal"–"health," the stem conserves its visual identity in spite of the change in sounds. The same is true in endings such as "kissed," "opened" and "wanted"—three words that have different end sounds, /t/, /d/ and /id/, respectively, are all spelled in the same way, with "ed," a unit of meaning that marks the regular past tense of verbs.

Finally, we also suggested that the linguistic connection does not tell the whole story. There are in English many restrictions on the use of letters by position, and when there is more than one option for spelling, as in "ay" or "ai," positional rules might be the crucial factor in indicating the correct spelling.

Research on children's learning of word reading and spelling, as well as teaching, has focused to a large extent on the connection between the surface of oral and written language. In this book, we argue that this focus on letter–sound relations is necessary for an understanding of how children learn to read and spell but not sufficient. Most children master simple letter–sound relations in word reading and spelling within one or two years from the beginning of their reading instruction but still have a lot to learn to become good readers and spellers.

The aim of this book is to go beyond studying how children learn simple letter–sound correspondences, in order to consider how children learn how to use more than one letter to represent a single phoneme and to use semiographs that do not correspond to phonological units. We will try to answer question like: Do children easily see that sometimes two or more letters are used to represent a single sound? Do they seem to learn form rules, such as no doublets at the beginning of words, independently of function rules, such as the need to double consonants when "ed" is added to a verb to form the past tense? When there are different options for spelling the same sound, such as "x" and "ks" at the end of words, do they learn each word separately or do they learn a rule that helps them choose the right spelling? How easy is to teach children about semiographic rules and what are the best ways of teaching these? Although all these are very important issues when children are learning to read and spell, there are not many sources of answers to these question. We provide some answers and invite you to explore them with us.

Chapter 2

From Letter–Sound to Grapheme–Phoneme Relationships

The case of consonant digraphs

Discussions about learning to read and write dwell disproportionately on how this learning begins. It is easy enough to find experts' opinions, and often some quite convincing evidence, on questions like "How do children first learn about the alphabet?" and "What experiences in nursery classes give children the best possible foundation for learning to read at school?" You will have a much harder job, however, if you are looking for equivalent ideas and discoveries about 9-year-old children's reading and spelling. There is some good and intriguing research on older school-children's reading and spelling and there are effective teaching systems for them too, but we have much less information on what children learn after they have taken the first steps into literacy, how they learn, and what forms of teaching are effective.

Our aim in this chapter is to examine what children learn about reading and spelling after they have taken the first well-charted steps into learning to read, but perhaps the best way to start is to consider the scope of these first steps. Naturally these first steps have a limited scope: there is no point in trying to teach children all the complexities of a very sophisticated system at the same time. On the whole, nowadays, teachers begin with the alphabet, showing children how individual letters represent sounds and at the same time how words consist of separable sounds. The teachers' aim is for the child to put these two facts together and thus to understand how the individual letters in a written word can represent the sequence of sounds in a spoken word. Children, who are beginning to read, work with words like "cat," "fun" "stop" and "pet."

These are words in which there is a direct correspondence between the number of letters in writing and the number of phonemes (phonemes are the smallest units of sound that can affect the meaning of a word) in speech. Thus, each letter represents a phoneme and the sequence of letters represents a sequence of phonemes which in combination add up to something like the spoken word.

In such words the relation between sounds and letters is at its simplest, and that is the reason why teachers use them a lot when introducing children to the alphabet. However, there are many words that do not take this form in English. The main reason for this is our heavy reliance on digraphs.

Digraphs and Grapheme–Phoneme Correspondence

Digraphs are pairs of letters, like "th" and "ea" that represent one phoneme. English spelling has to rely on digraphs to represent consonants and vowels because there are more sounds in spoken English than there are letters in the alphabet. No individual letter in the alphabet signifies the opening consonant in "this" and "that": so, the job has to be done by two letters "th." There is no single alphabetic letter to represent the vowel sound in "feet" and "leaf," which is why it is usually spelled as "ee" or "ea." These, and other digraphs, are "graphemes." There is one-to-one grapheme–phoneme correspondence between three phonemes and the three graphemes in the word "th-a-t," just as there is between the three graphemes and phonemes in "c-a-t."

Digraphs have other functions too. Some, such as "wh" and "ph," provide alternative spellings for sounds that are represented as single letters elsewhere. In English pronunciation, the sound that we usually write as "w," as in "wipe" and in "wasp," is represented by the digraph "wh" in words like "why" and "what." The "wh" opening reminds us that these words are interrogatives and relative pronouns, although, rather annoyingly, several other words, such as "white" and "whisky," which also start with this digraph, are nothing of the sort.

Note, however, that in some dialects the "wh" is aspirated and represents a different sound. We recognize that there are dialect variations in pronunciation but for the most of part these will not matter for this discussion. In all the different dialects of people who speak English as their first language, there are more vowel sounds than vowel letters in English, and therefore a need for digraphs.

Another type of digraph, which is of great importance in English, is the doublet or "the geminate" as it is called sometimes. The double "p" in "stopped" and the double "n" in "funny" are consonant geminates. Vowel geminates are restricted to double "e" and double "o": there are no geminate "a"s or "i"s or "u"s.[1] Consonant doublets have a function in English, but it is not an invariable function. In many words they signal that the preceding vowel sound is short. Thus the double "n" in "funny" is a signal that the preceding "u" represents a short sound, and not a long one as in "puny." We decided to use here the terms "long" and "short" vowels, which are in common usage, even though the vowels are not simply distinguished by length but also by quality. Another quite respectable way to make the same distinction is to describe them as tense (long) and lax (short), but we decided not to use these because they are not so well known.

What Do Children Learn about Digraphs?

The existence of digraphs means that children have to work with a system that is partly based on one-to-one letter–sound correspondences (single letters depict single phonemes) and partly on two-to-one letter–sound correspondence (pairs of letters in combination signify single phonemes). There is also some variation in this system of correspondences, as we have already seen. Some sounds can only be represented by digraphs, such as the "sh" digraph in "shoot" and the "ay," "ai" and "a-e" digraphs in "say," "sail" and "same." Other sounds are represented in some words by single letters and, usually less frequently in others by digraphs: thus "fan" and "phantom" begin with the same phoneme which is written as one letter in the first and as two in the second of these two words. This is a complicated system and probably, to young children at least, it may seem a capricious and unpredictable one as well. How well do they cope with it? We will look for an answer to this question by considering two kinds of evidence on consonant digraphs.

The first kind comes from studies in which children were asked to mark on written words the units that correspond to the sounds in these words: in some of these words there was a simple one-to-one

---

[1]   There are very few words with two "a"s, "i"s or "u"s in English. Some of these are imported into English, for example, "bazaar." In others, the repetition of the two letters results from adding a suffix that starts with a vowel to a stem that ends with the same vowel, for example, "skiing" and "Hawaiian." Finally, in some words each letter represents one sound—as in "vacuum"—and the repetition of the same letter does not form a digraph.

correspondence between the letters and the sounds, but there were digraphs in other words. The second comes from research on how children represent consonant and vowel sounds that should be represented by digraphs in their own writing.

A classification of consonant digraphs

Representing consonant sounds in English is a straightforward matter in many words because there are almost as many consonant letters as there are consonant sounds in the English orthography. There is also less variation across regional accents in the pronunciation of consonants than of vowels (O'Connor, 1982). However, although some consonant sounds are only ever represented by one letter, there are other consonant sounds that can be represented by a digraph too.

In order to organize the discussion of consonant representation in English, we distinguish three cases in the use of digraphs, which differ in terms of their function (see the form–function distinction in Chapter 1).

Obligatory digraphs

The first case is the one briefly mentioned in the previous section: some consonant sounds are typically (and almost always) represented in English by a digraph and not (almost never) by a single letter. For example, the end sound in "king" and the beginning sounds in "think," "cheese" and "shadow" cannot be represented by a single letter. The most frequent spellings (Treiman, 1993) for these sounds, though not the only ones, are "ng," "th," "ch" and "sh" respectively. We will refer to these as "obligatory digraphs." Our hypothesis is that children become aware of obligatory digraphs as spelling units more easily and use them more consistently than the other types of digraphs.

Doublets (geminates)

The second kind of the consonant digraph is the doublet or geminate: this is the use of the same consonant twice, as in "ll" or "pp." In English, doubling a consonant does not affect its pronunciation but it often affects the pronunciation of the vowel that precedes it. For example, if we added "ed" to "stop" without doubling the "p," ("stoped" instead of "stopped") and then read it, we would pronounce it as "stoaped"; if we added "er" to "sad" ("sader" instead of "sadder") without doubling the "d," we would pronounce it as "saider." However, not every use of double consonants falls into this category: "leter" and "letter" would probably be pronounced in the same way, just as "baloon" and "balloon." So, in English, doublet consonants vary: sometimes the form does have a function and sometimes it does not.

Extras: digraphs that are alternative spellings

We include in the third kind of the consonant digraph those pairs of letters that transcribe a sound for which there is a single consonant that could do the same job. For example, the letter "f" could be used in all words that contain the sound /f/, but it is not. In "elephant" and "telephone," the "f" is replaced with "ph" and in "laugh" and "cough," it is replaced with "gh." Similarly, the letter "r" could be used to represent the beginning sound in "write" and "wrap" and the letter "n" could be used to represent the beginning sound in "know" and "knife." These digraphs can be seen as "extras" because the consonant sound could be represented by a single letter. Extra digraphs might be entirely consistent or inconsistent, when you go from print to pronunciation. For example, "ph" is consistent and represents the /f/ sound; "gh" can represent the sound /f/ but it is inconsistent even when we limit the analysis to a certain position, such as following the letters "ou" and at the end of words: for example, it is pronounced as /f/ in "cough" and "tough" but not in "dough" or "through." "Kn" and "wr" differ from "ph" and "gh" in one way: the former might be seen as digraphs but also could be seen as spellings that contain a silent letter: we would read "nife" in the same way as "knife" and "rite" is read exactly as "write." In contrast, with "ph" and "gh," if we remove either the first or the second letter from the digraph, the word would sound quite different: "pone" or "hone" sound quite different from "phone."

Summary

There are three types of consonant digraphs:

1   Obligatory digraphs representing sounds that are not represented by single letters, such as the opening sound in "thin" and the end sound in "wash."
2   Doublet digraphs, or geminates, in which the same consonant letter is repeated, as in the medial sound in "hopping" or the final sound

in "kiss." In English, and in several other orthographies, words never start with a doublet (but this is legal in Spanish for some doublets, as in "llamo").

3   Extras, which are digraphs representing consonants in some words, while in others the same sound is spelled as a single letter: e.g. compare the spelling of the beginning consonants in "phantom" and in "fan."

What do children know about consonant digraphs?

We can now turn to the question of children's awareness of the use of more than one letter to represent a consonant sound. It is widely acknowledged that children often form concepts in everyday life without explicit teaching, and that these concepts may or may not be in line with scientific concepts that are referred to by the same words. This idea was stressed by many great developmental psychologists, including Piaget (e.g. 1954) and Vygotsky (e.g. 1986), and is probably by now part of how educators think about children. If spontaneous learning of this sort is an important part of children's learning of the alphabet, they might well use the terms that adults use but in an idiosyncratic way. Fortunately, studies by different researchers suggest that children in the beginning of their school years and adults use the word "letter" with a very similar meaning. Many pre-school children are able to identify letters by selecting them from a series of letter-like stimuli and reject other stimuli, which are letter-like but are not actual letters (see, for example, Ferreiro & Teberosky, 1983; Tolchinsky, 2003). Children know what a letter is and use the word "letter" easily. However, they do not use the words "grapheme" or "digraph." So, how do we know whether they extend the concept of letter–sound correspondences to grapheme–sound correspondences?

Ehri and Soffer (1999) set out to investigate whether children at different age levels and with different levels of reading and spelling proficiency realize that some sounds are represented by more than one letter and that some letters may be used in spelling though they do not represent any sounds. The children in their study were 78 2nd, 3rd, 5th and 6th graders (about 7 to 11 years of age) from New York, whose reading level was adequate for their age. Because the children were unlikely to know the word "grapheme," the researchers presented the task of grapheme identification in three phases. In the first phase, they wrote five words on the board, pronounced them, and showed the children how to mark the correspondences between sections of the written word and the smallest units of sound. The words used as example were "no," "fun," "see," "make," "this." The first two contain simple letter–sound correspondences; "see" has a vowel digraph ("ee"), "this" contains a consonant digraph ("th") and "make" was described to the children as containing a silent letter ("e"). The researcher circled the digraphs as one unit and put an X across the silent letter as she explained to the children how they should mark the correspondences between the spelling and the sounds in the words.

In the second phase of the procedure, the children were asked to mark on their own papers the correspondences between the spelling and sounds in the same way as the researcher had done, and then were asked to check their work by comparing it to the researcher's segmentation of written units that represented sounds. Finally, the children were asked to carry out the same task by marking the spellings of the smallest units of sound in 24 words. The list contained words in which each of the letters corresponded to one sound, plus other words with varying types of difficulty. Those of interest to us here were words with consonant digraphs.

The younger and less experienced readers were as proficient as the older and more experienced readers in matching letters to sounds when there was a simple one-to-one correspondence between them. The scores for correctly splitting 9 simple words into the right number of written segments were 7.2 for the younger group, 5.9 for the middle group and 6.6 for the older group. Although the younger children obtained a higher score, the difference was not statistically significant: so, we can conclude that children at the three levels of age and competence were equally capable of establishing these simple letter–sound correspondences.

However, younger and older children may have succeeded in the task for different reasons. It is possible that the younger and less experienced readers succeeded because they had little knowledge of how to establish correspondence between graphemes and phonemes that did not take the form of one-letter-to-one-phoneme correspondence, even after the demonstration and practice trials. In fact, the younger children continued to mark every letter as corresponding to one sound in 6.1 out of 15 words where this was not appropriate, in comparison to the intermediary and older group, who did so in 3.6 and 2.4 words, respectively. Thus the younger children were correct 80% of the time when the appropriate division was a letter-by-letter one and continued to use the same system for marking divisions in 40% of the words, where this was not appropriate. They showed a strong bias toward using one-letter-one-sound correspondence when marking the units on the written words, even though they knew the correct pronunciation of the written words. They over-extended the idea of one-letter-one-sound to words where this was not appropriate, but they used this simple correspondence more often when it was the right thing to do than when it was not.

The older children, in contrast, did not show a bias towards using simple letter–sound correspondences. They were correct approximately 70–80% of the time with both types of word, those with one-to-one letter–sound correspondences and those in which digraphs were used to represent one sound.

The other side of the coin—marking digraphs when this was appropriate—leads to the same conclusion of a bias among the younger children, which is that they treat single letters, rather than graphemes, as the units in spelling. The younger children correctly marked only a mean of 3.9 digraphs (out of 15), whereas the mean scores for the intermediary and older groups were 5.1 and 6.5, respectively. These differences were statistically significant, which indicated that the task of marking digraphs was much more difficult for the younger than for the older children.

The fact that the younger children correctly marked 26% of the digraphs as a single unit does not tell us too much about their ability to recognize digraphs, because they also marked 19% of the simple letter–sound correspondences wrongly by including more than one letter in the same spelling unit. This type of mistake included both circling rimes ("ed" in "red") as one unit and circling the onset plus the vowel ("ca" in "catch"). So, it is not possible to say, on the basis of this information, whether the younger children were actually developing an understanding of digraphs or whether they had simply failed to carry out a proper phonological analysis of the words when they marked more than one letter as a grapheme.

One more finding from the Ehri and Soffer study supports the idea that the younger children had a bias towards using single letters as the units in spelling and the older children did not. The children in the intermediary and older group were significantly more likely than the younger group to make the mistake of putting together two letters that represented two sounds into one unit. The percentage of words with errors of putting together two letters that should have been treated as separate units was 14% for the older children, 24% for the intermediary group, and 9% for the younger group. The younger children were less prone to make this type of error because of their one-letter-one-sound bias.

Ehri and Soffer further point out that there was a strong connection between the children's ability to identify a digraph as a spelling unit and their performance when spelling a consonant sound that must be represented by a digraph: among the younger children, 7 (out of 23) spelled the word "ship" as "sip"; 6 of these failed to circle the digraph "sh" correctly in the word "she," splitting the "s" and the "h" as separate units.

Finally, Ehri and Soffer found that children had a clear preference to mark the "w" in the digraph "wr" ("write") and the "k" in "kn" ("know") as a silent letter: 45% and 60%, respectively, marked the "w" and the "k" as silent letters, whereas only 20% and 18% marked these as part of a digraph. These examples suggest that, when a consonant sound can be represented by a single letter which is part of the digraph, the other letter in the digraph may be considered as a silent letter by children.

Summary

This pioneering study by Ehri and Soffer showed that children's everyday concept of spelling units and the concept of grapheme accepted as scientific wisdom do not coincide. However, even in the absence of explicit teaching about what a grapheme is, children do develop a conception that is clearly beyond a one-letter-one-sound idea as they become older and more proficient readers and spellers. Does this emerging, and not completely appropriate, conception of spelling units interfere with children's spelling performance?

Other Sources of Data

We turn now to other sources of data, about how children spell words that contain digraphs. Research on children's use of digraphs in spelling is relatively scarce but the little research that there is tells us important things about the development of children's spelling.

Rebecca Treiman (1993) analysed the spellings of a group of U.S. first graders learning to read and write in English. Their teacher encouraged them to write and did not stress spelling: Treiman indicates that the teacher told the children to spell the words as well as they could and did not tell them the correct spelling even if they asked. Treiman carefully analysed these first grade children's use of consonant digraphs, and reports several results that throw light on the development of spelling.

First, obligatory digraphs were spelled correctly by these first grade children in 70% of the words where they were the correct spelling. Although the children were correct 87% of the time when a single consonant was required, and the difference between these two percentages is statistically significant, the high levels of use of these digraphs is impressive, particularly if children do have a bias to think in terms of one-sound-one-letter. It is quite likely that, when it comes to obligatory digraphs, this bias is challenged by the fact that there is no letter to represent these sounds, and so the children realize that they need two letters to do this job. In contrast, extra digraphs resulted in significantly lower levels of success: for example, they were correct in only 21% of the words where "ph" should be used to represent the sound /f/.

Treiman's results are remarkably consistent with Ehri and Soffer's data on the way that children mark the graphemes on written words. "Sh," "th," and "ch" (or "ch" + "tch," in "catch") were identified as single units by between 72% and 81% of the children; in contrast, "wr" in "write" and "kn" in "know" were identified as single units by 20% or fewer children.

Finally, we note that, although children can use both form and function rules in learning about graphemes that involve more than one letter to represent consonant sounds, they find this a bit of a challenge, even if not a huge one. Nunes and Aidinis (1999) showed that children in their first years of school made significantly more errors in a spelling test when they had to spell words with the digraphs "sh" in "wish" and "ch" in "chin" than in spelling other three-phoneme words that did not contain digraphs: their level of success fell from 96% to 92%, a difference that was significant. The difficulty was considerably larger for poor readers: their accuracy level fell from 94% to 73%. The greater difficulty of the poor readers continued to be significant even when they were compared to young children who had the same reading age as they did. Previous work by Henderson and Shores (1982), Kibel and Miles (1994) and Henry (1989) had suggested that poor readers have greater difficulty in spelling words that include digraphs and consonant clusters but they had not compared the poor readers to children of the same reading age, only to those of the same chronological age. So it was not possible to know whether poor readers' difficulties with digraphs were simply a matter of them having less experience with reading or whether they resulted from a real difficulty with using correspondences that differed from the one-sound-one-letter system. The work by Nunes and Aidinis showed that poor readers do find these more complicated correspondences considerably more difficult than children who are younger but have the same reading age.

Summary

1   Even if young and inexperienced spellers do tend to use a one-sound-one-letter strategy in spelling, they seem to realize quite soon that there are no single letters to represent some sounds and then they learn the digraphs that are required for the job relatively quickly and without explicit instruction.

2   It is likely that the level of success reached by the children with obligatory digraphs indicates *rule learning* whereas their learning about optional digraphs depends on *word-specific learning*—that is, learning that "write" is spelled with "wr" and not just with "r" (as "rite"). However, there is presently no evidence relevant to digraphs to support this conjecture or to help reject it. Therefore, we do not dwell on the issue of word-specific learning in this section, but will raise it again when the relevant research is available.

3   The use of obligatory digraphs is a greater spelling obstacle for poor readers that for younger readers of the same reading level. This could either mean that poor readers do not realize that they need a consonant digraph for certain sounds because they are not completely aware of the sounds (e.g. they don't note clearly enough the difference between "sip" and "ship") or because they find conditional rules, even those as simple as obligatory digraphs, harder to learn.

Doublets: The Relative Importance of Form and Function in Children's Spelling

What about doublets? Do children spell these successfully or not? In Treiman's sample, the correct use of doublets is at a level intermediary between obligatory and extra digraphs: the children used the doublets correctly in 32% of the appropriate words, but very rarely—in less than 1% of words—where a single consonant should have been used. So, they use doublets much more often in the right than in the wrong place: however, this lack of use of doublets in the wrong place may not be a true achievement, because young children have a bias to use a single letter for a single sound. In about 50% of the words, the children used the appropriate single letter to represent the consonant sound (e.g. a single "t" in "kitten").

Learning doublets may actually be a mixture of rule learning and word-specific learning: in some cases, there is a rule about the need to use a doublet (as we mentioned previously, when you add the "ed" suffix, for example) but in other cases there is no rule (why should "letter" have two "t"s?). It would be really interesting if the children were using doublets more often when there is a rule that requires doubling than when the doublet is an extra, but the relevant information about the differential use of doublets is not presented by Treiman.

A second aspect of Treiman's work on doublets is related to the issue of form and not of function. The consonants "h," "j," "k," "q," "v," "w," "x" and "y" do not generally appear as doublets. The rest make legitimate doublets. Treiman observed 12 legitimate doublets in the children's writing. These were "bb," "cc," "dd," "ff," "gg," "ll," "mm," "nn," "pp," "rr," "ss," and "tt," which the children used in the right words 55% of the time and in wrong words 45% of the time. In contrast, only three of the total number of doublets that these children produced were doublets that do not normally occur in written English ("hhp" for "help," "rqqn" for "raccoon" and "yy" for "yours"). So these children may not have known *where* to use legitimate doublets, but they certainly had learned a form rule and hardly ever used doublets that were not legitimate.

Later, Rebecca Treiman and Marie Cassar (Treiman & Casssar, 1997) showed that children also learn about form in the case of doublets. English orthography contains doublets at the end and in the middle of words but not at the beginning. This is a matter of form, not of function, because having a double "s" at the beginning of a word would not change the way it sounds. These experimenters presented children with a pair of written pseudowords, one that contained a doublet at the end (e.g. nuss) whereas the other contained a doublet at the beginning (e.g. nnus). Note that both doublets are permissible in English. The children were asked to choose which one looked more like an English word. The participants in the study were in kindergarten, first, second, third, sixth and ninth grade, spanning the age range 5 to about 14 years. Even kindergarten children tended to choose the pseudowords with doublets at the end as more like English words than those with doublets at the beginning.

Is the children's knowledge of form aspects of doublets similar to their knowledge of the function of doublets? Treiman and Cassar had a second condition in their study, where they studied the children's understanding of the function of doublets. They spoke a pseudoword—for example, "sallip"—and asked the children to decide which spelling best corresponded to this pronunciation. One of the spellings contained a single "l"—i.e. the pseudoword was spelled as "salip"—and the other contained the doublet, and was spelled "sallip." The functions of doublets in English spelling, discussed in greater detail in the subsequent paragraphs, would indicate that these two spellings correspond to different pronunciations: in "sallip," the "a" should be short and in "salip," the "a" would be preferentially long. Although the children showed such good performance with issues of form, only the children in sixth grade (about age 11 years) and above displayed any knowledge of the correspondence between short vowels and spellings with medial doublets. Because the study did not include children in their fourth and fifth years in school, aged 9 and 10, it is not possible to conclude that the function of doublets is only learned at around the age of 11, but the evidence is that children aged about 8 years did not perform very well.

Thus, form, as well as function, does affect children's spelling development from an early age: the children in Treiman's studies seemed to know more about form (which doublets are allowed and which ones are not; the positions where doublets can appear in a word) than about function. They rarely used proscribed forms but they used acceptable forms wrongly only slightly less often than correctly.

Summary

1 Beginning spellers are slow to use doublets in their writing and for the most part write single letters where doublets are needed.
2 However, when they do introduce doublets into their spelling, they do so much more frequently when it is right to use doublets than when it is not.
3 There is a striking contrast between children's slowness in using doublets and their rapid learning about the form that doublets take. Young children soon understand that it is incorrect to start a word with a consonant doublet, and they rapidly form a clear idea of which consonant doublets are possible (e.g. "pp" and which are not e.g. "yy").
4 Finally, doublets are not as easy to learn as obligatory digraphs. This could be the result of the fact that consonant doublets in English affect the pronunciation of the vowel that precedes them, and this is a difficult rule, or could result from the fact that there are rules for some doublets but not for others: it could take children more time to find out that there are rules at all when there is also much unpredictability in the use of doublets.

Learning about the function of doublets

The question of the function of doublets in English orthography is interesting, but slightly difficult, because the function is rather a subtle one. The best way to express it is as follows: very few words indeed in English orthography have long vowels which are followed by a doublet: there are some exceptions like "gross" but these are rare (Carney, 1994). So, if you see any English word with a doublet, you can be fairly sure that the vowel that precedes it is a short one. However, when a short vowel is immediately followed by a consonant sound, this consonant does not have to be written as a doublet. There is a very large number of English words like "cat," "hop," "very" and "level" in which single consonants follow a short vowel.

Therefore, the functions of doublets are these: (1) if you are reading and you come across a word with a doublet, the vowel before that doublet is almost certainly a short one; (2) if you are writing a word with a long vowel in it, never (or hardly ever) put a doublet after that vowel. Thus there are two ways to measure children's understanding of this function. One is to see whether children read vowels as short more often when they come just before a doublet than when they come just before a single consonant letter. The other is to see whether they are more likely to spell a consonant as a doublet when it follows a short vowel than when it follows a long one.

Before we review the evidence on what children know about the function of doublets, we think it worth explaining why this type of rule about function is both complex and subtle. It is complex because of the nature of the rule. Thus far we have discussed mainly a simple correspondence rule: "a" on its own usually signifies one sound, "b" another, and "th" still another, and so on. But we are dealing with an entirely different kind of rule in the case of the function of doublets. Here, we have a "conditional rule." Vowel letters are often pronounced one way if they are followed by a single consonant ("hoping") and in another way if they are followed by a doublet ("hopping"). So, the sound that the vowel letter represents in these cases and in many others is conditional on the presence or the absence of a doublet immediately after it. This rule is subtle, as well as complex, because the function of doublets is an indirect one. Doubling a consonant has no effect on the pronunciation of the consonant itself: for example, the pronunciation of the /p/ sound in "hoping" and in "hopping" is the same. The effect of the doublet is indirect: it is on the pronunciation of the preceding vowel letter. It seems to us, therefore, quite possible that young children, who are taught a great deal about simple and direct correspondence rules when they begin to read, might find this new kind of rule much harder to handle. But this is a matter for empirical research.

Cassar and Treiman (1997) reported that children seem not to realize that there is a possible link between the presence of a doublet and the pronunciation of the preceding vowel until they reach the age of about 11 years. Claire Davis (2005) carried out longitudinal research, which suggested that children younger than that are to some extent aware of this link, but that this understanding remains imperfect for several years. The children, who took part in her project, fell into three age groups. At the start of the project these three groups consisted of 9-, 10- and 11-year-old children. She saw these children on two occasions, the second occasion taking place one year after the first.

In both sessions she looked at how the children read two-syllable words with and without doublets, her aim being to find out whether they pronounced these differently. She also gave the children a spelling task in which she dictated two syllable words in some of which the first vowel sound was short and in others a long one: she wanted to know whether they would introduce doublet consonants more often in the short than in the long vowel words.

Claire Davis worked with real words and with pseudowords (pseudowords are words which usually sound much like real words, but have no meaning, like "wef," "bip," "slinny" and "maping"). She formed lists of two-syllable real words and pseudowords that were made out of very similar pairs of words like "holy" and "holly" (real word list) and "haser" and "hasser" (pseudoword list).

In the reading tasks the children had to read these words, which were presented to them in a random order and not as pairs. Claire Davis wanted to know whether children would be more likely to read the first vowel as a long one when it came just before a single consonant than when it preceded a consonant doublet, and also whether they would be more likely to read the first vowel as short if it immediately preceded a doublet than when it came before a single consonant letter. The words that she used in the reading tasks are presented in Table 2.1.

In the spelling tasks the order of events was the other way round. Claire Davis asked them to write two-syllable words, and the first vowel sound in some of these words was short while in the others it was long. For that purpose she again formed one list made out of pairs of real words and pairs of pseudowords: the words in each pair sounded exactly the same, except that the first vowel was short in one of the words in the pair and long in the other. The question was whether the children

Table 2.1 The words used in Claire Davis's study of the effect of the presence or absence of a consonant doublet on children's reading of single words

Real-word Reading Task

| | Primary vowel letter | | |
	a	*i*	*o*
Real-word pairs	later–latter	diner–dinner	holy–holly
	stable–babble	tiger–digger	sober–robber
	ladle–paddle	piper–dipper	noble–cobble

Pseudoword Reading Task

| | Primary vowel letter | | |
	a	*i*	*o*
Pseudoword pairs	haser–hasser	hiner–hinner	doson–dosson
	baper–japper	fidy–liddy	lober–lobber
	satle–sattle	silow–tillow	poby–wobby

Note that these pairs of words were not presented as pairs. The order of the individual words in each list was randomized.

would be more likely to spell the consonant that immediately followed the first vowel sound as a singlet or as a doublet when that vowel was short than when it was long.

We shall describe her work with real words first. In both tasks (reading and spelling) the first vowel sound was short in all the real words with doublets, as one would expect, and it was long in all the words without doublets. The children did well in both tasks, as Figures 2.1 and 2.2 show. Indeed the oldest group made hardly any mistakes at all in the second session when they were 12-years-old. The two figures also present us with an apparent puzzle. The children found words with doublets easier to read but harder to spell than words with single consonants. In fact, it is quite easy to solve this seeming contradiction. The doublet words were almost certainly easier to read because the initial vowel sound in these words was short. At these ages children probably still associate vowel letters more easily with short vowels than with long

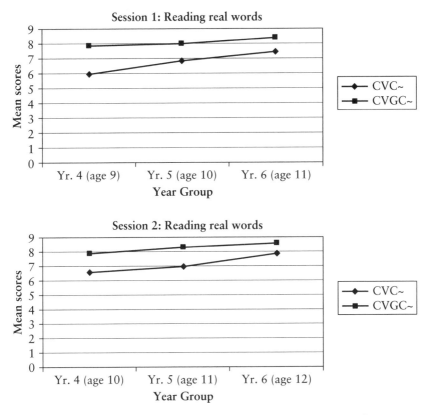

Figure 2.1 Correct reading of real words: the mean number of correct long vowel readings (out of 9) in CVC (single consonant) words and short vowel readings in CVGC (geminate consonant) words for all year-groups in Sessions 1 and 2

ones. Their preference for short over long vowels reflects what they are taught when they are first introduced to the alphabet—that the letters "a," "i," and "o" represent the short sounds which one finds in words like "cat," "pin" and "top." Conversely, the words with single consonants are easier to spell because at first children are much more at home with the idea that single consonant sounds are represented by single letters. They have not escaped completely from the simple idea of one-sound-one-letter correspondence.

The children's nearly complete success, by the age of 12 years, in reading and spelling both kinds of word demonstrates that most of

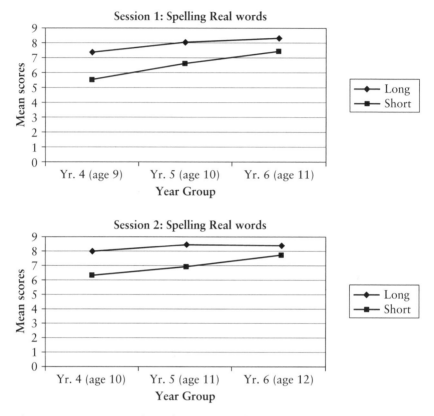

Figure 2.2   Mean number of correct single consonant spellings of long vowels and doublet spellings of short vowels (out of 9 real words) for all year groups in Session 2

them get over these obstacles, which therefore must be relatively small ones. However, this does not mean that 12-year-old children understand the abstract and rather complex rule about the function of doublets that we described earlier. When real words are used in reading and spelling tasks, there is always a non-rule-like explanation for children's learning. This is "word-specific learning."

There is no doubt that children and adults alike pick up a lot of knowledge about specific words which, just because it is specific, has nothing to do with rules. We know that "pain" is the correct spelling for one word, and "pane" for another, not because of some spelling rule, but because of what we have learned about these specific words' spellings. We learn about strange spellings, like "Gloucester" and "pint," without the help of any rules: since the spelling of these words does not conform to any rule, we just have to get down to learning them individually. So, we have to rely on word-specific learning when the spellings of particular words cannot be predicted or explained by any rule, and it is quite possible that we also learn how to read and write many other words through word-specific learning, even when their spelling is entirely rule-like. Thus, we may learn to spell the word "hopping" with a doublet and "hoping" with only a single "p" as two different and specific spellings for two specific words. To do this, we would not need to know about any general connection between the presence or absence of doublets in a written word and the length of the vowel sounds in that word.

How can we distinguish between rule-like and word-specific learning? The answer is to use pseudowords. They are a convenient and powerful way of testing people's understanding of spelling rules. If you find that children read the first vowel sound in the pseudoword "slinny" as short more often than the first vowel in "sapy," you can be reasonably sure that they know something about the doublet rule. They have never seen these pseudowords before, and thus could not have learned them by rote: if they treat pseudowords with and without doublets differently, they are probably using some form of the doublet rule.

Claire Davis used two-syllable pseudowords as well as real words in her longitudinal study, and she asked children to read and to spell these pseudowords. In the reading task they simply had to decipher pseudowords like "satle" and "sattle." In the spelling task she dictated pseudowords: the first syllable in some of these contained a short vowel and in others a long one.

The results were straightforward. It was clear that the children in all three age groups were much more likely overall to read vowel sounds as short than as long which, as we have already noted, may be due to prolonged teaching on the correspondence between vowel letters and short sounds. They almost always read the first vowel in the pseudowords with doublets as short: so, they hardly ever infringed the rule that vowels which precede a doublet are almost invariably short ones. They also were more likely to read the first vowel as a long vowel in pseudowords without a doublet. There were signs too that this difference in reading the vowel sounds between pseudowords with and without doublets increases with age. Figures 2.3 and 2.4 show that the number of times that children read the first vowel as long in pseudowords with doublets, always very low, was much the same for all three age groups in both sessions. However, there was a difference between the age groups in the

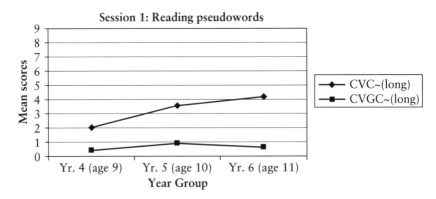

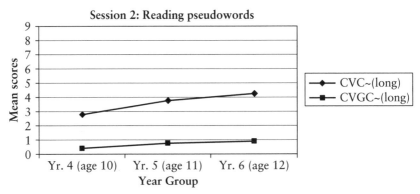

Figure 2.3 Mean number of words (out of 9) that were read as having long vowels in CVC (single consonant) and CVGC (geminate consonants) pseudowords by all year groups in Sessions 1 and 2

number of times that they produced the long vowel sound in response to the pseudowords with no doublets. The older children did so more often than the younger ones. This probably means that there was some increase between the ages of 8 and 11 years in the children's sensitivity to the function of doublets.

It might at first surprise some readers that even the oldest group of children pronounced the first vowel in pseudowords without doublets as short more than 50% of the time, but of course it can quickly be seen that this shows no misunderstanding on their part. There is nothing wrong with reading words without doublets in this way, since short vowel sounds are often followed by a single consonant letter in actual words like "level." The children broke no rule when they read the first vowel in pseudowords like "lober" as short, but the fact that they were

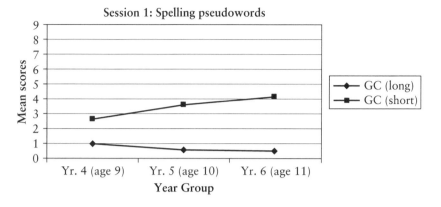

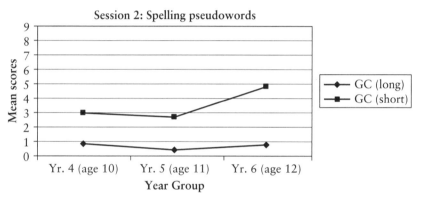

Figure 2.4 Mean number of geminate consonant (GC) spellings of long and short vowel syllables (out of 9 pseudowords) for all year groups in Sessions 1 and 2

much more likely to come up with a long vowel in these words than in pseudowords containing doublets does establish some knowledge on their part of what to make of doublets when reading words.

What about spelling? We have seen that the doublet rule is never to put a doublet after a long vowel. Children who know this should only write doublets in words with short vowels. Claire Davis tested this knowledge in the same two-year longitudinal study, again with two-syllable pseudowords which she dictated to the same children. She asked them to spell these pseudowords in what they thought to be the right way.

Figure 2.4 shows how often the children spelled the consonant that followed the first vowel as a doublet. You can see that in both sessions the children in all three age groups used doublets more often when the first vowel was short than when it was a long one. In fact, they hardly ever put a doublet after a short vowel. The figure demonstrates that the average number of times that the children introduced doublets into the long vowel pseudowords hovered between 0 and 1 (out of a possible 9) and hardly varied between the different age groups in both sessions. They used doublets in the short vowel pseudowords a great deal more often than in the long vowel ones, as the two figures clearly show.

There were also strong signs that the children learned about doublets over time. In both sessions the older children introduced doublets into the short vowel pseudowords more often than the younger children did. This cannot be dismissed as a matter of children becoming more willing to use doublets more readily as they grow older. The increase was selective. It happened with short vowel but not with long ones. The children had learned something about the function of doublets between the ages of 8 and 11 years.

Thus, we now have evidence that 8-year-old children have quite a good understanding of the function of doublets and use it when they read and when they write words. It is also clear that this understanding improves with age. At first sight, this might seem a rather dull conclusion, but in fact we think it to be quite remarkable. At the age of 9 years, many children are already quite proficiently using a rule that, as we have shown, is both complex and subtle, and are able to apply it to completely unfamiliar words. By the age of 12 years, their performance is about as good as it could possibly be. The result is particularly striking, at a time when many psychologists and teachers concerned with spelling tend to stress the importance of specific "retrieval" and "word-specific learning." No doubt word-specific learning is important too, but we must not underestimate the role that children's understanding of rules plays in their reading and writing.

Summary

1   In English, the function of the doublet is its effect on the pronunciation of the vowel sound that immediately precedes it. In most English words with doublets the preceding vowel sound is short. The first vowel sound is short in "hopping," but long in "hoping."

2   However, this rule is a subtle one, because vowel sounds do not have to be followed by a double consonant to be short. There are plenty of words, like "city" and "bus" in which short vowels are followed by a single medial or end consonant.

3   Nevertheless, English-speaking children do seem to learn about this function with very little obvious difficulty. Eight-year-old children are more likely to read vowel sounds in pseudowords as long when these are followed by a single consonant than when they are followed by a doublet. This difference is even more marked in 10-year-olds.

4   In their writing, English-speaking children also spell consonants in pseudowords as doublets much more often when these follow a long than a short vowel. Again this pattern is stronger in 10-year-old than in 8-year-old children.

5   Thus, these pseudoword studies establish that between the ages of 6 and 10 years children are managing to learn a subtle and complex conditional rule, despite receiving very little direct teaching about it.

Doublets in Finnish

The intriguing interplay of form and function in children's learning about doublets is apparent in other spelling systems too. In Finnish, doublets have a clear function which is a great deal more direct than in English. To understand this function you must first know that there are long and short consonants in Finnish words as well as long and short vowels. The distinction between long and short consonants does not exist in English or in many other languages, and so it is difficult for people from countries without this distinction to hear the difference between the two. Yet, it is important in Finnish because it affects the meanings of words and Finnish people are able to make this categorical discrimination as soon as they begin to speak and thereafter.

We can turn first to the function of doublets in Finnish. They signify long phonemes. So "tt" and "t" signify the same sound, but in the first case the sound is a long one and in the second it is short. Thus "mato" means worm and "matto" carpet. Although these two words may sound much the same to an English ear, they sound different to Finnish people and different meanings are attached to the two sounds. The differences in sound, and thus in meaning, are represented by the presence or absence of a geminate "t" in the middle of the word.

However, form also plays a part in the spelling of long Finnish consonants. Doublet consonants are not allowed at the beginnings of any Finnish words. When a Finnish word starts with a long consonant, the doublet rule does not apply and the consonant is represented by a single letter. Thus the spelling of long and short consonants is determined by form at the beginning of any Finnish words, and by function in the rest of the word. If Finnish children are sensitive to form, they will soon learn, as English-speaking children learn, that no words begin with double consonants. If they learn the functional rule, they will know how to spell long and short consonants in the middle and at the ends of words.

This clear positional difference makes it easy to compare children's understanding of form and function. Lehtonen and Bryant (2005) set out to do this by asking Finnish children in their first three years at school to judge which of two target words in a set of sentences was spelled correctly. In this experiment the children listened to the experimenter reading out 24 sentences. The second word in each of these sentences was a pseudoword, and the children were asked to choose between two spellings of each of these target words. The difference between the two spellings was that a particular consonant was spelled as a doublet in one and as a single letter in the other. In half the sentences this sound was at the beginning of the word (e.g. "suono" versus "ssuono") and in the other half it was not (e.g. "muosi" versus "muossi"). Notice that "suono" and not "ssuono" would always be the correct choice whether the opening sound was short or long. However, "muosi" would be the right choice if the consonant in the middle was short, while "muossi" would be right if this consonant was a long one.

The most interesting results in this experiment came from the youngest children who were in their first few months at school. When the target sound was at the beginning of the word, they chose the word with the doublet less often than the word with the single consonant, and they chose the word with the doublet far less often when the doublet was at the beginning of the word than when it was in the middle. This shows that although they were at the very beginning stages of learning to read and spell, many of them knew the formal rule—no doublet consonants at the beginning of a word. However, these same children showed no understanding of the functional rule. When the target sound was in the middle of the word, these children chose the word with the doublet spelling about half the time and chose it as often when the sound was short as when it was long.

The older children did much better with the functional rule. Those in their second year at school made the correct choice when the target sound was in the middle of the word and children in the third school year made the right choice on nearly every trial in this condition. They had plainly learned the rule, and this definitely was rule-learning because the choice words were pseudowords which meant that the children could not rely on their familiarity. Thus, we find that for Finnish children, just as for English children, knowledge about form definitely precedes knowledge about function. Right at the beginning of learning to read and write they have a working knowledge of a fairly sophisticated aspect of form in spelling. Function comes later.

Summary

1   In English, consonant digraphs raise issues both of form and of function. Some aspects of form are easily learned by children. For example, English-speaking children in their writing tend not to double consonants that are never doubled in conventional English spelling.

2   Functional aspects are more difficult to learn. It is particularly hard for children to learn the function of the digraphs known as "extras," like "ph" and "wr," which represent sounds that in other words are written as single consonants.

3   However, when the function of a consonant digraph is to represent a sound that cannot be represented by a single consonant, children seem to learn about this digraph in a rule-like manner. They show high levels of success in spelling these "obligatory" digraphs. This contrasts with the difficulties that children have with extra digraphs.

4   It is quite likely that they learn these "extra" digraphs by acquiring word-specific knowledge.

5   These two different learning processes, rule-based and word-specific knowledge, are characterized by different properties during the acquisition phase. Rule learning results in steeper learning curves than the learning of individual items. However, there is no systematic evidence on this comparison yet, and all we know is that the two types of digraph result in markedly different rates of success.

6   The use of doublets involves its own subtle and complex conditional rule about the pronunciation of the vowel letter that precedes the doublet. Despite the complexity of this conditional rule, there is evidence from pseudoword studies that many children are able to use it to some extent and do rely on it in reading and in spelling.

Chapter 3
Spelling Vowels
Digraphs and split digraphs

Representing Vowel Sounds by Two Letters

In the last chapter we showed how one of the main functions of digraphs is to provide spellings, like "th" and "ch," for particular consonants which are not represented by any single alphabetic letter. The same is true of English vowels, but here the problem of shortage of letters is much more severe than it is with English consonants.

The number of vowels sounds in English varies with different accents, but in the accent known as "received pronunciation" (RP) or "BBC English" one can distinguish 21 vowel phonemes (O'Connor, 1982). One of these is the schwa vowel: this vowel is not clearly pronounced; it appears in unstressed syllables (such as the last vowel in "magician" and "emotion" and the first and last vowels in "banana") and it can be represented in many different ways in English. We exclude this vowel sound from the table of English vowels because of its peculiar pronunciation.

In Table 3.1 (O'Connor, 1982) we list the remaining 20 vowel sounds using words as examples rather than phonetic symbols. In the top line of words in this table we give the vowel sounds that are typically represented by the five vowel letters in the alphabet. These, of course, are all short vowels. Each of the remaining words contains a vowel sound that is typically not represented by a single alphabetic letter.

The main aim of this table is to show the excess of vowel sounds over vowel letters in English, and we should emphasize at this point that much of what we write in this section will be strictly about English spelling and not directly relevant to other languages and orthographies. Many other European languages do not have this excess. In Greek, for example, it is the other way round. There are only five vowel sounds and seven single vowel letters (as well as several digraphs) to represent these five sounds.

Table 3.1 The 20 vowel sounds of BBC English (excluding schwa vowels) according to O'Connor (1982)

pat	pet	pit	pot	cut			
sale/pail	part	peat	pear	pine/sign	pier	port	pool
hole/foal	foul	foil	pour	poor	flute/root		furl

Table 3.1 shows how the English orthography's main tool for dealing with this imbalance between the number of vowel letters and the number of vowel sounds is the digraph. The usual way to spell the 15 vowels or so that are not typically represented by single alphabetic letters is to use digraphs which are either of two letters together (e.g. "pail") or split digraphs (e.g. "sale"). Vowel digraphs are similar in many ways but different in another way to the digraphs that represent consonants. With vowels, as with consonants, the first shift from understanding only letter–sound correspondence to learning about grapheme–phoneme rules takes the form of learning about digraphs. The big difference is that the vowel digraph system is more complicated than the consonant system, because it includes the split vowel digraphs.

Introducing the Split Digraph

The split digraph will play an important part in the arguments that we are going to develop in this chapter and later on in the book. Contrast "hop" and "hope," "pin" and "pine," "hat" and "hate," "cut" and "cute." All these are one-syllable words with three phonemes, and the words in each pair differ from each other only in their vowel sounds. There is one-to-one correspondence between letters and sounds in the first word in each pair. However, all the second words contain a split digraph. In split digraphs two vowel letters combine to represent one vowel phoneme, as in other vowel digraphs, but these split digraphs have three distinctive features:

1 The second vowel letter is always "e."
2 This "e" is always separated from the first vowel in the digraph by a consonant.
3 The vowel sound that the digraph represents is always a long one.

In effect, the addition of the "e" after the consonant has the effect of changing the preceding vowel.

There is another way to describe this spelling pattern, which is to refer to it as "the silent e." We believe this to be misleading since it implies that the final "e" has no function and plays no part in the transcription of the words' sounds by letters, in much the same way as the letters "p" in "psychology" and the "w" in "writing" are genuinely silent and quite irrelevant to the pronunciation of these two words. The split digraph is not like this, because the final "e" affects the pronunciation of the preceding vowel sound in a highly consistent way, and it does so as part of a combination of two letters or, to put it another way, as part of a digraph. Neither of the two vowel letters in "gate" or "grape" or "same" determines the vowel sound on its own: the digraph "a-e" does that (and it doesn't matter that the consonant gets between them).

How Children Deal with Spelling Vowel Digraphs

What do children make of all this complexity in the English system for spelling vowels? Do they recognize the difference between the 20 or so vowel phonemes described by O'Connor? In some of the vowel sounds listed by O'Connor, there is a change in vowel quality in mid-sound. For example, when you pronounce the vowel sound in the word "foil," you begin with an /o/ sound and then shift to /i/. Other vowel sounds contain only a single sound, as does the vowel in "pool." Do children consider vowels where there is a change from one vowel quality to another as a single vowel or as a diphthong—that is, as two vowels in sequence represented by two letters? O'Connor suggests that the second treatment of these vowels is possible but prefers to see them as a single unit in linguistic analyses. This is interesting, but it does not tell us anything about what children think.

The study by Ehri and Soffer (1999) showed that children were much less likely to treat vowel digraphs than consonant digraphs as single units. For example, the "ea" in "eat" was marked as a digraph by only 27% of the children even though this vowel sound cannot be represented by a single letter (contrast this with over 70% digraphs marked correctly when they stood for consonants that cannot be represented by a single letter). The "ea" in "eat" marks a long vowel, and perhaps children consider this as two vowels, and indeed 42% of the children circled the letters separately to indicate that each one represented one sound. Another 22% crossed out the letter "a," thereby indicating that they thought it was a silent letter (but note that "met" would not be pronounced as "meat," so the digraph has a different function from that of the single letter).

Ehri and Soffer found that children separated out the vowels in the digraphs more often when the digraph stood for a vowel where there was a change in quality than when there was no such change: 72% separated out "ay" in "play," which is considerably more than the percentage of children who separated out the "ea" in meat. Only 11% marked the digraph as a single unit and 15% marked the "y" as a silent letter. Thus, many children may treat vowel digraphs in which there is a change in vowel quality as sequences of two vowels, and they probably use this conception to learn the spelling of these vowels. Thus, in the word "boy," they may conclude that the letter "o" represents the beginning of the vowel and the letter "y" its end. This may be why children learn to use digraphs for these vowel sounds more easily than the digraphs for other vowel sounds where there is no change in the quality of the vowel.

Treiman (1993) observed that young children were more successful in spelling vowels that can be represented by a single letter than those whose most frequent spelling is a digraph. Her group of first graders produced 78% of the spellings correctly when the vowel could be represented by a single letter whereas only 37.5% of the spellings were correct when a digraph was the most common spelling of the vowel sound. She also showed that children's most frequent error in digraphs was to use a single vowel which was a possible spelling of the sound represented by the digraph—e.g. the letter "e" instead of the digraph "ei" in the word "their." This indicates that the children were attempting to represent the vowel sound, but were also maintaining the one-sound-one-letter principle in spelling. Treiman also points out that the children's errors revealed some word-specific knowledge: they were more likely to use only the first letter from the digraph (21% of the spellings) than to use another letter that could also approximate the representation of the vowel sound (10%).

We recently carried out a detailed study of children's vowel spellings by analysing the monosyllabic words that children used in stories which they wrote without help. Our aim was to see whether the children's spellings indicated that they were able to discriminate between different vowels and whether the spellings that they chose, even when incorrect, would have been appropriate representations of the vowel sounds. We worked with children's stories because this would allow us to obtain frequencies for words that children spontaneously wrote, not words that we chose. Finally, we analysed only monosyllabic words because

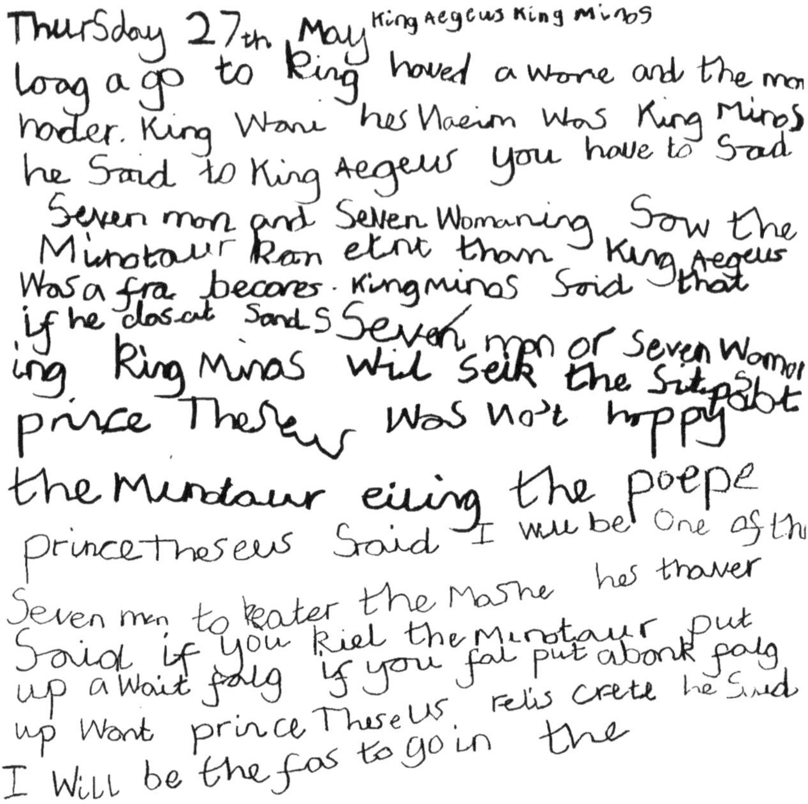

Figure 3.1 The first page of one of the stories analysed in the study of children's spellings of vowels in stories

there are no schwa vowels in these words: vowels are always clearly articulated in words with one syllable. Figure 3.1 presents one example of the first page of a story analysed in this study.

The corpus was obtained in eight schools in London in 1993, at a time when the children were not taught phonics extensively and were encouraged to read and write stories. In contrast to the teaching received by first graders in Treiman's study, the teachers of the children in this study provided them with the correct spellings when they later edited the children's productions. The children were sampled from three year groups: second (N = 27; mean age 6y11m), third (N = 52; mean age 8y6m) and fourth (N = 49; mean age 9y4m).

For each monosyllabic word, we entered in a data base both the child's spelling and the target word—that is, the word that we judged that the child was trying to spell. (We made these judgements on the basis of the observed spelling and the story context.) A trained teacher, who had studied English at university, carried out the data entry and consulted with another trained teacher when in doubt. The classification of words by vowel type were checked once again by Peter Bryant. All three are native English speakers.

Table 3.2 presents, for each year group, the percentage of correct spellings for each of the five vowel types that are typically spelled with a single letter. The value indicated by N for each year group is the number of different target words that contained that particular vowel sound. The most frequent target words with these vowel sounds that are spelled with digraphs are listed at the bottom of the table.

Table 3.2 Percentage correct of vowel spelling by type of grapheme in target word and year group

Vowel as in the words	Percentage correct spelling with one letter	Percentage correct spelling with digraph
Year 2		
pat – N = 158	97	Not applicable
pet – N = 336	82	64*
pit – N = 238	92	Not applicable
pot – N = 222	94	92**
cut – N = 151	92	92***
Year 3		
pat – N = 277	98	Not applicable
pet – N = 349	98	83*
pit – N = 186	96	Not applicable
pot – N = 309	99	94**
cut – N = 179	95	96***
Year 4		
pat – N = 277	99	Not applicable
pet – N = 337	93	80 (said)
pit – N = 233	96	Not applicable
pot – N = 357	100	99**
cut – N = 243	94	92***

Notes:
* said, says, read, dead, thread
** was, wash, want, what
*** some, come, one, touch

Some of the results in Table 3.2 are immediately obvious. First, the vowels in "pat" and "pit" were always spelled with a single letter across the different target words used by the children: there were no vowel digraphs in the target words classified as having these vowel sounds.

The most frequent word in the children's writing, and one that caused children considerable trouble in spite of being a frequent word in children's story books, was the word "said." It was misspelled 32% of the time by children in Year 2, 17% of the time by children in Year 3, and 22% of the time by children in Year 4. These percentages suggest a real difficulty in mastering this spelling and little progress is observed across the years. But in none of the misspellings did the children simply write "sed" or add a "d" or "ed" to "say" (writing "sayd" or "sayed"). A few (18% of the errors) of the younger children's errors were to spell it as "sad," using the first vowel in the digraph and omitting the second. All other spellings used digraphs, including the split digraph "a-e" ("sade"), "ea" ("sead"), and trigraphs such as "aia" ("saiad") and "aie" ("saied"). We believe that the children's spellings for "said" are sophisticated examples of attempts to achieve word-specific learning—but the children have not yet mastered the word. They seemed to know that transcribing the sound phonetically with the vowel "e" is not the right way to go and that more than one vowel letter is necessary but they still had not conquered the right spelling. The difficulty of this word suggests that word-specific learning is not an easy way to learn to spell, particularly if it goes against expectations generated for the word's spelling when other spelling knowledge is used: the rime "aid" is pronounced consistently in a different way, as in "aid," "maid," "paid," "afraid," "raid" and "braid." The word "said" is one of the five most frequent words in children's books, listed with a frequency of 16,115 per million, and surpassed in frequency only by "a," "the," "and" and "to" (see http://www.essex.ac.uk/psychology/cpwd/, consulted on 13.11.2007).

Table 3.2 also shows that there is an alternative and not unusual spelling for the vowel sound in "pot": the sequences "wa" or "wha." These spellings were used with the same level of success as the single vowel "o." The words used by the children which had the sound /o/ spelled with "wa" or "wha" were very frequent, particularly "was" (incidentally, only one child spelled "was" as "wos"). The children found "was" much easier to master than "said": even Year 2 children spelled words containing "wa" for the vowel sound /ɔ/ correctly almost all the time. The initial sequence "wa" is often, but not always, pronounced as /wɔ/, and perhaps this made it easier for the children to learn the spelling of "was" than of "said."

Similarly, the sequence "ome," an alternative way of spelling the vowel sound in "cut," appears in the children's spelling with consistent success. Very few errors were observed in the words "some" and "come."

What happens when a digraph is the most common spelling for a vowel sound? There are two issues to be considered. The first is whether the children realize that a single vowel will not do the job. The second is if they are able to choose the correct alternative, when more than one spelling is possible. These issues will be considered when we discuss the findings summarized in Table 3.3. Table 3.3 shows how well the children in different year groups spelled the different vowel sounds that are most commonly spelled with a digraph. It also shows the percentage of alternative spellings which would sound the same and were used in the wrong words by the children (e.g. spelling "tale" as "tail"). We will discuss in detail the first example and consider other examples in a more global manner.

The vowel sound in "pale" was represented in the target words in the sample produced by the children in three different ways: the split digraph "a-e," and the digraphs "ay" and "ai." Only three words ("eight," "reigns" and "great") had a different spelling. How did the children manage to make the correct choice most of the time, out of three possible spellings? In this case, the matter of form, rather than of function, might be what helps the children to make the right choices.

The split digraph "a-e" can only be used when there is a consonant in the word stem, after the vowel sound. So words like "play," "day" and "way" cannot be spelled with the split digraph. When this sound is in the final position in a stem, it is not spelled with the digraph "ai." The MRC database (http://www.psy.uwa.edu.au/Scripts/MRCDatabase/ccMRC.exe) only produces 26 words ending in "ai," most of which we had never encountered before. Those which we do know—e.g. Shanghai and Thai—are not pronounced like the vowel sound in "pale." So, for this vowel sound in the final position of a stem, the spelling should be "ay." The children used "ay" correctly at the end of stems in 96% of the words in this category.

The solution for spelling this sound when it is in the medial position is not as simple as for the final position. Yet the children were still correct much more often than by chance with such words. The words that were spelled with "ai" in this sample of children's writings were *aimed, brain, fail, faint, main, paid, pain, rain, sail, straight, tail, trail, train, wait, waited*. The words "aimed" (n = 1), "paid" (n = 1) and straight" (n = 4) were not spelled correctly. In the remaining words, the vowel sound is followed either by "n" or "l." According to the MRC

Table 3.3 Vowel sounds that are represented by digraphs and their representations in each year group

Appropriate vowel spellings	Year Group	Percentage correct	Percentage words with alternative digraphs	Percentage wrong
pail	2 – N = 165	84	4	12
	3 – N = 162	86	2	11
	4 – N = 146	95	0	5
part	2 – N = 29	90	0	10
	3 – N = 89	88	1	11
	4 – N = 74	95	2	3
peat/eet	2 – N = 63	79	4	17
	3 – N = 92	82	6	12
	4 – N = 127	91	2	7
pear/ai/a-e	2 – N = 51	72	10	18
	3 – N = 100	85	9	6
	4 – N = 60	80	8	12
pile	2 – N = 109	75	7	18
	3 – N = 149	90	4	6
	4 – N = 152	95	3	2
pier	2 – N = 10	60	0	40
	3 – N = 15	80	0	20
	4 – N = 16	100	0	0
port	2 – N = 107	71	5	24
	3 – N = 172	82	11	7
	4 – N = 176	97	1	2
pool	2 – N = 68	62	12	26
	3 – N = 74	72	2	26
	4 – N = 102	98	1	1
foal	2 – N = 134	89	5	6
	3 – N = 184	86	6	8
	4 – N = 174	96	1	3
foul	2 – N = 84	76	6	18
	3 – N = 123	93	1	6
	4 – N = 120	95	0	5
foil	2 – N = 15	73	13.5	13.5
	3 – N = 15	87	6.5	6.5
	4 – N = 7	100	0	0
poor	2 – N = 0	–	–	–
	3 – N = 2	100	0	0
	4 – N = 0	–	–	–
flute	2 – N = 57	67	17	16
	3 – N = 83	85	6	9
	4 – N = 62	87	11	2
furl	2 – N = 46	67	3	30
	3 – N = 79	78	13	9
	4 – N = 86	94	3	3

data base, the rimes "ain" and "ail" are more frequent than the rimes "ane" and "ale": they are used in about 54% and 63%, respectively, of the words ending in these sounds. This slightly greater familiarity of the forms "ain" and "ail" could have helped the children spell with the correct digraph. However, it is quite important to notice that the children produced 90% correct spellings when the word was spelled with the split digraph "a-e" and only 61% correct when the word was spelled with "ai"; spellings such as "tale" for "tail," "fale" for "fail" and "sale" for "sail" were observed in this sample.

In the majority of the words where the sound was deemed as not represented correctly, the children used the letter "a" by itself: this accounted for 70% of the errors. Perhaps they treated this letter as a correct representation of the sound, because of its name, or perhaps they made the mistake of using only the first vowel from the digraph. We cannot tell which strategy described the children's spelling because either possibility would lead to the same result. In 10% of the wrong spellings the children thought of a digraph but produced the wrong form: "whaly/waly" for "whale" and "striagt" for "straight." In the remaining mistakes the children used another single vowel, not "a," but we also observed isolated vowel omissions. Thus most of the mistakes in this category were examples of using a single vowel when a digraph is necessary to represent the vowel sound.

This detailed analysis shows that the children displayed a marked preference for spelling this vowel sound with the split digraph "a-e," which is a sensible preference as, in most cases, this is the correct spelling in medial position. However, the children were also aware that "ai" is a possible spelling in the middle of a stem and tended to use it more frequently when it is actually more frequent, in the rimes "ain" and "ail." Their high level of success with words ending in "ay" suggests some recognition that this is the spelling to be used in the final position. These spellings indicate that children master the representation of this vowel sound through a combination of explicit learning of the function of the digraphs and implicit learning of the forms. The children probably realize that the digraphs "a-e," "ai" and "ay" are used to spell this vowel sound and, indeed, they are explicitly taught this. However, they do not seem to be aware of the positional rules or the differences in frequency across rimes, which is something that they are not taught about.

An overall look at Table 3.3 shows that, on the whole, the younger children made the mistake of misrepresenting the vowel more often than the older children, whose mistakes were more about choosing a wrong representation for the digraph, when more than one option was possible. In many cases, the younger children used a single vowel (most often the first vowel in the digraph), but sometimes they also omitted vowels or inverted the order of the letters (e.g. "striagt" for "straight" and "hlaf" for "half").

The older children's weakest performance was with the vowel sounds like those in the words "pair" and "flute." The most common error they made with the first of these vowel sounds was to use "there" for "their." The word "there" was much more common than "their": "there" was observed a total of 132 times in the children's writing whereas "their" appeared only 18 times—and was spelled as "there" 12 times. Because both of these are function words, their discrimination is based on grammar, and it seems to remain difficult even for older students. It would be of interest to know whether explicit teaching can result in success in eliminating this error during revision, as suggested in the developmental theories of revision (Largy, Fayol, & Lemaire, 1996; Largy, Dédéyan, & Hupet, 2004).

The vowel sound exemplified by "flute" can be spelled in many different ways. Some of the examples observed in the children's writings were *blue, do, flew, flute, group, moon, shoe, through, two, too,* and *who,* which illustrate the great variety of spellings for this vowel sound. This great variety of possible spellings is, in itself, the possible explanation for why this remained a spelling problem for children: learning is most likely dependent on word-specific learning in many of the words that the children used.

The children's spellings revealed that, when they used the digraph "ew," they always did so in the right places. The words where the "ew" was used were most ofter the irregular past tense of a verb: "flew," "grew" and "drew," so one wonders whether this could have helped the children with their use of this digraph.

A mistake that was rather common (12 out of 23 errors made by the children) was to use the sequence of letters "ow," which we would expect to be pronounced quite differently. This could be an inversion error in words like "two" and "who" but it was also observed in "flew," "blue" and "through." The number of mistakes is admittedly small and it is the only consistent example of misspelling by using a digraph that is normally pronounced differently.

Finally, we would also like to comment on the vowel sound represented in "pier." In BBC English, this is a long vowel marked by the letter "r," which itself is not pronounced. One might expect that the most frequent error here would be to omit the "r," but this was not observed in any of the words. Mistakes were made in the choice of vowels (e.g. "bird" for "beard") but in every spelling the children used the letter "r."

Summary

1   Children seem to use single letters to represent vowel sounds accurately from the beginning of their literacy learning. The first graders in Treiman's study were correct 78% of the time. In our study, the children were correct at least 82% of the time from their second year in school, but for most of the vowels spelled with a single letter the level of correct spellings was above 90%.
2   Digraphs are more difficult. However, children learn to use digraphs more easily when the vowel sound contains a change in quality than when it does not.
3   When children do learn to represent specific vowels sounds with digraphs, they often have difficulty in remembering which digraph, especially when there is a choice.
4   These confusions between digraphs often involve choosing between an un-split and a split digraph. When they have to choose between the spellings "a-e," "ai" and "ay," they seem to use a form rule, and use "ay" correctly quite often at the end of words.

Using Pseudowords as well as Real Words

All the research on vowel digraphs that we have reviewed so far concerns real words, which means that we cannot be sure how much the children in these studies were using word-specific knowledge when they got the vowel spellings right or to what extent they relied on understanding the role of digraphs in spelling vowels. Of course, word-specific knowledge must be involved in spelling vowels. From the point of view of grapheme–phoneme rules "snail" and "snale" are equivalent, but only one of them is the correct spelling for this garden mollusc, and we have to rely on word-specific knowledge to know which one that is.

We have to turn to pseudowords, as we did before, to find out how specific or how general is children's learning about vowel digraphs. A pioneering study of children's reading and spelling of pseudowords containing the vowel sounds that are often represented by the split digraph was carried out in the late 1970s by George Marsh and his colleagues in Los Angeles (Marsh, Desberg, & Cooper, 1977; Marsh, Friedman, Welch,

& Desberg, 1980). Marsh and his colleagues found that children were able to read pseudowords containing the split digraph, such as "fise" and "jate," and differentiate them in pronunciation from pseudowords with the same consonant sounds but a short vowel, such as "fis" and "jat." They also found that children were able to distinguish these pseudowords in spelling. The children's ability to do so improved with age and instruction: children in second grade (approximately 7 years of age) did not do very well on this but those in grade five (approximately 10–11 years) succeeded quite systematically on this task, showing the same level of performance as college students.

Thus, Marsh's research provided clear evidence that, from at least about 10 or 11 years of age, children show some form of general learning about the split digraph. However, the number and choice of pseudowords in their study were insufficient for a good description of when and how well children begin to use the split digraph in pseudoword reading and spelling. We will discuss this work in greater detail later, in Chapter 4, when we consider different theories about the acquisition of the split digraph.

There is, as far as we know, only one study of spelling pseudowords that produces enough evidence for a precise description of what children learn about split digraphs. This was done by Megan Patrick (2006) with 7- and 8-year-old children. She gave these children both a reading task and a spelling task. In the reading task, she asked them to read some pseudowords, each of which ended in a split digraph, such as "sape." Since these pseudowords invariably consisted of a "consonant-vowel-consonant-e" sequence, they can be described as CVCe words. She also gave them some other one-syllable pseudowords to read, like "fap," which did not contain a split digraph (CVC words). In the spelling task, she asked the children to spell one syllable pseudowords which she dictated to them. The vowel sounds were long in some of these pseudowords and short in others.

Megan Patrick wanted to know whether, in the reading task, the children would pronounce the vowel sound as long in the split digraph pseudowords and as short in the other pseudowords. In the spelling task her aim was to see if the children would use the split digraph with long-vowel pseudowords but not with short-vowel ones.

If children rely just on word-specific learning in order to read and write split digraph words correctly, they would only be able to cope with words that are familiar to them. So, this kind of learning would be no use to them when they read and write pseudowords. They would not be able to apply what they have learned about specific words to these pseudowords which they have never met before. It follows that their reading and spelling of the vowel sounds in pseudowords would be completely random. On the other hand, if children learn a general and an abstract rule about the function of split digraphs, they should be able to apply it to completely new material, such as pseudowords, with no difficulty at all.

However, although success in these pseudoword tasks would certainly rule out the possibility that children learn to read and spell split digraph words entirely on a word-specific basis, it would not establish that they do use abstract rules. There is another possible way to read and write split digraphs successfully even in pseudowords, and that is to learn specific letter sequences. Children may simply learn a set of correspondences, this time between a number of specific letter sequences and the particular sound that they are associated with: they may learn that the letter sequence "-ate" usually represents one specific sequence of sounds, "-ame" another, "-ope" another, and so on. This is not abstract learning. Although each of these sequences occurs in several different words, children who just learn about the links between specific sequences that contain a split digraph will find out nothing in general about the effect of the final "e" on the preceding vowel sound. They will be very far from knowing anything like "the big idea" behind the split digraph.

A child's chances of learning specific associations like these would be bound to depend heavily on how often the child encounters them in reading. The more frequently she encounters a particular split digraph sequence, like "-ame," the more likely it is that she will associate it with the sound that it usually represents. On the other hand, if a child learns and uses an abstract spelling rule (the big idea) for the split digraph, frequency should make no difference. The rule applies equally to totally unfamiliar sequences and to sequences that crop up all the time.

In fact, the frequency of different letter sequences which contain split digraphs varies a great deal. For example, the number of times that the split digraph letter sequences "-ake" and "-ame" can be found in the words that appear in books for children is rather high: "-ake" occurs 3,882 times and "-ame" 3,007 times in one million words, according to the excellent word-count developed by a research team in the University of Essex (see reference to the site earlier on in this chapter). In contrast, other split digraph sequences such as "-ape" and "-age" occur far less often in children's texts: 228 and 208 times in 1,000,000 respectively.

Megan Patrick took advantage of these differences in frequency. In her reading task, she asked the children to read pseudowords with digraph sequences that are very common and other pseudowords with sequences that hardly occur at all. In much the same way, some of the pseudowords that she dictated in her spelling task ended in sounds that could be represented by very common letter sequences while others could only be represented by infrequent letter sequences. Her reason for comparing very common associations between specific letter sequences and sounds with very rare ones was, of course, to contrast specific with abstract learning.

The first, and probably the most important, result in this study was that these 7- and 8-year-old children did remarkably well. Despite working with entirely unfamiliar material, they read the split digraph pseudowords as long vowel words far more often than they did with the pseudowords that did not contain a split digraph. In fact, they hardly ever pronounced the vowel sounds in CVC words as long, though they did so often when they read the CVCe words. In the spelling task, in much the same way, they used the split digraph mainly in response to long vowel words. They almost never represented short vowel pseudo-words as CVCe words. This pattern of results shows that they depend on more than just word-specific associations to distinguish between long and short vowels both in reading and in writing.

What about frequency? This also had an effect. The frequent split digraph sequences were much easier to read and much easier to write than the infrequent ones. In reading and in spelling the vast majority of the children did better with the common than with the rare letter sequences. So, here is evidence for specific learning as well. The more often children encounter a particular digraph sequence in books and in the classroom, the better they are at deciphering it correctly and repro-ducing it in the right place.

An apparent mix of two quite different kinds of knowledge in young children naturally provokes the question: does one kind of knowledge lead to the other? In this case they may be independent, or they may not. Children are taught about the split digraph rule, and at the same time they encounter some specific split digraph patterns far more than others. Another possibility is that children initially learn about specific sequences and later use this knowledge to abstract more general rules. When, eventually, they learn the right sound, not just for "-ame" but also for "-ape," they could spot that these two sounds share a common vowel sound and that they are represented by two different letter se-quences which nevertheless share the same split digraph. We shall re-turn to this question in the next chapter, where we will discuss theories and the evidence relevant to how children learn about the split digraph. However, before we turn to these issues, we want to make one more point about split digraphs and see whether it really matters whether children learn them or not.

Summary

1 Pseudoword spelling studies are an essential tool in research on children's knowledge of the function of the split digraph.
2 Initial research by Marsh and his colleagues did establish that many children in their third year of learning to read had already established a rule-like knowledge of the split digraph.
3 Recent research has shown that 7- and 8-year-old English children learn associations between specific and common letter sequences like "-ame" and particular VC (rime) sounds.
4 This same research establishes that children of this age also learn a more abstract rule about the vowel sound in split digraphs: this is that, for example "-a," followed by any consonant, followed by "e" signifies the long vowel sound that we find in words like "blame."

The Importance of the Split Digraph in English

Some of the research that we presented in the previous sections in this chapter and in the previous chapter suggests that young literacy learners seem to have an initial bias to use one-to-one letter–sound correspondences and find it more difficult to work with grapheme–phoneme correspondences that differ from these simple ones. The need to use even consonant digraphs that are fairly consistent, like "ch," increases the number of spelling errors that children make. This increase in the number of errors made is even more noticeable if the children happen to be poor readers.

Among the different vowel digraphs, we paid special attention to the split digraphs, which involve a more complex rule than those where the two letters are written in sequence. We now want to make the case that this is not a minor detail in children's reading and spelling development: we argue that mastering the split digraph is a marker of great progress in word reading and spelling. If this is right, then a measure of the children's progress in reading and spelling the split digraph should be strongly related to a general measure of their reading and spelling ability, even though the general measure contains a large variety of words that present children with diverse types of reading and spelling difficulty.

The Schonell Word Reading and Spelling Test (Schonell & Goodacre, 1971) is a measure of children's general progress. It was not designed to identify children's learning of the split digraphs but relied on a completely different conception for the choice of words: because children find less familiar and long words more difficult to read and spell, the graded difficulty of the test is based on word familiarity and word length. The reading test starts with words like "tree," "little," and "book" and includes words like "evangelical," "grotesque," "homonym," "procrastinate," "metamorphosis," "somnambulist," "bibliography" and "idiosyncrasy" at the end—all of which can be read using simple letter–sound correspondences but are long and infrequent.

In order to see how well children's mastery of the split digraph relates to their general reading and spelling development, we analysed the connection between an assessment of their performance on the split digraph and their performance on the Schonell. We (Nunes, Bryant, & Olsson, 2003) developed an assessment of children's reading and spelling of words that contained the vowel sounds represented by the split digraphs "a-e," "i-e," "o-e" and "u-e" and presented this assessment to 468 children in eight schools in London. The children were in their third to sixth year of school and their age range was from about 7 to 11 years. The mean age of the children in the third year of school was 7y10m and this mean increased by about one year for each year of school; the mean for the children in their sixth year was 10y10m. The schools covered a range of abilities and the children's performance in the Schonell Word Reading Test showed this variation well.

Our assessment of the children's ability to read long vowels was designed to tap their decoding ability as much as possible. In order to accomplish this, we chose words which contained the split digraph and which, if the vowel were misread, would still result in reading another word. Our words were: "cuter," "huge," "fate," "taped," "site," "hope" and "cute," which, if misread, would be pronounced as "cutter," "hug," "fat," "tapped," "sit," "hop" and "cut." We chose to use these words because we did not want the children to use information extraneous to the decoding process itself when pronouncing the word. For example, if a child encounters the word "grape" and misreads the split digraph, "grape" would be read as "grap." The child would know that "grap" is not a word, and could try to find a plausible word for this spelling by varying the pronunciation of the vowel, and through this process manage to read "grape." The child's success in this item would be a product of two things: some decoding skill, used to deal with the consonants in the word "grape," and lexical knowledge, i.e. knowledge of what is a word and what is not a word. Research actually shows that children use lexical knowledge in decoding: when they are shown two pseudowords, one that sounds like a word (e.g. "poast") and one that does not (e.g. "loast"), they are much more likely to say that those that sound like real words are actually words (Johnston, Rugg, & Scott, 1988).

Thus, choosing the right type of word for our test was an important part of our attempt to tap decoding ability directly as possible. These seven words were part of a longer list of 30 words, which included also simple words that could be read using one-to-one letter–sound correspondences and words with other digraphs (e.g. "dishwasher") as well as doublets (e.g. "hopper"). Thus the children were not being cued into looking for the split digraph as it was not prominent in the list.

We also asked the children to read seven pseudowords: "smaped," "sofe," "duter," "pive," "daver," "mive" and "dape." The pronunciation of pseudowords cannot be corrected by using lexical knowledge—and the children were well aware of the fact that these were invented by us, that they were not words which they had encountered before. Again, the pseudowords were part of a longer list of pseudowords, some of which could be read by using simple one-to-one letter–sound correspondences and others which required the use of grapheme–phoneme correspondences where the grapheme was composed of more than one letter (e.g. "kished"). Thus, the assessment of long-vowel reading included 7 words and 7 pseudowords, and produced a score that could vary between 0 and 14, by adding together the number of correctly decoded words and pseudowords.

In order to test whether the children's progress in reading the split digraphs is important, we analysed the relationship between the children's scores in reading these 14 items and their scores in the Schonell Word Reading Test. If our assessment is a marker of important progress in word reading in general, we should find a strong relationship between our assessment and a general word reading test.

The strength of the relationship between tests is measured by correlations. A perfect relationship, where all the scores in one test can be predicted if you know the scores on the other test, corresponds to a statistic—termed a correlation—with the value of 1. The complete absence of a connection between two tests corresponds to a correlation of 0. But a correlation of 1 between two tests is a great rarity. Even when we give the same test twice to the same group of children, the correlation is not equal to 1. We gave the Schonell Word Reading Test twice to the whole sample of children in this study with an interval of four months between the two testing occasions. The correlation between the children's results on the first and the second occasion was .95. This is a striking result: most tests do not show such strong test–retest correlations, particularly when the testing occasions are separated by four months, because children's performance on tests can fluctuate for several reasons (e.g. they may be more tired, or more distractible, or less motivated on one occasion than the other). When we examined the correlation between our assessment of the children's ability to read words with long vowels and the Schonell Word Reading Test, we found that, when the tests were separated by the same interval of four months, the correlation between our assessment and the Schonell was .83. This means that our test gave a very good indication of how well the children would perform on the Schonell four months later. Many test–retest correlations obtained by giving the same test twice four months apart will not show an association stronger than this one.

This strong relationship between our assessment and the Schonell Word Reading Test means that our assessment picks up something important about children's progress in reading between the ages of 7 and 11 years. We think that the assessment is sensitive to the fact that the children's ability to work with more complex grapheme–phoneme correspondences is developing during this period: our long-vowel reading test is one way of measuring this development.

We observed similar results when we asked the children to spell a list of nine words, all of which contained split digraphs. In some of these, the split digraph came at the end of the word (e.g. "white") and in others in the middle of the word but at the end of a root-word (e.g. "baseball," "pavement"). For the purposes of this analysis, we considered only whether the child had used the split digraph correctly. For example, if when children spelled "pavemunt," with the split digraph correctly but the suffix "-ment" incorrectly spelled, we still gave them a point for the correct spelling of the split digraph.

The correlation between the children's scores on our spelling assessment of the use of the split digraph and their performance on the Schonell Word Spelling Test four months later was very high (r = .82). This confirms our conclusion that children's progress in the split digraph is indeed an indicator of an important progress, and now we can say that this is true of progress both in word reading and spelling.

Summary

The importance that we attributed to children's progress in the split digraph was justified. This is not a small detail in the growth of their ability to read and spell words correctly. It is a sign of significant progress in decoding and spelling skills.

Poor Readers and Split Digraphs

In Chapter 2, we referred to a study (Nunes & Aidinis, 1999) which showed that poor readers were much worse than normal readers of the same reading age—who were, consequently, younger than the poor readers—at spelling words that include the consonant digraphs "sh" and "ch." In that study, we used data from a standardized test, and that did not give us sufficient information to compare good and poor readers on the split digraph.

However, we were able to give our assessment of children's perform-ance on the split digraph to a group of 59 poor readers and to compare their performance to that of the normal readers who participated in our earlier study (Nunes, Bryant & Olsson, 2003). The poor readers were selected (for an intervention study, which we report in Chapter 7) on the basis of their having very low reading and spelling ages for their chronological age, in spite of an average performance in an intelligence test. Their average chronological age was 10y9m with a range of 8y10m–11y1m. Their reading age (assessed by the WORD Reading Test) was in the range of 6 years–9y6m and their spelling age (assessed by the WORD Spelling Test) 7y3m–8y9m. Their average reading delay was 2y3m and their average spelling delay 2y5m.

In order to compare the poor readers with good readers of compar-able reading ability, we selected from the previous study all the children whose chronological age was within the same range of the poor readers' reading age and whose own reading scores did not show a delay (i.e. there was not a large and negative discrepancy between their reading age and their chronological age). This selection resulted in a sample of 236 normal readers, to be compared with the 59 poor readers. The mean age of the normal readers was 8y5m: that is, they were on average 2y4m younger than the poor readers.

Our reading assessment produces two scores: one for the children's performance in reading words that do not involve the split digraph, which we call *basic reading score*, and one for their performance in reading words with split digraphs. Similarly, our spelling assessment provides two scores, one for spelling words without the split digraph, the *basic spelling score*, and one for words with the split digraph. We wanted to know whether the poor readers would score significantly lower than the normal readers in words with the split digraph than one would expect from their performance in the basic reading and spelling assessments. Putting it another way, the question was whether the poor readers make significantly more mistakes in words with the split digraph than one would expect from their basic level of reading and spelling.

In order to answer this question, we obtain scores that are the difference between how well we expect each child to read or spell words with split digraphs, given the child's own scores in the basic reading and spelling assessment. This discrepancy score would be 0 if the children managed in the split digraph tests just as well as we would expect from their scores on the basic tests; it would be negative if the children did less well on the split digraph than expected, and positive if the children did better on the split digraph than expected.

The results of the comparison between normal and poor readers can be summarized quite easily. The normal readers' discrepancy scores on the split digraph tasks did not differ much from what was expected of them, given their basic reading and spelling ability. Their discrepancy scores were, on average, equal to zero (to be precise, -0.01 for reading and -0.09 for spelling).

The same was true of the scores of the poor readers in *reading* words with the split digraph: the average discrepancy score for them is also close to zero (more precisely, 0.07). Their score did not differ much from what was expected from their basic reading ability. In contrast, their scores in *spelling* words with the split digraph were significantly worse than what we would expect from their basic spelling ability: their discrepancy score for spelling words with the split digraph was -0.35, which is about four times larger than the discrepancy score for the normal readers (a difference that was statistically highly significant). This means that poor readers do find it much more difficult than normal readers of the same reading ability to spell words with the split digraph.

The specific reason for poor readers' unexpected and extra difficulty with split digraphs is not known yet. However, this finding has a clear educational implication: poor readers probably need larger amounts of specific teaching about the split digraph than normal readers need in order to conquer this aspect of English spelling. Our next chapter considers how this specific teaching might be offered to children.

Summary

1   Children learn to represent vowels with single letters in English before they learn about digraph spellings for vowel sounds.

2 The system of using digraphs to represent vowels is a relatively complex one, partly because there are so many vowel sounds and so few single letters to represent vowels and partly because of the existence of split digraphs (e.g. "a-e" as in "tame" and "o-e" as in "hope").

3 One problem for children is to choose between different digraphs that represent the same vowel sound (e.g. "sope" vs. "soap"). Children need to rely on their word-specific knowledge to make these choices but in some cases they can also use other information: when they must choose between "a-e," "ai" and "ay" and the vowel sound is at the end of the word, they can use a form rule which indicates that "ay" is the correct choice.

4 Research done with pseudowords shows that children learn about the split digraph in a relatively abstract way and also rely on more specific learning. They learn to associate particular sequences, especially common ones, like "-ame" with particular VC (rime) sounds, and, at a more abstract level, they also begin to learn that "a-e" and "o-e" sequences, for example, represent long *a* and long *o* sounds, whatever the intervening consonant letter.

5 There is a striking relation between children's general progress in reading and spelling and their understanding and correct use of the split digraph. This suggests that the step that English-speaking children take when they conquer the split digraph marks a crucial change in the process of their becoming literate.

6 Children who have fallen behind in learning to read and spell have a particular difficulty with the split digraph: they make more mistakes in spelling split digraph words than one would expect from their spelling of other words. This particular difficulty is a matter of concern, but it also strengthens our conclusion about the importance of the split digraph in the development of children's literacy.

Acknowledgements

We are very grateful to Melanie Good and Deborah Evans for their work on the analysis of children's vowel spellings described in this chapter.

Chapter 4

How Children Learn and Can Be Taught about Conditional Rules

We have seen that it takes children some time to learn how to interpret digraphs and how to use them in their own writing. This learning is a mixture of specific and rather abstract knowledge. For example, young children learn a great deal about specific split digraph sequences, especially common ones like "-ame." However, they also pick up some fairly abstract knowledge about the role of the final "e" in the split digraph, and this is what allows them to read and write some split digraph sequences which are so unusual that they have probably have never come across them before.

These observations prompt an obvious but important question. We need to know how children learn in this mixed way. What experiences underlie this learning? How do they manage to take this major developmental step? If we can find an answer to these questions, we will be in a much better position than before to teach children about graphemes and phonemes, and thus to help them over a hurdle which some of them find quite difficult.

We begin this chapter with a review of the early work on how children master the step from letter–sound correspondences to grapheme–phoneme correspondences. In the second section of the chapter, we describe work that gives some insight into the processes that support children's mastery of this important developmental step. Finally, we review past work on teaching and present our own recent work, carried out in interaction with teachers and aimed at answering their questions about how to teach spelling as well as our own theoretical questions about processes in the development of spelling.

Different Ideas that Children Need to Use to Master Word Reading and Spelling

Both teachers and researchers have been interested in how children learn to read and spell words for more than a century. However, as often happens in education, teachers taught reading and spelling for many years before there were any systematic attempts to formulate explicit theories about how children learn to read and spell and about the connection between reading and spelling. It is only possible to develop such systematic knowledge when we have measures that can be used to describe children's progress—and these were not available until Fred Schonell (Schonell & Schonell, 1950), a pioneer in the study of English spelling, produced standardized tests of word reading and spelling. His tests contain 100 words each, which are graded in what he expected to be levels of difficulty. When children make 10 consecutive errors, we interrupt the test as it is unlikely that they will get any more words right.

An analysis of his choice of words suggests that his implicit model of what made words more difficult to read and spell was based on word length and familiarity. Both the reading and spelling test start with short and frequent words; word length increases and familiarity decreases as the test progresses. Subsequent research does show that these are important aspects in determining item difficulty in reading and spelling. In Chapter 3, for example, we described how the frequency of different rimes is related to children's success in reading and spelling pseudowords that contain split digraphs. Thus there is clear support for the idea that less familiar items are more difficult than more familiar ones. There is also support for the idea that word length affects spelling success in English: we (Nunes & Aidinis, 1999) observed that both normal and poor spellers make more mistakes in long words than in short words, even if the long words' spelling is entirely predictable from letter–sound correspondences. So Schonell's assessments continue to be of value in providing a measure of children's general word spelling and reading ability. However, there are now different models of progress, which take other factors into account and are based on the different types of regularity of English spelling and children's mastery of these different sorts of rules.

Some researchers—for example, Linnea Ehri, George Marsh and Uta Frith—proposed that the first words that children learn to read and write may be learned as wholes. Most of us will know children who can, for example, write their own names correctly and recognize some written words (for example, Merry Christmas) when they see them, without much knowledge of how to read and spell other words. This is described as "logographic" knowledge of words, to indicate that the words are known as wholes, without the support of analytic processes that can facilitate the transfer of knowledge from these words to other, similar words. There is much controversy regarding whether this is a proper first step into reading and spelling or just the learning of isolated items, which has no role in further learning and thus is not necessarily observed in many children. This controversy does not need to concern us here, as we are focusing on children's word reading and spelling beyond the first steps.

It is actually uncontroversial that children do not continue to learn to read and spell words simply by rote, even if some approaches to the teaching of spelling are based on the idea of rote learning (for a comment on this, see Nunes & Bryant, 2006). Different arguments and sources of evidence converge to support the idea that words are not learned singly and by rote. Claiborne (1989), for example, argued that there are about 450,000 English words in current use, and it would be a monumental task to learn all of them by rote. This is a convincing argument, but there is also empirical evidence to support the idea that children learn basic consistencies in letter–sound correspondences and use this knowledge to read and spell words which they have never seen in print before—and, therefore could not have learned by rote. As we showed in Chapters 2 and 3, children can correctly read and spell pseudowords, i.e. made-up sequences of sounds which are not actual words in English—and this means that they must be able to use grapheme–phoneme correspondences as they have never seen these made-up words before. Furthermore, although familiarity is important, as indicated earlier on, letter–sound regularity is more important than familiarity. Marsh and his colleagues (1980) showed that children in second (about 7 years) and fourth grade (about 9 years) were better at reading and spelling pseudowords with regular letter–sound correspondences than real words which they had encountered before but which contained more difficult patterns of correspondence or were irregular. So it is also uncontroversial that children form basic concepts about how oral and written words are connected to each other and use these concepts to read and spell words as well as pseudowords. There are so many reviews of the importance of children's learning of letter–sound correspondences that we do not dwell on this issue here (see, for example, Ehri, 2005; National Reading Panel, 2000; Torgerson, Brooks, & Hall, 2006).

However, there is some controversy regarding the nature of the concepts that they form and whether the changes in the children's reading and spelling should be described as "developmental stages." In this section, we consider first the different types of concepts that the children need to form in order to master word reading and spelling in English and only later discuss whether or not there is a case for thinking about developmental stages.

In Chapters 2 and 3 we suggested that there are two types of units that children need to use in reading and spelling: one-to-one letter–sound correspondences and grapheme–phoneme correspondences that are not one-to-one. We think that these different types of correspondences are different concepts of how spoken and written words relate to each other. The one-to-one correspondence conception is termed in the literature "alphabetic" in order to reflect the idea of letters representing sounds in a simple way and we will use here the expression "alphabetic conception" for the sake of brevity.

When children use concepts that go beyond this simple correspondence, different terms have been used in the literature—for example, "conditional rules"—which is the term we use here—or "orthographic stage." In the previous chapters we focused on doublets and digraphs— "sh," "ch" and the split digraphs "a-e," "i-e," "o-e," and "u-e"—as examples of reading and spelling consistencies that require children to go beyond the alphabetic conception and we referred to these cases as involving a conditional rule, i.e. a rule that requires looking beyond the letter in order to know how it is pronounced in reading or in order to make a decision about spelling. We hinted previously that there are different types of conditional rules—some based on the words' sounds and others based on morphemes—but we will consider only phonological conditional rules in this chapter. From the analysis of children's reading and spelling in those chapters, we concluded that young children have a bias towards using an alphabetic conception in reading and spelling but that this is not all that they do. Children in their second year of school already recognize, for example, that certain sounds cannot be represented by a single letter and use digraphs more often than single letters to represent these sounds. However, they do make more mistakes with these words—and particularly with the split digraph—than with words that can be written alphabetically. So the use of conditional rules does represent a stumbling block for children. Are there other examples of conditional rules and are they also more difficult for children?

Other examples of conditional rules in reading and spelling have been studied previously. Marsh and his colleagues analysed whether children were able to use the "C-rule" in reading (1977) and in spelling (1980) pseudowords. In reading, the "C-rule" is that, when the letter "c" is followed by "e" or "i," it is pronounced as /s/; when it is followed by "a," "o," "u" or a consonant, it is pronounced as /k/. The participants in these studies were in grades 2 (about 7 years), 5 (about 10 years) or in college. The second graders were significantly worse than the other participants in using simple alphabetic correspondences both in reading and spelling but the fifth graders and college students did not differ from each other in the use of alphabetic correspondences. Second grade children were also significantly worse at using the conditional "C-rule" in reading than using simple alphabetic correspondences but fifth graders and college students used alphabetic rules and the conditional C-rule equally well.

Marsh and his colleagues also showed that young children have a strong bias towards pronouncing the "c" as /k/: there was little difference in the number of correct responses given by the younger and older participants when the letter "c" should be pronounced as /k/ but a large number of errors was observed among the younger children when it had to be pronounced as /s/. The younger children seemed to work with an alphabetic conception when they generated the pronunciation of the pseudowords and attributed the pronunciation /k/ to the letter "c." This could be an effect of familiarity, since the letter "c" appears much more often before "a," "o" and "u," when it is pronounced as /k/ than before "e" and "i," when it is pronounced as /s/. In the MRC data base, we found over 3,300 words where the "c" appeared before "a," "o" or "u" and less than 2,000 where it appeared before "e" and "i." If we remember that "c" is also pronounced as /k/ before consonants and at the end of words, it is clear that it is much more often pronounced as /k/ than /s/. The young children's bias towards this pronunciation is, therefore, justified in terms of familiarity. However, they were not always wrong and did get some of the "ce" and "ci" pseudowords right. The older participants were better at using this conditional concept, and they were consequently more able to read correctly the pseudowords where the "c" was followed by "e" or "i."

So Marsh's work with a different type of rule that requires going beyond simple correspondences confirms the idea that children have a bias towards working with an alphabetic conception in reading, and become more skilled at looking beyond it later in their school lives.

The "C-rule" is more complicated in spelling than in reading. Almost all the words that contain the sound /k/ followed by "e" or "i" are spelled with the letter "k" (with very few exceptions: e.g. "scheme") but if the sound /k/ is followed by other letters, one could use either the letter "c" or the letter "k." The letter "c" is the most frequently used of the two: for example, "ka" appeared in 51 unique words in the MRC data base whereas "ca" appeared in 991 words in the same data base; "ko" appeared in only 12 words whereas "co" appeared in 1,960; and "ku" appeared in 8 words whereas "cu" appeared in 381. Marsh and his colleagues did not design their study in order to analyse the use of the "C-rule" in spelling properly. They only asked the participants to spell pseudowords where the /k/ sound was followed by the letters "a" and "u." So both "k" and "c" would be correct in this context. The fifth graders and college students used the letter "c" significantly more often than the second graders, but this does not provide evidence for the "C-rule." In order to show that the older participants were using the "C-rule," Marsh and his colleagues would have to demonstrate that they used "k" more often before "e" and "i." So we cannot be sure that this result really shows the use of a conditional rule in spelling. This could be simply the result of familiarity.

We want to introduce another type of conditional rule—and a much more complex one—that was described by Henderson (1990; first published in 1985) on the basis of observations of difficulties displayed by individual children, and later on, more systematically, by Schlagal (1992): syllable juncture. Syllable juncture requires the children to "think across syllables, anticipating the effect that the addition or deletion of a specific letter will have upon the target word" (Shlagal, 1992, p. 46). We mentioned briefly the issue of syllable juncture in Chapter 2 when we referred to the doubling of a final consonant in a verb to preserve the vowel pronunciation in the past form—for example, "tap"–"tapped" and "hop"–"hopped." Davis' work with doublets (see Chapter 2) did not cover these cases because she was working with pseudowords: so she only looked at the conditional rules involved in the pronunciation and spelling of long and short vowels before single consonants or doublets. The examples considered by Shlagal differ because the children will know a base form—for example, the present tense of a verb—and may well know that it has a single consonant. What they need to learn is that by adding a suffix to it, the pronunciation will change, unless they change the spelling of the stem.

The conditional rules of syllable juncture can be about doubling consonants but also about dropping letters (or, less often, the substitution of letters, e.g. "y" being replaced by "i"). For example, if we added the suffix "ed" to the verb "dance" to form its past without dropping the "e," we would have the form "danceed," and this would change the vowel pronunciation and shift the stress in this word. The final "e" in the stem is dropped when the suffix that is added starts with "e" or "i" and would thus create a vowel digraph: for example, we need to drop the final "e" in the words "dancer," "dancing" and "hedging": otherwise we would end up with the vowel digraphs "ee" and "ei." In contrast, we need to retain the "e" in "graceful" and "manageable" in order to maintain the pronunciation of the "c" and the "g."

Although the concept of syllable juncture involves morphemes—it is called into play exactly when a prefix or a suffix is added to a base form—syllable juncture concepts are about preserving the pronunciation of a word, and thus we consider them in this chapter. Unfortunately, there is a paucity of work on syllable juncture. The little work that there is suggests that it is difficult.

Shlagal indicates that the children in the schools where he carried out his work received instruction on syllable juncture, both doubling and the e-drop operation, from second and third grade on. However, these errors were prominent throughout primary school. Schlagal does not present his results by grade level but by level in spelling development. The children made progressively fewer errors with the e-drop rule as they progressed in spelling: these errors represented 15% of the spelling errors at their level III of spelling development and only 3% at level VI. In contrast, consonant doubling errors did not decrease in importance across spelling levels.

The interpretation of Shlagal's findings is not straightforward because the words that the children spelled at the different levels were not the same. However, the results suggest that looking across syllables was more difficult for the children in this study than looking at digraphs, and that the split digraphs were also more difficult than the digraphs where the letters are not split.

Summary

1 The development of children's reading and spelling is not simply a matter of becoming able to deal with longer and less familiar words: they need to master different ideas about how to approach word reading and spelling.
2 Three types of concepts are necessary for word reading and spelling. The simplest concept, the alphabetic one, involves looking at letters one at a time and considering their one-to-one correspondence to sounds. The second concept involves looking beyond one-to-one

correspondences, to the next letters, and using conditional rules. The third conception involves looking beyond the syllable.

3   Young children have a bias towards using an alphabetic conception in reading and spelling words. However, this is not all that young children can do: as early as their second year in school, they realize that some sounds cannot be represented by a single letter and they can also make some use conditional rules, but they find it significantly more difficult to do so than to work with an alphabetic conception.

4   Familiarity plays an important role in the learning of sequences that require going beyond the alphabetic conception: children learn specific things as well as more abstract rules at the same time.

5   Finally, the little evidence to date on syllable juncture suggests that this is an even bigger challenge to children: even children who were taught about syllable juncture in school continued to make mistakes throughout primary school with some aspects of syllable juncture, though they showed improvement with the e-drop rule that avoids the inappropriate use of digraphs.

We now turn to the question of whether these are developmental stages or not.

Is it useful to think of progress in word reading and spelling as representing different developmental stages? It cannot be doubted that children's learning about conditional rules is an important part of their intellectual development. Naturally, therefore, we should try to understand how this change happens and what makes it happen. Over the years, several psychologists and educationalists have responded to this theoretical challenge, and many of their theories about children's growing knowledge of grapheme–phoneme rules have taken the form of stage theories. Stage theories hold that the vast majority of children go through an orderly sequence of changes in learning how to spell as they grow older.

The general idea of developmental stages was a common and widely accepted one at the time that most of these theories were first produced. It remains a powerful idea today, but it is less popular than it was and it has fallen out of favour with many psychologists who argue that it gives a misleading account of children's development. So, it is worth spending a bit of time considering the advantages and disadvantages of the idea of stages before going on to stage theory accounts of learning to spell.

Jean Piaget was certainly the most persuasive and most successful champion of the idea that human development consists of an ordered sequence of stages. The object of children's learning in his theory was logic and the question was whether children think logically from birth or whether their ability to think logically develops. To use one of Piaget's best-known studies, we consider briefly children's willingness to make inferences about numerical equivalence without counting. When two sets of objects are in one-to-one correspondence, for every item in one set there is an item in the other and vice versa: when this is the case the two sets, of course, are the same in number, and will be so however you rearrange them, provided that you don't add any objects or subtract any from either set. Piaget claimed that it takes children many years to understand this necessary relation between one-to-one correspondence and numerical equivalence—a claim that is still controversial. However, the important point here is that there is a contradiction between believing that sets that were in one-to-one correspondence are no longer numerically equivalent when you move the elements about without adding and subtracting anything and seeing the necessary equivalence between them. Going from not seeing this equivalence to believing that it is necessary is a qualitative change. It is a change from believing "not A" to believing "A." This notion of qualitative changes was at the heart of Piaget's theory of intellectual development and also at the heart of his theoretical explanations for development: children develop as a result of perceiving contradictions or conflicts between two different ideas.

We think that it is not possible to import Piaget's conception of developmental stages to the analysis of the development of word reading and spelling without modifying it. We argued in the previous section that children need to consider one-to-one correspondences between letters and sounds *as well as* conditional rules. Conditional rules do not contradict the alphabetic conception of the script but rather refine it. When children become more at ease with conditional rules, they do not abandon previously learned letter–sound correspondences but encompass these into a broader system. If we recognize this difference, a stage theory of the development of word reading and spelling could simply indicate that the majority of children find alphabetic correspondences easier than conditional rules and conquer alphabetic correspondences before they master conditional rules. Consequently, young children would show a bias towards treating word reading and spelling in accordance with the alphabetic conception.

But there is one further point to make about stage theories of spelling. They fall into two categories. One kind of stage theory simply describes a sequence of stages in children's spelling. The other kind describes an ordered sequence of stages too, but also makes a statement about what causes children to make their way from one stage to another. We will present an example of each kind of theory.

A good example of a non-causal spelling theory was one of the first on the scene. This was Gentry's hypothesis that children go through five stages in spelling. Table 4.1 sets out the typical ways in which children in these stages would spell digraph and split digraph words. The first stage, the pre-communicative stage, need not concern us. The child simply writes letters apparently haphazardly that have nothing to do with the words' sounds. In the next two stages the child appears to write a phonetic transcription. At first (the semi-phonetic stage) she does so incompletely, representing some of the sounds with appropriate letters ("ac" for "lake"), but leaving other sounds out. Later (the phonetic stage) she writes letters for all the sounds, usually assigning a letter to each phoneme ("nam" for "name"). In this stage, the child ignores conventional spellings and orthographic rules, and therefore fails with digraphs. This pattern of spelling works well with simple words like "cat" but fails with digraphs.

Gentry called the fourth stage in his theory "transitional." The child who has reached this stage has learned and has begun to use digraphs (which he refers to as "orthographic conventions") but not always the right ones and in the right place. She is likely to write "feal" instead of "feel" and "stail" instead of "stale." The final stage ("correct spelling") is perfection or near perfection. The children use orthographic conventions and rules and apply the right conventions and rules to the right

Table 4.1 The five stages in Gentry's hypothesis about spelling

1. Pre-communicative	letter-like written symbols stand for words	
2. Semi-phonetic	partial sounding out	"am" for "name"
3. Phonetic	accurate sounding out	"lit" for "light" "eg" for "egg"
4. Transitional	some orthographic and morphemic conventions used, but not always correctly	"eeg" for "egg" "naem" for "name"
5. Correct	coherent understanding of phonemic and morphemic spelling rules and of orthographic conventions	

words. Although Gentry does not make this clear, the difference between the last two stages must depend quite heavily on word-specific knowledge. In terms of orthographic rules, the two spellings "feel" and "feal" are both quite appropriate, because the digraphs "ee" and "ea" are equally good ways of spelling the same sound. The only way any one can say which of the two is right is through specific knowledge of the spelling of that particular written word.

In our view, the main thrust of this theory is the idea that children learn to use the traditional letter–sound relationships on a one-to-one basis, before they do anything else. Until they can represent each phoneme in the word with a reasonably appropriate alphabetic letter, they pay no attention to digraphs or to any other spelling sequences or to the spelling of specific words or to any orthographic rules. In fact, some of the evidence that we have reviewed in the previous chapter suggests that this part of the Gentry theory is most unlikely to be right. Patrick's (2006) study showed that even beginning spellers manage to learn specific split digraphs that are very common fairly well and also show some glimmerings of knowledge about the split digraph rule. A theory of stages is about the more abstract knowledge that children develop about word reading and writing but evidence suggests that it must leave room also for specific knowledge of familiar letter sequences and very common items, even if these are not yet connected to more abstract knowledge of rules.

Some doubt has also been expressed about one of Gentry's five stages. Varnhagen, McCallam and Burstow (1997) looked at stories written by Canadian children whose ages ranged from 6 to 11 years and reported that they could find no evidence for the transitional stage—the stage at which Gentry claimed that children began to produce orthographic sequences like digraphs, but often used the wrong sequence (e.g. by writing "hope" as "hoap") when they did so. In the Canadian study, however, when the children did use digraphs to represent a vowel, they tended to use the right one. We also observed (see Table 3.3, Chapter 3) that, for all of the vowels that must be represented by a digraph, the children's most frequent choice was the correct one, not an alternative spelling. This is a remarkable observation, and it is worth noting that it demonstrates that the children had to be relying largely on word-specific knowledge. The sequence "-oap" is a perfectly respectable way of spelling the rime sound in "hope." It just happens to be the wrong sequence for "hope," and the only way to know this is to remember the particular digraph that belongs to this specific word.

Varnhagen and her colleagues also criticized the Gentry stage theory, and by implication other stage theories, on the grounds that the spellings in their collection of children's writing were frequently incon-sistent. Often the same child would write some split digraph words correctly but would leave out the final "e" in others (e.g. "cam" for "came"). These experimenters argued that, from the point of view of Gentry's theory, children like this are neither fish nor fowl, since they show signs of being at two quite different stages at the same time. However, stage theories have always dealt easily with evidence that many children respond at quite different levels at roughly the same time. According to Piaget, who first suggested the idea of stages in cognitive development, some children are consistent, others not. Piaget reported that when children first acquire a new intellectual capacity, like under-standing one-to-one correspondence, they use it only intermittently and inconsistently and they are easily dissuaded from doing so by quite flimsy and illogical arguments. Even later on, when they appear to be settled and confident with the new intellectual level, they will occasion-ally lapse into their old ways of dealing with things. A child who has shown that she understands and can use one-to-one correspondence between two sets when comparing numbers extremely well, will never-theless sometimes incorrectly make such comparisons on the basis of the area occupied by the two sets, particularly when this misleading spatial cue is made a very obvious one. Thus the stages in the theory are separate, and well defined, but individual children often operate at more than one level. In all his empirical books, Piaget presented a great deal of evidence to show these inconsistencies. This last point is important because children's spelling is nearly always inconsistent, but this would not mitigate against stage theories of spelling development. Children can draw on specific word knowledge, they can use knowledge of famil-iar rimes, and they can also have more abstract knowledge of condi-tional rules.

In our view, the Gentry theory captures some of the developmental changes in children's spelling quite well, but its description of these developments is too much on the surface. For example, as we have already noted, it must be the case that children's progress towards correct spelling involves word-specific knowledge. How else could they know that the same sound is spelled one way in "hope" and another way in "soap"? The question that this observation raises is whether this is all that the children learn beyond the basic one-to-one letter–sound rules. Do they just learn these specific spellings, or do they also learn more abstract patterns, such as that one legitimate way of spelling the long "o" sound is with the digraph "oa" and another with the split digraph "o-e"? There is no answer to this question in Gentry's theory.

Summary

1   Stage theories in cognitive development can take different forms. This is also true in the context of the development of children's reading and spelling. Some researchers have assumed that a developmental theory means that at each stage in development children's spelling is all guided by a single principle. This type of theory does not seem to fit the data presently but it is not necessary to make this assumption to view a stage theory as useful. A stage theory might simply assume that children have a bias to do things in a particular way, and in order to do things differently, they need to change. This type of theory would actually fit with current views that children at first have a bias towards using a one-letter one-sound approach to reading and spelling words.

2   Other researchers assume that the main question in development is whether children can or cannot use a particular way of thinking at specific stages in development. We think that this type of theory remains too much on the surface. Developmental theories should go beneath the surface, and look at causal connections between different things that children learn about reading and spelling.

A Different View on Stages in the Development of Reading and Spelling

Theories that account for the causes of developmental changes are more likely to go below the surface because many possible causal factors, like phonological awareness, are not directly observable. We turn now to a stage theory that sets out a series of ordered stages and also an account of what prompts children to progress from one stage to the other. This is Uta Frith's (1985) theory of the development of reading and spelling.

Frith made the claim that children go through three broad stages in learning about reading and spelling. The first is a *logographic* stage, the second an *alphabetic* stage and the third an *orthographic* stage. The logographic stage concerns the first encounters that young children have with print before they master the alphabet, and is not directly relevant to the discussion here. We will concentrate on the alphabetic and the orthographic stages.

The alphabetic stage is a time when children learn about the phonological basis of reading and writing. During this stage, according to Frith, children become more sensitive to the sounds in spoken words and at the same time learn how to represent these sounds alphabetic-ally. To some extent this is like Gentry's phonetic stage, but it is a bit broader than that because Frith included learning about digraphs as well as about single letter–sound connections in the alphabetic period. Frith also made a causal claim about this stage.

The alphabetic stage, she argued, begins with spelling. At the begin-ning of the alphabetic stage children start to spell words out letter by letter, even though at the same time they are still reading words in non-alphabetic ways, particularly by recognizing words as unanalysed wholes. Only later on during the alphabetic stage do they extend their knowledge of alphabetic correspondences between letters and sounds to help them to read the words as well.

This claim boils down to two statements. One is that children use phonological correspondences in spelling before they do so in reading, and the second is that their experience of using grapheme–phoneme correspondences in spelling eventually leads to them to begin to rely on these correspondences in reading as well. The evidence on these two statements is still a little thin. According to the first statement there should be a time when children's ability to analyse the sounds in words will be related to the progress that they make in spelling but not in reading. This has never been found. Predictive studies have always shown a strong connection between children's phonological awareness and their success in reading as well as in spelling.

There is, however, some evidence that does suggest that there is a time when children use the alphabetic code more in spelling than in reading English words. Bryant and Bradley (1980) gave 5- and 6-year-old children the same words to read and to spell at different times, and then looked at which individual words children could read or failed to read and which they could spell or failed to spell. They found that most children were able both to read particular words correctly and spell them correctly as well, and also that most were quite unable either to read or to spell other words (of course, precisely which words fell into these categories varied between individual children).

Bryant and Bradley also found that the majority of the children could read some words which they failed to spell correctly. This specific dis-crepancy is not particularly surprising: adults as well as children are very familiar with the experience of being uncertain about how to spell specific words which nevertheless they recognize with no difficulty at all when they are reading. However, the study produced another discrep-ancy which certainly was surprising. About one quarter of the children could spell particular words which they failed to read. This two-way discrepancy demonstrates a certain independence between reading and spelling, which is interesting in its own right. The question is whether the words that children spell correctly but fail to read are more likely to be those that can the spelled using the letter-by-letter or alphabetic approach, whereas those that the children read but do not spell correctly are words that are not successfully read using the same approach. If this turns out to be the case, there will be some support for Frith's hypothesis.

The words that children often read, but failed to spell properly were almost always words which did not conform to single letter–sound correspondences. The words which were most commonly read but not spelled were "school," "light," "train" and "egg." None of these words has a one-to-one correspondence between letters and sounds as they include digraphs (e.g. the "oo" in "school") and doublets (the "gg" in "egg"). In contrast the words that the children typically managed to spell, but failed to read were "bun," "mat," "leg" and "pat," all of which conform to single letter–sound connections. This result does provide some support for the first step in Frith's claim that young learners use letter–sound correspondences more consistently in spelling and may draw on visual strategies that rely on other sorts of chunks in reading. The discrepancy between the numbers of words that the children could spell and not read decreased with the children's increasing proficiency, which is also in agreement with Frith's hypothesis.

Subsequent research by Claire Fletcher-Flinn and her colleagues (2004) partially confirmed these results, even though the specific words that the children in their study spelled but did not read were not exactly the same ones: they were "ran," "bag" and "bun," all of which, again, can be spelled using simple letter–sound correspondences. However, the words most frequently read correctly but not spelled were "cut," "pen," "from," and "milk"; "cut" and "pen" could also be spelled using simple letter–sound correspondences even if "from" and "milk" might be more difficult because they contain consonant sequences that young learners might find difficult to analyse. It is not clear in their report what happened to words like "school" and "light"—whether the children read and spelled them correctly because these are, according to the authors, highly frequent in the children's printed materials, or whether they failed both to read and write them. The children in their study were being instructed by a phonics method—and thus might not have had the same visual strategies at their disposal which were available to those in the study by Bryant and Bradley, who were being instructed by an eclectic approach, combining visual strategies and phonics. The children in the Fletcher-

Flinn study failed to both read and spell on average 4 more words (out of 30) than those in the Bryant and Bradley study, which means that they might have failed to read words that could be read using visual strategies but not letter-by-letter strategies.

One more point should be made about these findings. Bryant and Bradley reasoned that, if the children were able to use an alphabetic approach to spelling, they should be able to do so also in reading, but because they had other strategies at their disposal, they may have used these instead. So they went back and asked all the younger children to read some pseudowords. They told the children that these were made-up words, which they would not recognize. In the middle of this list of pseudowords were the words that the children had previously spelled but not read correctly. They did not tell the children how to solve the pseudoword reading task but they predicted that the children would now adopt an alphabetic approach and so they would now succeed with these words. A comparison condition was also used, in which the children saw the same words again but embedded in a list of frequent and meaningful words. Here they predicted that the children would not feel that they had to rely on an alphabetic approach to the task: so there would be no difference in how they would approach these words. Their results were in agreement with their predictions. Reading the previously not-read words in the middle of a list of words did not alter the children's level of success but reading them in the middle of a list of pseudowords significantly improved the children's performance: out of an average of 4.9 words that had not been read successfully, they now read on average 3.5 correctly. So the children had not failed to read the words for lack of skill in using the alphabetic approach: they had failed because they had other ways to approach word reading, and these had gotten in the way of their alphabetic reading. This is a very important lesson about what stages might mean in word reading and spelling: as we indicated earlier on, they might reveal more a bias in how a task is approached than a lack of other skills. If we have a bias to do something in one way—say, to approach reading and spelling as a letter-by-letter task—we might fail to use alternative solutions to the task. In this case, we might get a bit stuck when we encounter a digraph, though this will not necessarily mean that we know nothing about digraphs.

Frith's hypothesis involved two claims: that children use different strategies for reading and spelling when they are just beginning to learn (and, as we saw, this statement would not be supported in this radical form) and also that children's experiences with grapheme–phoneme correspondences in spelling prompt them after a while to use these correspondences in reading as well. This second claim has not been tested. It would not be difficult to test this idea in a longitudinal study, but so far no one has done that.

Frith's theory is that during the next stage, the orthographic stage, children acquire several different kinds of knowledge that take them well beyond simple alphabetic correspondences. They learn about written words like "pint" and "Gloucester" that do not conform to simple grapheme–phoneme correspondences: they learn too about common orthographic sequences, like "-ight" which also transcend simple grapheme–phoneme correspondences. They also begin to understand and apply conditional rules like the split digraph rule and the rule about the function of consonant doublets during this stage.

The causal claim about this stage is the opposite of the one that Frith made about the alphabetic stage. Here she argues that reading takes the leading role. At first children become familiar with orthographic sequences and conditional rules in texts that they read, and later on they extend this new knowledge to their spelling. Thus at this stage the experiences that children have in reading eventually determine how they spell.

This claim has been tested. In a recent longitudinal study of children's understanding of the split digraph rule, Davis and Bryant (2006) gathered data on how well children used this rule both in reading and spelling. This allowed them to track the relation between how children read and spell split digraphs over time. This was a two-year longitudinal study of school children whose ages ranged from 7 to 11 years.

Davis and Bryant saw the children in this study on three separate occasions, and there was an interval of about a year between the first and the second and between the second and the third of the sessions. In each session they asked the children to read and to spell real words and pseudowords with long and with short vowels. The correct spelling for all the long vowels in the real words was the split digraph. In the reading tasks all the long-vowel words were split digraph words.

In the reading tasks they found that the children read the short vowel words better than the long ones, which means that it was relatively hard for them to read split digraphs, as we have already seen happening in other studies. The difference between long and short vowel words was far greater with pseudowords than it was with real words. So, the children had much more difficulty in deciphering the split digraph in totally unfamiliar words than in familiar ones. This strong result suggests that much of what children learn about split digraphs, at least at first, can be counted as word-specific knowledge. They learn how "lake" is spelled, for example, but often cannot generalize this knowledge to unfamiliar pseudowords like "nake."

Nevertheless, even the 7-year-old children did have some relatively abstract understanding of the split digraph rule. In this session and in later sessions the children in both age groups consistently read pseudo-words as words with long vowels much more often when these contained a split digraph than when they did not. This is something, as we have already noted, that Megan Patrick also found in her study. It is clear that by the age of 7 years, children's knowledge about split digraphs transcends word-specific knowledge. This knowledge is incomplete, since the children certainly did not read all the split digraph pseudowords as words with long vowels. In fact, at 7 and 8 years, the children treated split digraph words in this way less than half the time. However, the consistent demonstration that 7-year-old children assign long vowels more often to split digraph pseudowords than to other pseudowords is a clear indication of some abstract knowledge in this age group of the function of these particular digraphs.

The spelling tasks in Davis and Bryant's study produced rather similar results. The children were better at spelling short vowel than long vowel words. In fact, they made relatively few mistakes in spelling the real words or the pseudowords with short vowels: their main problem was in representing long vowels with digraphs or split digraphs. This difference between short and long vowel words was far greater in the case of pseudowords than of real words, which means in effect that the big difference between the real and the pseudowords' spelling scores was in the long vowel words. Some of children's use of split digraphs, therefore, must depend on specific knowledge of the spelling of particular words.

We can turn now to the causal side of the Davis and Bryant study. The study produced two results which strongly supported Frith's causal hypothesis that reading plays the leading part in the orthographic stage. We have illustrated the first of these results in Figures 4.1 and 4.2, which contrasts how well children read split digraph pseudowords as words with long vowel with how well they spelled long vowel pseudowords with split digraphs. Between the ages of 7 and 8 years, the children's reading scores improved more rapidly than their spelling scores. Between 8 and 9 years, the improvement in the children's reading and spelling of the split digraph was roughly the same. From 9 to 10 years, the improvement in reading tailed off, but the children's spelling scores continued to get better at much the same rate as in the previous year. Thus the children seemed to get to grips with the split digraph rule first

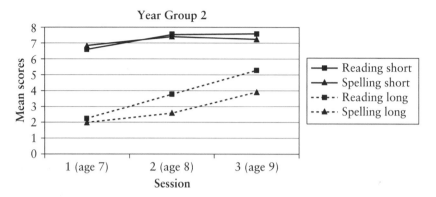

Figure 4.1   Mean scores (out of 8 pseudowords) for Year Group 2's reading and spelling of long and short vowels in each session

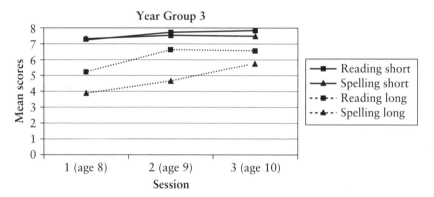

Figure 4.2   Mean scores (out of 8 pseudowords) for Year Group 3's reading and spelling of long and short vowels in each session

in reading and later in spelling, and this pattern is consistent with the hypothesis that their experiences in reading laid the basis for their learning, later on, how to spell long-vowel words.

The other result in the Davis and Bryant study is even stronger evidence for the idea that what children learn about orthographic rules when reading lays the basis for how they use these rules in spelling. Since this was a longitudinal study, Davis and Bryant were able to correlate the children's reading and spelling scores over time. Such correlations are a great help in testing causal hypotheses. If children's orthographic experiences in reading really do lead the way, as Frith claims, the children's reading scores early on in the study should predict their spelling scores later on: in contrast the children's initial spelling scores should not predict their later success in reading orthographic sequences in later sessions nearly as strongly.

The Davis–Bryant study established this pattern, at any rate between the ages of 7 and 9 years. Figures 4.3 and 4.4 show that, from 7 to 8 years and also from 8 to 9 years, the children's reading scores were a great deal better at predicting their spelling a year later on than vice versa. Notice, too, that this effect appears to be over at 9 years: in the following year the children's spelling was a better predictor of their reading a year later than the other way round, though not significantly

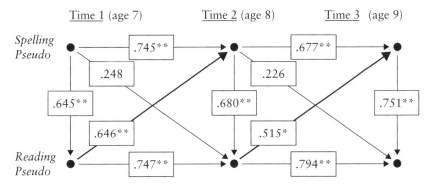

Figure 4.3 Cross-lagged partial correlations (controlling for age and outcome measure) in Year Group 2 for their appropriate reading and spelling of CVC and CVCe pseudowords

Note: correlations are significant at **$p < .001$, *$p < .01$

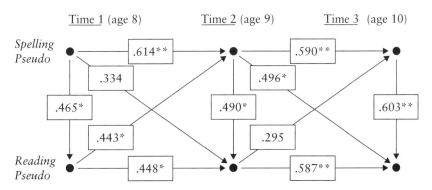

Figure 4.4 Cross-lagged partial correlations (controlling for age and outcome measure) in Year Group 3 for their appropriate reading and spelling of CVC and CVCe pseudowords

so. What is happening between 9 and 10 years is not clear, but in the previous two years we have a strong and consistent result which supports the idea that children initially learn about the split digraph rule mainly through reading and then apply this learning to their spelling as well.

Summary

1 A detailed look at children's word reading and spelling convincingly shows that children's knowledge changes quantitatively and qualitatively over time. Word-specific learning, either in terms of whole words (e.g. learning that the garden mollusc is spelled as "snail" not "snale") or in a more analytic form (e.g. learning about specific rimes, such as "ame") is quantitative: the children know more items as they progress through school.

2 Learning how to deal with different types of regularity—one-to-one letter–sound correspondences, digraphs, and syllable juncture rules—is about qualitative progress because it is learning about distinct categories of spelling rules, not just more instances of the same thing.

3 Some interpretations of the idea of stages in development are of the type "can children do this or can't they?" This is less helpful than analyses that investigate whether children's approaches to word reading and spelling change qualitatively as they go through primary school, and whether one way of thinking about spelling forms the foundation for other, more sophisticated ones. When children are starting to learn to read and write, they have a strong bias to use one-to-one correspondences, but when there is no single letter to represent a sound, do not find it too difficult to go beyond single letter–sound correspondences.

4 More complex functions—such as those served by the split digraphs and doubling letters—take longer to learn, and may be learned exactly because reading words with the split digraph by using a one-to-one correspondence leads to errors that the children can themselves identify. They can use other cues beyond letter–sound knowledge in reading: for example, they can reject the pronunciation "grap" because this is not a word and then give the right pronunciation to the word "grape," and this may be the reason why they learn about the split digraph first in reading.

5 There is clear evidence that their learning about the split digraphs from reading lays the foundation for later spelling: children progress more quickly in reading than in spelling and their progress in reading is a strong predictor of how well they will learn to spell these digraphs.

Finally, it is worth commenting on whether the idea of stages or phases in the development of word reading and spelling is a useful one. In order to come to a conclusion about this, it is necessary to make the point that a theory of stages does not imply complete homogeneity in children's word reading and spelling. Children may use different types of knowledge at the same time—as we have been indicating, some more concrete and specific as well as some more abstract and general know-ledge—and thus show variation in behaviour. In spite of this variation, we think that a theory that allows us to recognize qualitative changes in children's spelling is helpful, both for understanding the child and for designing appropriate instruction to promote the child's progress. Let's do a thought experiment: a teacher asks the children in her class to spell the word "know" in the context of a sentence that makes the meaning of the word clear. What sorts of mistakes might children make? Let's imagine that the teacher observes the following mistakes: "no," "now," "kow" and "knaw." The spelling "no" is the one that differs mostly from "know"—it misses out two letters—but the teacher should be more worried about a child who spelled "kow," where only one letter is missing, because missing out the "n" may indicate that this child needs help with phonological analysis and letter–sound correspondences. If the same type of error is observed in other spellings, there will be confirmation of the need for phonological instruction. However, a child in a later grade who still spells "know" as "no" should also give the teacher some cause for concern. This alphabetically adequate spelling in the first year of school means something quite different in a later grade. This is why the idea of stages may be useful: putting children's errors in the context of development helps understand the child's production and whether or not specific instruction is required at the time.

The interest in instruction and its coordination with theory leads us into the third section of this chapter. We know that children learn both specific things about word spelling and more abstract ideas. As the work of Megan Patrick suggests, learning about specific words and rimes is to a large extent promoted through the amount of reading that children do. What about learning the more abstract ideas that are in-volved in English orthography? How do we design teaching that helps them move on with the more abstract ideas?

Teaching Children about Split Digraphs

Over the past decade or so, we have worked closely with teachers in discussing word reading and spelling, exchanging our doubts and

queries, designing research, and implementing teaching studies. Sometimes we carried out the teaching studies ourselves: sometimes the teachers
carried out the experiments. We have described elsewhere the ideas
behind this collaboration (Nunes & Bryant, 2006) in detail. Suffice it
to say here that some of the questions asked in these studies were raised
by us and some were raised by the teachers, and we can no longer say
who first raised each specific question with precision. In general, the
teachers asked practical questions, and in doing so prompted the design
of experiments that address practical and theoretical questions.

When we were working on a project designed to compare the effectiveness of different forms of instruction to improve children's word
reading and spelling (reported in Nunes, Bryant, & Olsson, 2003), one
of the teachers asked us whether we thought that the children should be
given practice separately on short vowels and long vowels or whether
they should practise long and short vowels at the same time. Should
they have a block of time—for example, three days—dedicated to prac-
tising reading and spelling words with "a" and then a similar amount
of time dedicated to words with the split digraph "a-e" or should they
be taught the two spelling patterns at the same time? In our discussion, there was support for both views. Those who thought that the
practice should be separate expected that the children would form specific letter–sound connections between the words with "a" and also
specific letter–sound connections between the words with "a-e." This
would be learning of the sort we referred to earlier as "specific and
concrete." Those who thought that the children should be given practice with both types of words at the same time thought that the children should be learning more abstract rules, and would learn more
effectively about these rules if taught to focus on the discrimination
between the sounds and associate this distinction with the different
spelling patterns.

In order to see what guidance teachers had on this matter, we looked
at the government proposals and analysed what was at the basis of
suggested approaches to the teaching of split digraphs. Neither the
advice from papers published by the government in England (The
National Literacy Strategy, 1998) nor the report on the effectiveness
of synthetic phonics published in Scotland (Watson & Johnston, 1998)
took an explicit position on this. However, they appeared very similar
in treating the acquisition of the split digraph as a specific form of
letter–sound connection, without proposing that teachers should use a
contrast between short and long vowels and try to teach ways of using
a rule for distinguishing between them in spelling.

The National Literacy Strategy offers an explicit definition and detailed instructions: split digraphs are defined as containing "letters which are modified by "e," e.g. "ate," "hope" (The National Literacy Strategy, 1998, p. 28), and are used to "represent the long 'a' in a medial position" (p. 30). Teachers are instructed to get the children to "investigate and classify words with the same sound but different spellings" (e.g. "ai" and "a-e" in the middle, "ay" at the end of words) but there is no mention of the idea of getting the children to classify *different* sounds with different spellings, as in the contrast between "hat" and "hate." The classification of words with the same sounds and different spellings would imply that the aim is for children to acquire word-specific knowledge, not to learn a rule that helps them differentiate sounds and their spelling with or without digraphs.

Ruth Miskin's (2004) *Teacher's Handbook* is much the same in so far as the phonics lessons are concerned: split digraphs are introduced along with other digraphs and there is no attempt to create discrimination learning exercises. However, Miskin includes exercises which aim at making an explicit connection between the different split digraphs: the children should be taught that these are called "split graphemes," where the two vowels are split but still function together. This approach to teaching prompted a new question: do children benefit from making this connection across the different split digraphs? Again, there were different views in our discussion groups. Some people thought that the children are really making specific connections between graphemes and sounds: thus there is no reason for the children to have to learn more than one thing at the same time. Others thought that, if children learn split digraphs at a more abstract level, then they would actually benefit from learning the different split digraphs one after the other. In other words, there would be transfer of learning from one digraph to the other because of this more abstract connection through a concept of "split digraphs."

We concluded that there were three issues here that needed investigation. The first is whether children learn these digraphs as abstract rules or as specific connections between graphemes and sounds. If they learn them as specific connections, they would be best learned in separate blocks, as proposed in the National Literacy Strategy. The second is whether the children can transfer learning across the split digraphs; if this is the case, there would be further support for the idea that there is some abstract learning, and that children benefit from achieving it. The third issue is that rule-learning is not sufficient to distinguish between the spelling of words where the same sound is spelled by different digraphs, such as "pail" and "pale." Whatever children learn about rules does not help then with this distinction because "ai" and "a-e" have the same function. However, the form rule related to position, and explicitly taught in the National Literacy, would at least help when this sound is at the end of words, as in "pay."

After considering different proposals for teaching, we realized that there was no answer to our query about the teaching and learning of more abstract spelling rules in the guidance that teachers receive, though the assumption seems to be that children learn specific associations. So we decided that it was necessary to investigate whether there is a role for rule learning here.

Do Children Benefit from Learning Digraphs as a Discrimination Rule?

We ran three experiments to analyse how variations in teaching affect children's learning of the use of digraphs versus single letters. In all three experiments, there is a rule that can help the children make the distinction—even though the rule does not cover word-specific learning. The first experiment was about the contrast between the vowels in "hat" and "hate," the second about the vowels in "hop" and "hope" and the third about the spelling of the final consonant in "beak" and "brick." The reasons for the use of the split digraph have already been discussed: the split digraphs have a function in representing the vowel sound. The difference between "beak" and "brick" is one of form rather than function: the final consonant sounds the same, irrespective of its spelling as "k" or "ck." The form-based rule is that, if the rime (i.e. the part of the syllable that starts with the vowel) only has one letter before the representation of the /k/ sound, then the /k/ sound is represented by "ck"; if the rime has two letters—as in "beak," "peak," "book," "park," "brisk" and "pink"—then the /k/ sound is represented with a "k."

There is, of course, one more case, when the "k" is followed by the letter "e" because the word contains a split digraph—as in "make," "smoke" and "like"; in this case, the spelling is also with "k." However, we excluded this case from our teaching because we wanted the spelling of the final /k/ sound to be unrelated to the other two spellings. The reason for this will become clear in the next paragraph, where we describe the design of our teaching experiments.

In each of our teaching experiments, we needed to have a taught group and a control group. The children would be randomly assigned to one of these two groups. The two groups should have the same amount of practice in learning about spelling and the same amount of individual attention from the experimenters in order for these factors to be controlled when we compared the teaching outcomes of the two groups. We also wanted to make certain that the children in both groups had a positive experience in learning spelling. So we used an overall design where the children were assigned to three learning groups: the first group was taught the "o" vs "o-e" spelling rule, the second the "a" vs "a-e" rule, and the third the "k" vs "ck" rule. The third group, which was taught about the form-based rule "k" vs "ck," was a control group for the other two because it was learning an unrelated spelling rule.

A total of 124 children from five different schools in Oxford or London participated in this study. They were in their second or third year in school and their mean ages were 7y2m (in Year 2) and 8 years (in Year 3). Their literacy teaching followed the National Literacy Strategy, which places emphasis on phonics; the teaching of the split digraph was described earlier on in this chapter. Both the children in Year 2 and Year 3 had been taught about the two split digraphs in the classroom; they had not been taught about the different spellings of the /k/ sound previously. So we expected that our experiment would show stronger effects for the different ways of spelling the /k/ sound at the end of words than for the split digraphs, because of the "k" vs "ck" distinction, this would be an entirely new learning experience for them.

The children were randomly assigned to one of six groups, which were defined by the type of rule being learned—"a" vs "a-e," "o" vs "o-e" or "k" vs "ck"—in combination with one way of teaching—block teaching, where each word type was trained separately, versus mixed teaching, where the two types of words in the rule were randomly mixed within each session. The amount of practice that the children would receive was the same so that differences between the groups taught in blocks and the groups taught with the word types mixed could not be explained by the amount of practice. Figure 4.5 shows a schematic representation of the design of our study.

The study followed a pre-test, immediate post-test, delayed post-test design. At pre-test, before the children had been taught anything, they were asked to spell 36 words and 36 pseudowords; 12 words and 12 pseudowords assessed the discrimination between the use of "a" and "a-e"; 12 words and 12 pseudowords assessed the discrimination between "o" and "o-e" and 12 words and 12 pseudowords assessed the discrimination between "k" and "ck." These assessments were repeated at the immediate and delayed post-test in order to see how much progress

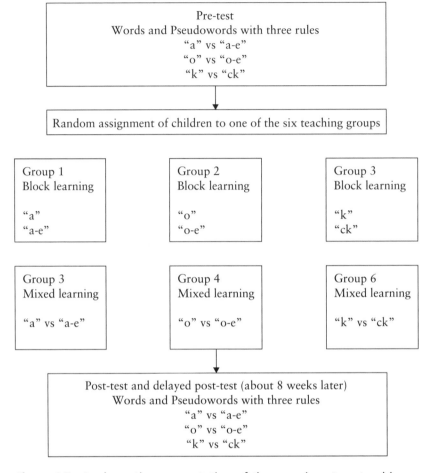

Figure 4.5 A schematic representation of the experiment on teaching digraphs

the children in each group had made. The testing sessions were carried out by an experimenter who worked with the children on a one-to-one basis. The words and pseudowords to be spelled were presented in sentences. The children spelled always the words first, then the pseudowords in a separate session. At the end of the delayed post-test, we also gave the children a brief interview, and asked them to explain to us why they had spelled some pseudowords in particular ways. In the case of the split digraphs, where the spelling has a function and thus affects the way the pseudowords should be read, we also asked them why they had read some pseudowords in particular ways. Our aim was to see whether the ability to explain the rule was related to the way they had been taught and also to a higher level of performance in the spelling test.

The teaching sessions were carried out over two days. On the first day, the experimenter explained to each child the rule that the child would be learning. The first session included only words and the second only pseudowords. The practice trials were presented on a computer screen and introduced as games by two animated characters that appeared on the screen, a boy and an animal—a reptile. During the whole teaching, the boy always said words; the reptile always said pseudowords.

Each session was divided into two parts. In the first session, the boy would appear on the screen and say a word; the word then appeared on the screen but the letters relevant to the training were missing. For example, for the word "hat," the screen would display the letters "H" and "T," separated by a box, with another box following the letter "T": the display looked somewhat like this but in colour:

H		T	

The same display was used for the word "hate" so that the child had no clue from the display whether there would be an "e" at the end of the word or not.

During the first part of the session, the child would provide oral responses, and say whether or not the word required an "e" at the end. Feedback would then appear on the screen, with the missing letter(s) flashing on and off and then staying on for the child to check her own answer. In the second part of the session, the procedure was very similar but the children wrote the words and checked the spelling when the word appeared on the screen.

The structure of the second session was exactly the same but the children worked with pseudowords dictated by the reptile. Figure 4.6 illustrates the method.

An important feature of these experiments was that the words and pseudowords used in the tests and those used in the training were all different. This means that any improvement in the children's performance could not be a result of word-specific learning during the teaching sessions. Also, there should be no "word-specific" learning of pseudowords, even in the eight-week interval between the immediate and the delayed post-test. So these studies were designed to help us focus on rule learning, not on word-specific learning.

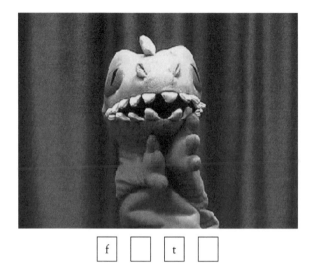

Figure 4.6 Example of a screen showing the reptile and the display for the pseudoword "fote"

At pre-test, the children in Year 2 did not differ from the children in Year 3 in the spelling of any of the three rules. Actually, the children in Year 2, who had recent practice with the split digraphs, scored slightly better but the difference was not significant. The overall mean number of correct spellings for words and pseudowords, out of 24, was 15.7 for the "o" vs "o-e" words, 15.3 for the "a" vs "a-e" words, and 12 for the "k" vs "ck" rule. There was great variation between the children, but only 4 children (out of 124) obtained full scores in at least one of the three rules. These children were allowed to participate in the teaching sessions and to work with a rule on which they had not obtained full marks but their data were not included in the analysis. The children performed significantly better on the words and pseudowords with the rules that they had already been taught in the classroom than on those with the "k" vs "ck" rule, which they had not been taught. However, even with the rules that they had been taught in the classroom, the pre-test results showed that there was room for further learning for most children.

In the subsequent sections of this chapter, we examine the results of each of the three experiments in greater detail. In all the experiments, the children's spelling was typed into the computer. A marking criterion was defined and then applied using a computer resource for scoring each item.

1. Learning the distinction between "o" and "o-e"

In the scoring of words with "o" and "o-e," the children were given a point if they correctly spelled the target portion of the words and pseudowords—with "o" or "o-e." If they made a mistake elsewhere— writing, for example, "nole" instead of "mole" or "scole" instead of "spole," they would still be given a point. The vowel marking in *words* was only considered correct if they used the split digraph "o-e" and did not use extra letters (e.g. "molle" and "moale" would be scored as incorrect). It was more difficult to decide how to handle the *pseudowords*, because there are different ways of marking the long /o/. In principle, "spoal" or "spole" would both be correct spellings of the pseudoword we had spelled as "spole." We looked at the proportion of spellings with "oa" and "o-e" at pre-test; 5% of the children used an alternative spelling for the long /o/ (e.g. the spelled the pseudoword "grode" and "groad" or "growed") whereas 49% used the split digraph; the remaining spellings failed to mark the long /o/ and used a single vowel or an inappropriate digraph (e.g. "oi" or "oo"). We then decided to consider as correct only those pseudoword spellings that used the split digraph. We had two reasons to make this decision: first, our aim was to teach the children the use of a spelling rule that relied on the split digraph; second, alternative spellings were so uncommon that they could be overlooked.

Before analysing the effects of the intervention, we examined the children's performance at pre-test, in order to know what it would tell us about their use of "o" and "o-e" in words and pseudowords. The results of this pre-test analysis are presented in Table 4.2.

The children's performance at pre-test showed that, even in their second and third year of school, they still had a tendency to use a one-letter grapheme more accurately than the two-letter grapheme. They

Table 4.2 Mean correct out of six (standard deviation in brackets) for each type of word and pseudoword at pre-test

	Words	Pseudowords
With "o"	5.2 (1.2)	4.6 (1.2)
With "o-e"	3.7 (2.0)	2.4 (2.0)

Note: The effect size for the difference between spelling "o" pseudowords and "o-e" words was large: Cohen's *d* = 0.6 SD.

performed better with "o" words and pseudowords than with "o-e" words and pseudowords.

They performed significantly better, overall, when spelling words than pseudowords. However, if we look at "o" words and pseudowords only, the difference between words and pseudowords tends to disappear (the level of significance is $p = .06$): they spelled pseudowords with "o" almost as well as they spelled words. In contrast, they spelled pseudowords with "o," which they never saw before, significantly better than words with "o-e," even though they were spelling words that are frequent in children's books. These results are completely in agreement with those by Davis and Bryant mentioned previously: what the children need to learn is to use the split digraph in order to mark the long /o/, which is not spelled with a single letter, because their bias is towards spelling with a single "o," which is appropriate for the short vowel.

These results indicate that the appropriate measure of progress from pre- to post-tests in the experiment is their progress in use of the "o-e" spelling, as there was not much room for progress with "o" words.

In order to analyse whether there was a difference between the groups, we compared the two taught groups—the children who received the teaching in separate blocks and those who received mixed teaching of "o" and "o-e" words—with the control group, who had received teaching on the "k" vs "ck" rule. We used the children's overall score for words and pseudowords with "o-e" as the dependent variable and we ran an analysis of covariance, in order to control for pre-test scores. Both taught groups performed significantly better than the control group at the immediate post-test and they did not differ from each other significantly. The children who received the training performed at more than 0.6 of a standard deviation above the control group in the immediate post-test, even though this training was quite short, as it was offered for only two days with a total of less than one hour of instruction. At the delayed post-test, about eight weeks after they had received teaching, both taught groups continued to spell "o-e" words and pseudowords significantly better than the control group; their advantage over the control group was now smaller but it was still quite noticeable: 0.45 of a standard deviation.

At delayed post-test, the children were asked to spell and read two further pseudowords and asked to explain why they read or spelled them the way they did. For each pseudoword, the children were given two points if their explanation included a reference to the correct vowel contrast and they had spelled the pseudoword correctly, 1 point for a correct spelling or reading with a partial explanation, and no points if they did not refer to the vowel sound or if they spelled the pseudoword incorrectly. Incorrect spellings with correct reference to the vowel sound were not observed. Examples of explanations scored as 2, 1 and 0 are presented below:

> I don't know this but I think that this is right.
> I just know.
> Smop is right because it has the oh sound (we used "oh" to represent the child's pronunciation of this vowel and "o" to represent the pronunciation of the vowel in "floke").
> It is floke because it has an e at the end. If it didn't, it'd be flok.

We analysed whether the teaching had a significant impact on the children's explanations by using an analysis of covariance with their pre-test scores on the spelling of "o-e" words and pseudowords as the covariate, the intervention group as the independent variable, and the score in the explanation task (out of 4) as the dependent variable. This analysis showed that the children in the taught groups scored higher than the children in the control group—their average score was about 0.8 points higher than the score for the children in the control group—but the difference between the taught and the control groups did not reach significance ($p = .08$).

In this study, the children were being taught a rule that they had already learned in the classroom. In spite of their previous learning, the groups that received teaching in our experimental sessions performed better than the control group both at the immediate post-test and the delayed post-test in spelling words and pseudowords with "o-e." However, they were not able to show a similar advantage when explaining the basis for distinguishing between the use of "o" and "o-e." This suggests that they improved more in their implicit knowledge than their explicit knowledge of the rule.

The two taught groups received the same amount of teaching and the same teaching trials and, under these circumstances, the use of a block teaching versus a teaching that mixed the two types of words did not make much difference.

2. Learning the distinction between "a" and "a-e"

In the scoring of words with "a" and "a-e," the children were given a point if they correctly spelled the target portion of the words and pseudowords. If they made a mistake elsewhere in the words or pseudowords, as explained for the previous experiment, they would still be given a point. The vowel marking as "a-e" in words and pseudowords was only considered correct if they used the split digraph and did not use extra letters (e.g. "nayde" was scored as incorrect for the pseudoword "nade"). Although in principle, "naid" or "nayd" would be both correct spellings of the pseudoword we had spelled as "nade," we considered, as in the previous experiment, that the alternative spellings for the long /a/ represented a very small percentage of the children's spelling: at pre-test; 5% of the children used an alternative spelling for the long /a/ whereas 56% used the split digraph; the remaining spellings failed to mark the long /a/ and used a single vowel or an inappropriate digraph (e.g. "ae" or "ee"). Consistently with what we had decided for the previous experiment, we considered as correct only those spellings that used the split digraph.

As in the previous study, before analysing the effects of the intervention, we examined the children's performance at pre-test, in order to know what it would tell us about their use of "a" and "a-e" in words and pseudowords. The results of this pre-test analysis are presented in Table 4.3.

The results at pre-test replicate very closely those in the previous experiment. The children had a tendency to spell with "a" much more often than with "a-e," so the difference between the correct number of spellings was significant. Overall, the children performed better with words than pseudowords, but they actually performed better with pseudowords with "a," which they had never seen, than with words with "a-e." So, the measure of progress in this experiment, as in the previous one, is the number of correctly spelled words and pseudowords with "a-e," controlling for the children's own performance when they were tested before the teaching started.

The comparisons between the taught groups and the control group showed that, in this experiment, only the group that had been taught

Table 4.3 Mean correct out of six (standard deviation in brackets) for each type of word and pseudoword at pre-test

	Words	Pseudowords
With "a"	4.4 (1.4)	4.1 (1.5)
With "a-e"	3.6 (2.0)	3.2 (2.0)

Note: the effect size for the difference between spelling "a" pseudowords and "a-e" words was large: Cohen's d = 0.6 SD.

with the "a" and "a-e" words mixed performed significantly better than the control group at the immediate post-test. At the delayed post-test, the group taught in blocks and the control group had virtually the same means; the group with the words mixed during the training performed better than the control group but this difference was not significant.

We scored the interviews in the same way as they were scored in the previous experiment. Neither of the taught groups was able to explain the rule better than the control group.

So, in the comparison between teaching methods, this experiment gives results a bit different from the previous one. The group that received teaching with "a" and "a-e" spellings mixed did better than the control group at immediate post-test but not at the delayed post-test. The group taught in blocks never showed an advantage over the control group. This suggests that the teaching with the two types of words mixed is more effective but it must be admitted that the effect is weak, as it disappeared after eight to ten weeks.

We explored our data a bit more to try to understand why this difference between the studies appeared. It became clear that the control group in this experiment had started out significantly higher than the experimental group: they were ahead of the taught groups by almost one standard deviation at pre-test. This is unexpected when children are assigned to groups randomly but can happen when the numbers in each group are small. The control group thus probably had very good spellers and, even without explicit teaching, these good spellers continued to make progress. The group taught with the two types of words mixed made sufficient progress within the short time of the training to overtake the good spellers. However, in the subsequent period, the good spellers' progress was sufficient to catch up with the taught group.

This turns out to be a very interesting result, even though it was the consequence of a mismatch between the groups at the start of the experiment. It suggests that weak spellers benefit from the comparisons afforded by the teaching sessions where they had to decide whether a word or a pseudoword should have an "a" or an "a-e." It is also interesting because, as indicated earlier on, the children had been taught about this rule in the classroom, but those in the experimental group had not learned sufficiently from the classroom experience.

3. Learning the distinction between "k" and "ck"

As in the previous experiments, we awarded points for correct spellings by considering only the relevant part of the word, the use of "k" or "ck" at the end. In this study, however, it was more difficult to score the pseudowords because the rule is about form, not function. The pseudoword "sook" would sound the same if spelled with "ck" at the end but it would be incorrect if the form rule is considered: there is one letter between the first vowel in the rime (the first "o") and the spelling of the /k/ sound. If the child used the "oo" spelling, we considered "soock" as well as "sooke" as incorrect. If the child used a different digraph followed by the letter "k"—spelling, for example, "souk"—we considered that the form rule was obeyed, and gave it a correct mark. However, if the digraph was replaced by a single letter—"sok"—this was considered incorrect. In the pseudowords that were to be spelled with "ck" at the end, the vowel sound was always one that can be spelled with a single letter; using "ck" here would be treated as correct and "k" as incorrect.

As in the previous studies, we started our analysis by examining the children's performance at pre-test, in order to know what it would tell us about their use of "k" and "ck" in words and pseudowords. Table 4.4 presents a summary of these results.

In contrast to the previous comparisons between single-letter graphemes and the split digraphs, the children showed a better performance in the words and pseudowords that end with the digraph "ck" rather than the single letter "k." But this does not mean that they had a preference for using the digraph over the single letter. In order to get a point for the "k" ending, the children had to use both a vowel digraph (e.g. "hook") or a vowel followed by a consonant (e.g. "risk") and then the "k"; furthermore, the "k" should not be followed by an "e," although this is a possible spelling in English. So they had to meet two criteria to get a point for using "k" at the end: there should be a letter between the vowel and the "k" and there must not be an "e" at the end. In contrast, words ending in "ck" are not preceded by digraphs and "cke" is not an ending in English. So the higher number of correct spellings for words and pseudowords with "ck" at the end cannot be interpreted as reflecting a preference for a digraph.

Table 4.4 Mean correct out of six (standard deviation in brackets) for each type of word and pseudoword at pre-test

	Words	Pseudowords
With "k"	2.9 (2.2)	2.3 (2.0)
With "ck"	3.6 (2.1)	3.2 (2.1)

The children's performance was actually not very good either in words or pseudowords and there is considerable room for improvement through training.

An analysis of covariance, controlling for the children's scores at pre-test, showed that both taught groups performed at the immediate post-test significantly better than the control group (formed by the children who had learned the "a" vs "a-e" rule and those who had learned the "o" vs "o-e" rule). Their advantage was equal to 0.6 of a standard deviation, which is a very good advantage to have after such a short training period. At the delayed post-test, only the group that had been taught mixing the "k" and "ck" items continued to perform significantly ahead of the control group. Their advantage over the control group was still 0.4 of a standard deviation. So the group taught mixing the two types of items showed greater and more sustained improvement than the group taught with separate blocks for the "k" and the "ck" ending items.

The interviews about the spelling with "k" and "ck" differed from those in the previous studies because this is a formal rule: there is no difference in the pronunciation of the pseudowords. Here the children were presented with a pair of pseudowords to be spelled with "k" or "ck" at the end, asked to spell them, and then were asked to explain why they spelled them differently, if they had done so. If they had not done so, they were asked when the other ending that they had not used was appropriate. This interview yielded a pass-fail score: either the children were able to explain the rule or not. So when we analyse the difference between the groups, we focus on the percentage of children who were able to explain the rule in each group.

In the control group, to our surprise, 2% of the children were able to explain this form rule. We say "to our surprise" because none of their teachers had been able to formulate a rule when we started discussing the use of "k" or "ck" at the end of words. In the group taught with separate blocks of words, 42% of the children produced a correct explanation and in the group taught with the items mixed 54% were able to explain the rule correctly. A statistical test that assesses whether this distribution can be expected by chance (the Contingency Coefficient) indicated that the probability of this distribution appearing by chance is less than 1 in a thousand ($p < .001$). So we conclude that the teaching was effective and that the children who were taught the rule were able to explain it better than those who were not taught.

The results of this study suggest that teaching rules is an effective way of improving children's spelling. Although the taught groups did not differ between themselves, only the children who had received teaching with both types of words mixed showed robust learning, which could still be measured against the performance of a control group after eight to ten weeks.

This experiment, like the one with the "a"–"a-e" rule, suggests that children benefit more from teaching that focuses on differentiating between the cases distinguished by the spelling rule than from learning each type of word separately in blocks. However, there were still occasions when the children who were taught the words in separate blocks showed a measurable advantage over the control group.

The Role of Awareness and Rule-Learning in Spelling

These three studies allow us to address one further question: does the children's awareness of the rule tell us anything about how well they can spell?

At delayed post-test, we asked the children both to spell words and pseudowords and to explain each of the three rules that we were investigating. This allows us to see whether the children who were able to explain the rule produced significantly more correct spellings than those who were not able to do so. In other words, we can test whether the children who are aware of the rule to the point of explaining it verbally perform significantly better than those who are not.

Unfortunately, we did not assess the children's awareness of the rules at pre-test. So we can only look at the connection between rule awareness and spelling performance on the third occasion of our study, in the delayed post-test.

The first step in this analysis is to see how well the different measures of the children's spelling correlate at pre-test, immediate post-test and delayed post-test. These correlations are presented in Table 4.5.

It is clear from these correlations that there is a stronger relationship between the different measures of accuracy in spelling than between the children's awareness of the rules and their spelling accuracy. However, simple correlations do not tell us whether awareness makes a difference. What we need to know is whether the correlation between rule awareness and accuracy in spelling at the delayed post-test continues to be significant when we partial out the connection that both of these variables have to the children's spelling performance at the beginning of the experiment.

Table 4.5 Correlations between the measures of the children's performance on the different occasions for each of the spelling rules

"o" vs "o-e"

Accuracy of spellings at	Immediate post-test	Delayed post-test	Rule awareness
Pre-test (N = 124)	.78	.72	.38
Immediate post-test (N = 124)		.71	.52
Delayed post-test (N = 122)			.50

"a" vs "a-e"

Accuracy of spellings at	Immediate post-test	Delayed post-test	Rule awareness
Pre-test (N = 124)	.81	.72	.52
Immediate post-test (N = 124)		.74	.55
Delayed post-test (N = 122)			.55

"k" vs "ck"

Accuracy of spellings at	Immediate post-test	Delayed post-test	Rule awareness
Pre-test (N = 124)	.84	.76	.23
Immediate post-test (N = 124)		.78	.43
Delayed post-test (N = 122)			.40

Note: All correlations were significant at $p < .001$ level.

We obtained these partial correlations for the three rules. The partial correlations between spelling performance at the delayed post-test and rule awareness, after subtracting what they had in common with pre-test performance, were: for the "o" vs "o-e" rules, $r = .31$; for the "a" vs "a-e" rule, $r = .23$; for the "k" vs "ck" rule, $r = .37$. In all three cases, the correlations remained significant. Thus rule awareness has an important connection to spelling performance which is independent of the children's performance in similar spelling measures.

We were also able to analyse the connection between rule awareness and spelling performance in a different way for the "k" vs "ck" rule. Our interview with the children led to a pass–fail score for this measure: the children were either able to explain the rule or not. So we looked at the distribution of scores in the spelling test for the children who passed the awareness question and for those who did not pass the question. These distributions are presented in Figure 4.7.

There are two salient features of these distributions that we wish to comment on. The first is that the lowest score for the children who passed the rule awareness test is 10 whereas the distribution of scores for the children who failed the rule awareness starts at 0. The second salient feature is that the distribution of scores for the children who failed the rule awareness test is a normal distribution, with a mean of approximately 12.5. This is very close to the mean expected if children were performing at chance level: because there are basically two alternatives—"k" or "ck"—and there are 24 items, the mean number of correct spellings obtained by chance would be 12. The distribution of scores for the children who passed the rule awareness question is quite different. This distribution has a mean of 18.8 correct responses but the majority of the children (12 out of 22) scored above 20 spellings correct.

These differences suggest that, for this rule, awareness is a sufficient, though not a necessary, factor for reaching high levels of accuracy. However, it is important to be cautious here: these results are based on correlations and correlations do not mean causality. Things could be quite the other way around: when you reach "expert" performance, you tend to become aware of rules that guide your spelling.

Transfer of Learning across Rules

One final question that we discussed with teachers was whether there could be transfer of learning across rules. When we speak of "split

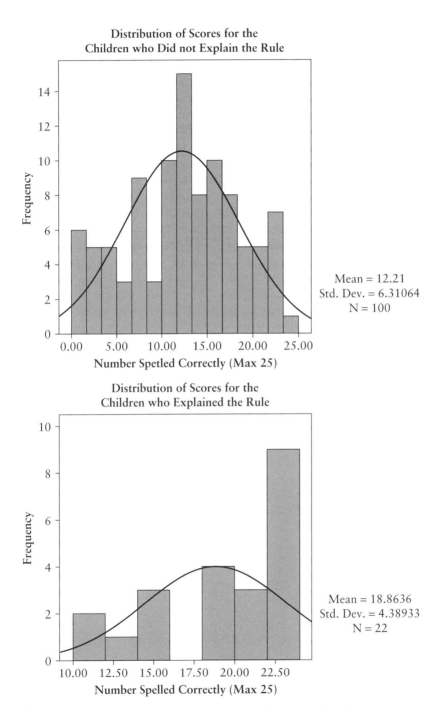

Figure 4.7 Distributions of scores in the spelling test (maximum score = 25) for the children who either failed or passed the rule awareness question

digraphs," we put into the same category rules that are in many ways different if we think of the connections between letters and sounds that children need to make. The vowels in "hat" and "hate" are quite distinct from those in "hop" and "hope." Yet we put these phonological contrasts and their spellings into the same bag. Is there good reason to do so or is the learning of each of these pairs independent from the other?

Our partners in answering this question were the teachers from Lauriston Primary School, in London. Using the design and the materials of the studies we described in the previous section, they set up a study to analyse whether there is transfer of learning across rules. The design that they used is described in Figure 4.8.

In Phase 1, the teachers gave all the children the same learning task: the children worked with the "a" vs "a-e" rule. In Phase 2, they gave the children in the Transfer Group a task which we think is related to the first one, learning the "o" vs "o-e" rules, and to the Control Group they gave an unrelated task, learning the "k" vs "ck" rule. Because the two tasks are related in the Transfer Group, it is expected that, at post-test, the Transfer Group will outperform the Control Group in the learning task that they both learned in Phase 1—the "a" vs "a-e" rule. Although both groups had the same learning experience in this task, the Transfer

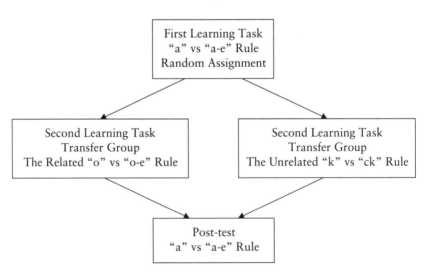

Figure 4.8 Schematic description of how the design of learning transfer studies was applied to the spelling rules

Group's learning was reinforced by learning the second, related task, whereas the Control Group's learning was not reinforced.

The 60 children who participated in this study were in their second or third year in school. Their mean age was 7y3m. The teachers adapted the procedure so that they could use the same materials for teaching in the classroom. They used the same scoring criteria as we had used in the previous studies.

We first analysed the children's performance at pre-test. Table 4.6 shows the results of this analysis. It is quite clear from Table 4.6 that the same trends observed in the previous studies were observed here. The children's performance was much better when they spelled words and pseudowords involving rules that they had been taught in the classroom—the "o" vs "o-e" and the "a" vs "a-e" rules—than when they were spelling words and pseudowords involving rules that they had not been taught—the "k" vs "ck" distinctions. They were also significantly more often correct with the single-vowel spellings that with the split digraph. In the "k" vs "ck" rule, they were at chance level, like most of the children in the previous study.

Because there was still room for improvement in all types of words and pseudowords, we decided to use a combined score for words and a combined score for pseudowords, adding across both types of items (i.e. adding "a" and "a-e" words and also adding "a" and "a-e" pseudowords). In order to analyse the effects of transfer, we carried out two analyses of covariance for the immediate post-test and two for the delayed post-test, with the scores in words and pseudowords separately as the dependent variable. The covariate was the children's performance in the same measure at pre-test. The independent variable was the group to

Table 4.6 Mean number of correct responses (SD in brackets) at pre-test for each type of item (words and pseudowords are added together: maximum number correct = 12) by group

Item type	Transfer Group (n = 28)	Control Group (n = 30)
Words and pseudowords with "a"	9.48 (3.23)	9.90 (1.99)
Words and pseudowords with "a-e"	4.22 (3.93)	5.03 (3.87)
Words and pseudowords with "o"	8.41 (3.04)	8.93 (2.88)
Words and pseudowords with "o-e"	5.63 (4.47)	5.63 (4.28)
Words and pseudowords with "k"	4.31 (3.98)	5.50 (3.65)
Words and pseudowords with "ck"	5.44 (4.57)	6.87 (4.30)

Table 4.7   Mean adjusted number of correct responses (controlling for pre-test scores) for words and pseudowords with "a" and "a-e" by group at each testing occasion

Group	Immediate post-test		Delayed post-test	
	Words	Pseudowords	Words	Pseudowords
Transfer Group	6.4	7.0	6.5	6.9
Control Group	5.9	5.4	4.9	6.6

which the children had been assigned, either Transfer or Control group. The mean number of correct spellings in words with "a" and "a-e" for each group and at both occasions is presented in Table 4.7.

The transfer group performed better than the control group on both measures and both testing occasions, supporting the idea that there is transfer across the split digraphs. However, the differences were not always significant. In the immediate post-test, the difference was significant for pseudowords but not for words; the opposite pattern was observed in the delayed post-test, when the difference between the groups was significant for words but not for pseudowords.

The results lend support to the idea that children learn a more general rule about split digraphs than specific associations between the "a" and "a-e" spellings and the sounds that they represent and the "o" and "o-e" spellings and the sounds that they represent. Teachers refer to this more general rule as: "when there is an 'e' at the end of the word, the letter says its name." Although this is a very abstract conditional rule, it seems that children can make use of it when learning to spell.

Summary

1   There are currently different approaches to teaching children about split digraphs: to teach each one independently from the others, and treat this learning as specific and concrete, or to teach children a more abstract rule, that helps them form the concept of "split digraph." There is also a third approach, which is to teach it through word-specific learning: children learn different words that have the same sounds and are spelled differently (e.g. the split digraph "o-e" or the digraph "oa." In none of these current ways of teaching are the children encouraged to make the contrast between "a" and "a-e" or "o" and "o-e" explicitly.

2 Our studies show that there are advantages to making this contrast explicit: children who are exposed to the two types of words in the same learning sessions on the whole showed a more robust learning, which could still be measured at delayed post-test. However, even the children who learned the distinction in separate blocks taught on the same day performed better than a control group.

3 Children who can explain the rules for choosing between the single letter and the digraph perform better in the spelling test; this correlation remains significant even when at post-test we partial out the overlaps that spelling and explaining the rule have with spelling correctly at pre-test.

4 The distribution of scores for children who were able to explain the rule was quite different from that observed for the children who could not explain the rule: the latter seemed to be at chance level.

5 Finally, children benefit from learning related spelling rules in sequence, on different days. Learning a second rule that has some connection to one previously learned seems to reinforce the learning of the first rule without further teaching. This is a result that we think has great educational significance and was previously not known.

Conclusion: Learning Conditional Phonological Rules

In this chapter, we considered the complex but necessary idea, at least in English orthography, of conditional phonological rules in reading and spelling. The idea of a conditional rule is that sometimes one needs to look beyond a grapheme to know how to read it or how to spell a particular sound. Conditional rules can be expressed as "if . . . then" rules: for example, if the letter "c" is followed by "a," "o," "u," a consonant (other than "h") or is at the end of the word, it is pronounced as /k/; if it is followed by "e" or "i," it is pronounced as /s/.

In Chapter 2, we argued that children start learning to read and spell with a bias towards a one-letter-one-sound conception or how oral and written words are related. We also argued that there are some words which confront the children with the need to modify this conception quite early on in their reading instruction because they contain sounds that cannot be represented by a single letter, such as those represented most often by "sh," "th" and "ch." So children need to modify the strict one-letter-one-sound correspondence rule and use more than one letter to represent some sounds: they need, for example, to look at what comes after the letter "s" in order to interpret how to read it. As we saw in Chapter 2, children do so without too much struggle in the case of obligatory consonant digraphs: 70% of the first graders in Treiman's (1993) study used these digraphs correctly in their spellings. This is a step towards understanding that the orthography they are learning is not solely based on one-to-one correspondences between letters and sounds. But this might be a modest step: Ehri and Soffer showed that the majority of the children in their study (72% of the younger ones) thought of these digraphs as single spelling units. So young children might learn digraphs in the manner we called concrete learning: they might learn simply the letter–sound correspondences between these two letters, when they appear in sequence, and the sounds that they represent. But they might also be taking a very small step beyond the concrete learning of what each digraph represents: they might be learning a general rule—that sometimes a grapheme is made of more than one letter.

There is a clear contrast between these obligatory consonant digraphs, where two letters represent one sound, and the "c" rule: the letter "c" and the one that follows it each represent a different phoneme. So it would be inappropriate to treat "ca," "ce" and "ci," for example, as graphemes, and this is why the "c" rule is a conditional rule.

Other examples of departing from the one-letter-one-sound rule lie between these two contrasting cases. Split digraphs and consonant doublets which maintain the phonological properties of the vowel that precedes them are cases that lie between digraphs and conditional rules.

Consonant doublets do not need specific rules for pronunciation: in English, they are pronounced as if there was a single consonant. In this sense, they are a digraph—two letters that represent one sound—but one can learn a more abstract rule to deal with them. Children do not need to learn specific grapheme rules for the pronunciation of "bb," "ff," "pp," etc.; they can learn the more general rule that doublets sound the same as the single consonant by itself (but here the "c" rule applies again: contrast "accord" with "accent"). However, this is not the difficult part of doublets: the difficult part is the conditional rule that goes with them, that they affect the pronunciation of the vowel that precedes them. So to teach children about consonant doublets as if they are simply digraphs (as some phonics schemes do) is to be economical with the truth about them: it is to teach them the easy part and leave the more difficult one for them to discover on their own.

Similarly, the split digraph can be seen as any other digraph: there are two vowel letters representing a single vowel sound. However, the vowel letters do not appear together, and this makes it is more difficult to perceive them as a unit. Indeed, there are different ways of describing split digraphs, and one way teachers often describe it is by creating a conditional rule: "if there is an 'e' at the end of the word, then the vowel says its name."

The research we reviewed in this and the preceding chapter leaves no doubt that conditional rules are difficult for children. Fortunately, this research also gives some clues about how children learn these rules and how we might help them through teaching.

Summary

1 It seems that children can start to learn words and rimes that contain these rules in a specific and concrete way: they learn examples without necessarily learning rules. They read and spell words with conditional rules correctly more often than pseudowords with the same rules. The implication of this finding for a theory of instruction is mostly about assessment: if we want to test whether the children have learned a word reading or spelling rule, it is not sufficient to ask them to spell words, we need to ask them to spell pseudowords also.

2 They seem to learn to recognize these words and rimes, producing correct pronunciations, before they can spell them correctly. Reading not only precedes but also predicts spelling: children who are better at reading words and pseudowords with specific rules at age 7, for example, will be better at spelling them at age 8. This finding has a counter-intuitive implication for instruction. It means that, in order to improve young children's *spelling*, it pays to give them reading *exercises*. Perhaps long spelling lists to be memorized are not what young children need in order to master these rules.

3 Conditional rules are about contrasts: "if A then X and if B then Y." Although our findings were not completely consistent, they pointed in the direction of better learning when the children learn the conditional rules by contrasting the cases, not as separate blocks in which the different sides of the rule are practised separately. Our studies only included three conditional rules, the "a"-"a-e," "o"-"o-e," and the "k"-"ck." It would be worthwhile investigating the consonant doublet rules for pronunciation.

4 When there is a connection between rules, as in the case of the split digraph, children seem to be able to transfer learning across the specific rules, and benefit from learning about them on consecutive

days. This is indeed a very important finding. If we think of reading and spelling in terms of specific and concrete examples, there is a very large number of graphemes to be learned—for example, if we count each consonant doublet as one grapheme. However, if children can learn that doublets sound the same as the single consonant, the number of specific facts to be learned is immediately reduced.

5   Finally, our studies showed that children who are aware of rules also perform significantly better than those who are not when spelling words that involve these rules. A word of caution is necessary here: our study did not allow for testing a causal connection between explicit knowledge of the rules and spelling achievement. In later studies, presented in subsequent chapters, we tested for this connection. But they deal with a different type of conditional rule, rules based on morphemes and grammar, and these will be the focus of Chapters 5 and 6.

Chapter 5

Morphemes and Spelling

Morphemes are to be found in all spoken languages, though there are striking variations between languages in the relationship between words and morphemes. For example, some parts of speech form separate words of their own in English but are affixes in other languages, which therefore tend to contain relatively long words. These languages are, quite charmingly, called "agglutinative." Finnish is one of them. It takes three one-morpheme words to say "in our house" in English: in Finnish it takes one three-morpheme word. That word is "talossamme": "talo" is its stem which means "house," and "ssa" and "mme" are two affix morphemes which mean, respectively, "in" and "our."

There are two kinds of affix morphemes. These are called "inflectional" and "derivational." Inflectional morphemes, which are often called "inflections," tell us about the grammatical status of the words to which they are attached. Thus, whether an English noun is plural or not is usually signalled by the presence or absence of an /s/ or a /z/ or an /iz/ sound that is added to the end of the stem ("cats," "trees" and "glasses"). Nouns with one or other of these added sounds are in the plural: nouns, or at any rate regular nouns, which have no added sound, are in the singular. The past tense inflection is another clear and important example of an inflectional morpheme. The effect of adding the sound /t/ or a /d/ or an /id/ sound to the end of a verb stem is to make it into a past verb ("kissed," "killed," "waited").

Here, too, there are striking differences between languages: some have many more inflected words than others. For example, every noun, adjective and verb in Greek is inflected. The inflection tells you whether the noun is singular or plural, and nominative, genitive (possessive) or accusative. This is quite a contrast to English in which inflections only appear at the end of nouns when these are plural ("the boys") or possessive ("the boy's game") nouns. So, Greek singular nouns end in an inflection which signifies that they are singular, but English singular nouns carry no inflection at all. In the same way there are no inflections in English to tell us whether a word like "boy" is accusative ("I surprised the boy") or nominative ("The boy surprised me"). Greek accusative nouns end in inflections which clearly mark them as accusative: English accusative nouns do not.

It is the same with verbs. English present verbs are not inflected, unless they are in the third person singular: we say "I smile," "we smile," "you smile" and "they smile," but "she smiles." The "s" at the end of "she smiles" is the active third person singular present tense inflection. Greek present verbs, in contrast, have a different inflectional ending for first, second and third persons both in the singular and in the plural: six different endings.

The other kind of affix is the derivational morpheme, and its use is widespread in most languages. Derivational morphemes are linguistic building bricks for creating new words out of old ones. They have this effect either by changing the grammatical form of the original word or by changing its value (positive or negative)—and, in all cases, by changing the word's meaning. We have already seen how "un" added to "kind" transforms the meaning of the adjective and how the "ness" turns this adjective into a noun. These are two derivational morphemes, and it is easy to think of others. Many English words for what people do are formed by adding "agentive" derivational affixes to nouns or verbs. These are the "-ian" ("magician," someone who does magic), "-ist" ("artist," someone who does art), and "-er"/"-or" ("painter," someone who "paints"/"instructor," someone who instructs) endings. Abstract nouns, too, are often built on a combination of a derivational morpheme and a one-morpheme adjective or verb. Thus the noun "education" is created by adding "-ion" to the verb "educate" and "sadness" by adding "ness" to the adjective "sad."

Morphemes and Literacy

The importance of this morphemic structure in children's reading and writing is immense. In reading, for example, it is an essential aid to children encountering a word which they have never seen before and sometimes have never even heard before. A child who knows and can read the word "instruct" and also knows how the derivational affix "-or" changes a verb into an agentive noun is in a good position to read and understand the word "instructor" even when it is entirely new to her.

We shall return later to the possible significance of children's knowledge about morphemes to their reading. Here, we will concentrate on the role of morphemes in children's spelling. The connection between morphemes and spelling is powerful and important and it is easy to summarize. The point is that spelling patterns represent morphemes, as well as sounds, in written English and in many other written languages as well.

This connection between spelling and morphemes sometimes supplements and sometimes conflicts with grapheme–phoneme relationships. Let us begin with the supplementary role of the spelling–morpheme connection. There are two ways, for example, of representing the two phonemes /ks/ at the end of a written English word. One is to use the letter "x" to represent these phonemes, as in "fox": the other is to add an "s" to the preceding representation of /k/, as in "socks" or "bakes." If one thinks just of grapheme–phoneme relationships, both spellings are perfectly legitimate, and the speller therefore has to be familiar with these specific words to know which spelling to use, in much the same way as she must rely on word-specific knowledge to know that she must write "soap" and not "sope."

However, once one brings morphemes into the equation, there is no longer any need for this reliance on word-specific knowledge. The /ks/ ending in one-morpheme words like "fox" and "fix" is always spelled as "x" or as "-xe" ("axe"). In two-morpheme words it is spelled as "-cks" or as "-kes," because in these words the letter "s" represents the second morpheme. This final "s" invariably represents the plural inflection ("cats," "socks") in regular plural verbs and the inflection for third-person present verbs ("he waits," "she thinks"). This is an entirely consistent spelling rule and it is a morphemic one.

Morphemic rules are instances of the indirect connection, which we discussed in Chapter 1, between oral and written language, via an abstract grammatical representation. The use of the same letter, "s," to represent the plural in words that sound different at the end is an example of the semiographic principle at work—"cats" has an /s/ sound at the end and "trees" has a /z/ sound but both are spelled with "s."

Morphemes settle spelling choices in many other scripts as well. In French, for example, the sounds of the endings of the past imperfect "je parlais" ("I was speaking") and the past perfect "j'ai parlé" ("I spoke") are exactly the same but spelled differently. There is one spelling for the imperfect and another for the perfect past tense inflection.

It is the same in Greek. The Greek script is a highly consistent one, but the spoken language has only five vowel sounds, as we noted in

Chapter 2, and three of these vowels can be written in more than one way. The fact that there are more ways of spelling Greek vowels then there are vowels in the spoken language means that anyone writing the language is constantly faced with choices between two or more legitimate spellings for the same sound. There is no rule for sorting out which is the correct spelling when these vowels are part of the word's stem; one has to rely on word-specific knowledge. However, this word-specific-knowledge is quite unnecessary when the vowel is the whole of or part of an inflectional morpheme. In this case there are strict rules about which of the candidate spellings is the right one.

Thus, when Greek words end in an /ɔ/ sound, this sound usually represents an inflectional morpheme. At the end of a verb, the sound signifies that the verb is in the first person singular and in the present tense. At the end of a noun, it tells us that this is a singular, neuter noun. There are also two ways to spell the /ɔ/ sound in Greek, which are "ω" and "o." The two spellings and the two inflections come together. It is an absolutely inflexible rule that the correct spelling for the present verb /ɔ/ ending is "ω," while for the singular, neuter noun ending it is "o." There are many other instances in Greek spelling, as we shall see, of morphemes determining the correct choice between different possible spellings. It seems that, in Greek as well as in English, it might help the budding speller to know something about the morphemes in the words that she is writing.

Thus far, we have looked at examples of morphemes settling the choice between two possible spellings which are both legitimate ways of spelling the sound in question. There are also cases where for entirely morphemic reasons words are spelled in ways that actually flout normal grapheme–phoneme correspondence rules—again, an example of the semiographic principle at work independently from the phonographic principle. The most obvious of these is the "-ed" spelling for the past tense inflection. In different regular verbs this "-ed" ending represents three entirely different sounds which are /t/ as in "kissed," /d/ as in "killed" and /id/ as in "waited." None of these endings, according to the grapheme–phoneme correspondence rules, should be spelled as "ed." The "ed" ending therefore is a direct link between morphemes and spelling which has little to do with correspondences between graphemes and phonemes.

Sometimes spelling even represents morphemes and morphemic distinctions that are not actually pronounced in spoken language. This happens quite a lot in French. In French, singular and plural nouns and adjectives, and singular and plural third person present verbs, usually sound the same as each other. The nouns in the sentences "la maison blanche" and "les maisons blanches" sound exactly the same and so do the adjectives: only the definite articles in these two phrases have different sounds. The sounds of the verb in "il aime" and "ils aiment" are also just the same. However, although these singular and plural words have the same sounds as each other, they are spelled differently. The difference is that the plural words are given an added ending in writing which is not pronounced in speech. French-speaking children, therefore, have the difficult task of learning the conventions for representing a basic morphemic distinction which is not part of their own speech.

Readers and speakers of English have much the same dilemma with the distinction between plural ("boys") and possessive ("boy's") nouns. They too sound exactly the same, even though the distinction between them is clearly signalled in writing by the presence or absence of an apostrophe. Our colleague Nenagh Kemp once saw a notice in the entrance of a block of flats which said "Residents refuse to be put in the bins." This notice, it turned out, was not a call for a basic human right, but an injunction about where the residents should put their rubbish. The caretaker had forgotten to put an apostrophe at the end of "residents." His difficulty is shared by a large number of people. The morphemic difference between plural and possessive nouns, being silent, is one of the great traps in English spelling.

Summary

Morphology affects spelling in a large number of alphabetic orthographies. It does so in three different ways:

1 When there are alternative spellings for the same sound, morphology often determines which spelling the writer should choose. The /ks/ ending is invariably spelled as "-x" or "-xe" in one-morpheme and as "-cks" or "-kes" in two-morpheme English words. In Greek words the /ɔ/sound is always spelled as "o" when it is the ending for neuter singular nouns but as "ω" when it is the first person singular present tense verb ending.

2 When the same morpheme is pronounced differently in different words, the way it is spelled is often the same across these words despite the variation in pronunciations. The pronunciation of the past tense endings of regular English verbs varies ("kissed" "killed" and "waited") but they are always spelled in the same way.

3   Spelling sometimes represents morphemic differences when speech sounds do not. There is no auditory difference between the French nouns "la maison" and "les maisons" but the difference between is represented by the absence (singular) or the presence (plural) of the final unpronounced "-s."

Slow learning of two basic morphemic spelling rules

The examples that we have given you demonstrate that English spelling, and spelling in many other alphabetic scripts, are based on correspondence between graphemes and morphemes as well as between graphemes and phonemes. The obvious importance of grapheme–morpheme links naturally prompts a suggestion about teaching and learning. It seems quite possible, even probable, that some knowledge of grapheme–morpheme correspondence might help children to learn how to spell.

We must start by treating this suggestion as a possibility, not a certainty. Morphemic spelling rules clearly exist, but this does not mean that children learn them. There is, as always, the spectre of "word-specific knowledge." We must recognize that a child may learn that "kissed" has an "-ed" ending and "education" an "-ion" ending simply by becoming familiar with the spelling of these specific words. In principle, the child could learn the spelling of all regular past verbs and all abstract nouns derived from verbs without any idea that "-ed" represents the past tense inflection or that "-ion" is a derivational morpheme that converts verbs into abstract nouns.

There are really two questions here. One is "How well and how quickly do children learn to write words like 'kissed' and 'education,' whose spelling is determined in part by morphemic spelling rules?" The second question is "To what extent do children rely on morphemic spelling rules in order to learn to spell such words?"

The answer to the first question is clear. On the whole it takes children a quite long time to learn how to write words whose spelling is determined by morphemic spelling rules, especially when these spelling rules flout grapheme–phoneme conventions.

We will document this claim in the following section, but before we do so, we want to make a disclaimer. The difficulties that young children have with morphemic rules about spelling do not mean that they are ignorant of morphemes or even of the connection between morphemes and spelling. It is quite possible that they know something about these things but are thrown off course by the conflict with grapheme–phoneme rules which they have had to work so hard to master.

We can start with some basic, and pervasive, rules for spelling inflections in English. When English-speaking children start to write words, they soon begin to use grapheme–phoneme correspondences to do so, as we have already seen. One cannot say the same for grapheme–morpheme correspondences. Many children at first by-pass even the commonest grapheme–morpheme correspondences. Take, for example, the common "-ed" spelling for the past tense inflection. In Figure 5.1 we present part of a charming story by an 8-year-old girl. You can see that she spells the past tense endings phonetically—"trict" for "tricked" and "killd" for "killed." Incidentally, you can also see that some of the segmentations used by this girl were phonographic rather than semiographic, and thus do not follow the usual conventions: "nomatte" for "no matter" and "a way" for "away." She also used apostrophes in "babby's" (line 2) and "egg's" (line 8)—in both cases, improperly so. All of these examples illustrate how a perfect phonological representation may be at fault because of semiographic rules.

Figure 5.2 presents a second example of phonological representations, by a 7-year-old boy, which also violate semiographic rules: "under grownd" exemplifies a different spelling and segmentation than the conventional "underground" and "killd" and "fritend" show a phonographic representation that is unconventional due to semiographic rules.

These children's spellings are typical. Not all 7- and 8-year-olds write this way, but these are not exceptions. We have already seen in Chapter 2 how Varnhagen et al. (1997) found that over 75% of Canadian Grade 1 children (6-year-olds) wrote the past tense ending phonetically (e.g. "helpt" for "helped" and "grabd" for "grabbed") and that none of them at all used the correct "-ed" spelling. More recently, Walker and Hauerwas (2006) showed that American school-children also find the "-ed" spelling a difficult one. Children in the first grade only managed to spell this ending correctly in around 25% of the past verbs that the experimenters asked them to write. An interesting part of this study is that these children did twice as well at spelling another inflectional ending, which was the present progressive ending "-ing." This large difference is almost certainly due to the fact that the "-ed" ending always flouts phoneme–grapheme principles while the "-ing" ending never does. It sounds the way that it is spelled.

What happens later on? We found the answer to this question when we did a large-scale longitudinal study some time ago (Nunes, Bryant, & Bindman, 1997a). The children who took part were either 6, 7 or 8 years-old when the study began. During the following three years we took measures of their progress in learning to read and to spell, and

my favourite Book is
Jemimma padel Dubk
By Beatrix potter
it is abowt   a Duck
she   cannot   have BaBBy's
nomatke Wher she Hids her Egg-
s   Thar awas Being Fohd oneDay
she Ran a Way   To The Wood-
s   and She maet a Fox The
Fox TowD her She   can place
her Egg's at his Howse so She
want to his Howse Bat he
Trick her   he Dat her In a
Sack Bat Loakaly she got Freey
and   a man came and killd
The Fox and she Had BaBBy's
areFad ahl
              The End

Figure 5.1 A girl's writing about her favourite book

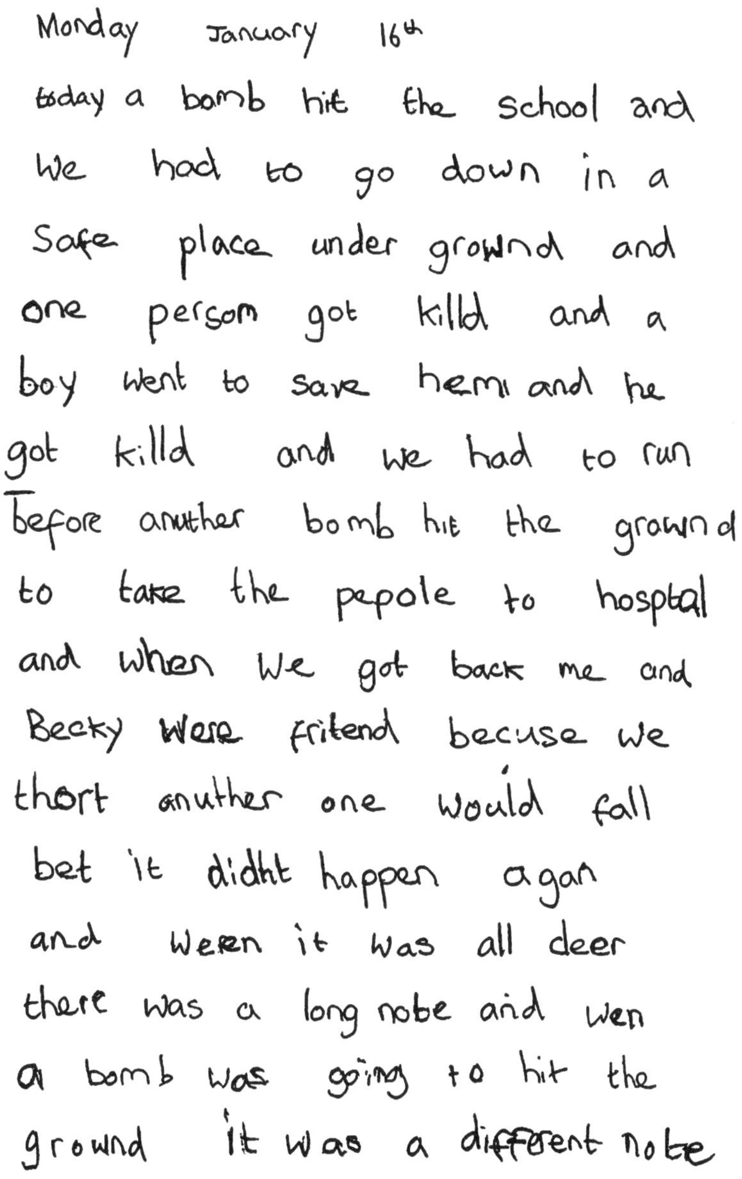

Monday   January   16th

today a bomb hit the school and
we had to go down in a
Safe place under grownd and
one persom got killd and a
boy went to save hemi and he
got killd and we had to run
before anuther bomb hit the grownd
to take the pepole to hosptal
and when we got back me and
Becky were fritend becuse we
thort anuther one would fall
bet it didht happen agan
and weren it was all deer
there was a long nobe and wen
a bomb was going to hit the
ground it was a different nobe

Figure 5.2 A boy's story (imaginary) about how a bomb hit the school

also of what they knew about the role of morphemes in spoken language and in spelling.

Table 5.1 gives the words that we asked them to write in one of our main measures of spelling. Notice that all these words end either in a /t/ or in a /d/ sound, and also that they are divided into three sets. In the first set, the words are all one-morpheme words and their /d/ and /t/ endings are all spelled phonetically. In the second set, all the words are irregular past tense verbs. Irregular verbs do not conform to the "-ed" spelling rule, and so in this set too all the /d/ and /t/ endings are spelled phonetically. Finally, all the words in the third set are regular verbs, and so their endings are spelled as "-ed" whether the final sound is /d/ or /t/.

Thus, the sounds of the endings were the same in all three sets. But these two end sounds were spelled according to grapheme–phoneme correspondence rules in the first two sets (non-verbs and irregular past verbs) and according to grapheme–morpheme correspondence rules in

Table 5.1 The words ending in either in a /t/ or in a /d/ sound that we asked the children to spell

/d/ ending	/t/ ending	
bird	belt	
cold	except	
field	next	Non-verbs—mean frequency: 287.1 in one million
gold	paint	
ground	soft	
found	felt	
heard	left	
held	lost	Irregular past verbs—mean frequency: 319.3 in a million
sold	sent	
told	slept	
called	dressed	
covered	kissed	
filled	laughed	Regular past verbs—mean frequency: 285.6 in a million
killed	learned	
opened	stopped	

Note: Frequencies obtained from http://www.essex.ac.uk/psychology/cpwd/ on 04/07/2007
Source: Nunes, Bryant, & Bindman (1997).

the third set. So, our purpose was to compare the children's use of the phonographic and semiographic spellings.

We asked them to spell the words at different times during the first two years of the project, and since their ages ranged from 6–8 years at the beginning of the project, we ended up with scores on this task for children between 6 and 10 years of age.

Figure 5.3 shows an example of how two different children spelled a portion of the words that we dictated and Figure 5.4 shows how the children managed.

Their spellings led us to two firm conclusions. The first, and perhaps the most important, is that the children were more at home with grapheme–phoneme correspondences than with grapheme–morpheme correspondences. It is hard to find any other explanation for the fact that the non-verb and the irregular past verb endings were so much easier for the children than the regular past tense "-ed" ending. It is most unlikely that this difference is due to any reliance on word-specific knowledge, because the frequency with which the words appear in children's texts is roughly the same for all three sets. The difference must be due to children having a far better understanding of the link between sounds and letters than of the link between morphemes and letters.

This conclusion is bolstered by the fact that the majority of the mistakes that the children made in spelling the endings of regular verbs were "phonetic" errors; when they erred, they tended to spell "kissed" as "kist" or "kisst," for example, and "killed" as "kild" or "killd" (see Figure 5.3). Their mistakes confirm the irrelevance of word-specific knowledge to the differing levels of success with the three sets: the children had never seen "words" like "kild" and so they did not make this kind of error because of anything that they had learned about specific words.

The second, inescapable, conclusion from the results presented in Table 5.1 is that the children got better at spelling the word endings in all three sets of words as they grew older. The improvement over age was slightly more rapid with the difficult set of regular past verbs than with the other sets, but this may be due to the fact that many of the children began to produce perfect scores with the words in the first two sets quite early on and therefore left no room for improvement with these easier words. At any rate, the children made few mistakes indeed in spelling the two easier sets of words by the time that they reached the age of 9 and 10 years, whereas even at this age the average score for the regular verbs still fell well below 80%. The "-ed" ending continued to cause many, though certainly not all, of the children a lot of difficulty,

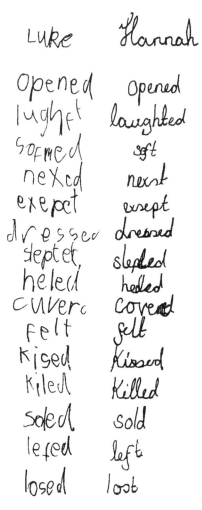

Figure 5.3 Two children's spellings of a sample of the words we dictated

despite having had so much teaching and so much experience of reading and writing.

The past tense ending is a striking example of the problems that children have at first with the connection between morphemes and spelling, and it is not a special case. Some recent evidence suggests that young children may have rather similar difficulties in understanding how plural words are spelled. The plural inflection in regular nouns is "-s."

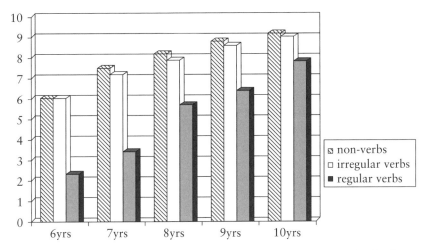

Figure 5.4 The children's mean correct spelling scores (out of 10) of regular and irregular past tense verbs and non-verbs between ages 6 and 10 years (N = 90)

Sometimes this spelling coincides with the sound of the plural inflection. The sound of the plural inflection in the word "cats," for example, is /s/ and that sound, according to the basic grapheme–phoneme correspondence rules, is usually spelled as "s." In other plural words, however, the sound and the spelling of the plural inflection do not agree so well. The sound of the plural inflection in "dogs" and "trees," to take just two examples, is /z/, but of course, obeying grapheme–morpheme correspondence rules, it is spelled as "s" in both these words and in every other /z/ ending plural noun (there are a great many of these).

Until recently the general opinion was that this conflict between the sound of the inflection and its conventional spelling was not much of a problem. The great linguist Charles Read found little evidence of children spelling /z/ ending plurals as "z" and cited this as the first sign of some recognition on their part of the connection between morphemes and spelling. Treiman (1993) accepted the observation about children's reluctance to write plurals as /z/, but argued that this might be due not to an understanding of the morphemic spelling rule for plural endings, but to the fact that the letter "z" appears infrequently in English texts and that "s" represents the /z/ sound in many common English words, such as "easy." No doubt it was this last fact that prompted King Lear to berate the letter "z" as "unnecessary" with such passion. ("Thou whoreson zed: thou unnecessary letter").

Now, however, it appears that children really do have a lot of difficulty with /z/ ending plural words, or at any rate with some of them. Kemp and Bryant (2003) asked children in the age range 5y10m to 8y11m to spell plural words that ended in a /z/ sound. We read out each word and then repeated it in the context of a sentence to make sure that the children understood that it was in the plural. Then we asked the children to write the word. Sometimes the /z/ ending in the plural word came immediately after a consonant ("*fibs*. The naughty boy told *fibs* to his mother") and sometimes it followed a vowel ("*fleas*. That poor little dog has got *fleas*").

We found that the children made a lot of mistakes in writing the ending of the plural words in which the sound before the /z/ ending was a vowel (e.g. "fleas"). They only managed to spell the /z/ ending correctly 73% of the time. They spelled 20% of these plural endings either as "-ze" or as "-se": these are the wrong spellings for plural endings but the right spellings for one-morpheme words in which the /z/ ending is immediately preceded by a long vowel ("freeze," "please"). So here was evidence of quite a lot of confusion about the plural ending even with words that were familiar to the children who took part in this study. Kemp and Bryant also analysed whether the better spellers in this age range would show excellent performance on these plural words ending in /z/. We divided the children into two groups, one of weaker spellers, whose mean spelling age was 6y11m, and a second of more proficient spellers, whose mean spelling age was 9y6m. There was a significant difference in the percentage of children in the two groups who spelled the /z/ sounding plurals with "s," and, as one would expect, the proficient spellers did significantly better. However, even their performance was not perfect: only 82% of their spellings were correct, which is not at all impressive given that the rule is so simple and the group's mean spelling age was above 9 years.

These children did much better with the other set of plural words—the "fibs" type words in which the sound just before the /z/ ending is a consonant. They spelled the plural ending correctly as "s" 91% of the time, and they hardly ever used the singular "-se" (1%) or "-ze" (2%) singular endings with these words. This is an interesting difference but it need not detain us long because the reason for their success with the "fibs" words is almost certainly due to the children detecting a specific pattern in English spelling. Virtually every word in the English language in which the /z/ sound follows a consonant is spelled as "-s." This is because virtually every English word of this sort is a two-morpheme word—either a plural word or a third person singular present tense verb (e.g. "(he) runs"). There are a few exceptions, but their number is small and they are all words which are unlikely to be part of a child's linguistic world—words like "adze" and "bronze." Thus, children probably do well with these "fibs" words by learning a simple but specific rule that the /z/ ending is always spelled as "-s" when it follows a consonant. It is fascinating that they pick this knowledge up, especially since no teacher ever tells them about it, but it is a far cry from a general morphemic spelling rule that the plural inflection in nouns is always spelled as "s."

No specific rule exists to help children with /z/ ending words in which a long vowel sound comes just before this ending. In some of these words the /z/ ending is spelled as "-s" because they are two-morpheme words ("trees," "he sees"). In others it is spelled as "-se" or as "-ze" and these are all one-morpheme words. Therefore, children have two possible ways to spell the endings of these words correctly. They can rely either on word-specific knowledge or on the morphemic spelling.

The fact that there are these two possible routes to success raises a question about the difficulty that the children have with words like "fleas" in the experiment that we have just described. Although these words are difficult, the children did manage to spell the plural ending correctly more often than not and the number of times that they got the endings right was much better than one would expect by chance. This relative success (73%), however, is not hard and fast evidence that the children had any knowledge of the spelling rule. Once again we must wonder about the impact of word-specific knowledge. When the children got the ending of "fleas" right, this could have been because they had seen the written word before and could remember it.

We have already explained that there is a simple way to eliminate word-specific knowledge. Ask children to spell pseudowords which are either obviously in the plural or obviously singular. One can make this clear by embedding the pseudowords in sentences which make it clear whether they are plural or not. We did this (Kemp & Bryant, 2003) in a further experiment with children in the same age range as in the first study. Again we asked children to write a series of words, and we embedded each of these words in a sentence. The only change in the new tasks was that the children had to write pseudowords rather than real words. All of these new words had /z/ endings. There were three sets of these words:

1 Plural words: the /z/ ending followed a consonant (correct spelling "-s") Example "*stogs*. There are five *stogs* in my garden."

2   Plural words: the /z/ ending followed a long vowel (correct spelling
    "-s") Example: "*prees*. How many *prees* can you see up there?"
3   Singular words: the /z/ ending followed a long vowel (correct spelling
    "-se" or "-ze") Example: "*preeze*. That man keeps a big *preeze* in
    his cupboard."

Again the young children found it hard to produce the right spelling for
the endings of the words with vowel sounds just before the /z/ sound
(the prees/preeze words in sets 2 and 3). In fact, these words were much
more difficult to spell than the equivalent real words had been in the
first study. On average in set 2 the children only spelled 37% of the
plural words with the correct "-s" ending. In set 3 they spelled only
49% of the one-morpheme pseudowords with the correct "-se" or "-ze"
endings. They did much better, as in the earlier study, in spelling plural
words with a consonant just before the /z/ ending (the *stogs* words in
set 1): here they were right 74% of the time.
     These two studies demonstrate that, at best, children at the early
stages of learning to read and spell are uncertain about the rule for
spelling plural inflections even though it is one of the most basic and
most pervasive of all the connections between morphemes and spelling.
The studies also show that children ingeniously discover for themselves
a spelling pattern, which helps them with some plural words ("fibs" and
"stogs") though not with others ("trees" and "prees"). In general, the
research that we have just described on spelling the past tense and the
plural inflection is clear and strong evidence that children tend not to
follow morphemic spelling rules during the first few years of learning
to read and write. Whether they know anything about these rules is
another question, and we shall deal with it later.

Summary

The way that school children spell two basic and much used inflectional
morphemes demonstrates that it takes a long time for them to learn
about and use morphemic spelling rules: it is not until the age of about
10 years that the majority of children attaches the "-ed" ending to
regular past verbs.

1   Part of the difficulty that they have with this spelling rule is the
    result of a clash between the morphemic rule and grapheme–
    phoneme correspondences. This is why some children persist in

spelling past verbs according to grapheme–phoneme correspondence ("kisst") instead of adopting the correct morphemic spelling.

2   Reliance on grapheme–phoneme correspondences is probably the reason why children often do not spell the plural ending with the appropriate "-s" in words in which it is pronounced as /z/.

3   In this case, children appear, spontaneously and somewhat perversely, to adopt a rule based on frequency. They note that whenever a word ends in the /z/ sound and that ending is immediately preceded by a consonant, the final /z/ sound is spelled as "-s." This odd rule works for some /z/ ending plural words but not for those in which the /z/ ending is immediately preceded by a vowel. That is why children spell "dogs" about as well as they do "cats" and both of these words far better than "fleas." The rule is not a morphemic one.

Research on Using the Apostrophe

Learning about English morphemic spelling rules is not all of a piece. English-speaking children learn about different rules at different times. By the age of 11 years, they are doing reasonably well with the past tense ending, as we have seen. Yet, at the same age their understanding and use of another morphemic spelling rule are, at best, decidedly patchy. This is the notoriously treacherous possessive apostrophe. Almost certainly its difficulty is due to a fact that we mentioned in the beginning of the chapters. Most words that differ by just one morpheme are also different in the way that they sound. The word "cat" sounds different from "cats" because we sound out the plural inflection in the second word. However, although there is a crucial morphemic distinction between plural and possessive nouns in English, they sound exactly the same. The morphemic distinction is signalled in writing, but not in speech; "cats" sounds just the same as "cat's" in spoken language but the two words look different in writing.

Children in schools in England are introduced to the possessive apostrophe when they are around 9 years-old. In what we think was the first ever scientific investigation of the apostrophe, we looked at how well 9-, 10- and 11-year-old children understand the role of the apostrophe, and we also tried to find out if it is possible to improve this understanding (Bryant, Devine, Ledward, & Nunes, 1997).

In the first of two studies our basic task was a set of 16 written sentences that we gave to each child. A word was missing in each sentence and there was a blank space where the word should have been.

We dictated each sentence including the missing word and it was the child's task to write this word into the space provided for it. The missing word was a plural, nominative or accusative, noun in half the sentences (e.g. "The dogs are barking") and a singular, possessive, noun in the other half ("Is this the boy's football?"): the missing word is underlined in both examples. Our question was whether the children could work out whether each word was plural or possessive and assign the apostrophe accordingly.

We found that the children were right most of the time with plural words and wrong most of the time with the possessives. They represented the final /s/ or /z/ sound as "s" with both kinds of word, but they usually left out the apostrophe. The 9-year-olds' scores were the worst: they hardly ever wrote any word with an apostrophe, and on the few occasions when they did use apostrophes they were as likely to do so with the wrong words as with the right ones. The 10- and 11-year-olds also tended to leave the apostrophe out, but at least they did write more possessive than plural words with apostrophes.

The children's performance was so unimpressive that we thought at first that we had given them too difficult a problem. However, we soon found that this pessimism was quite unjustified because we also established we could quite easily help them to do a great deal better. We taught some of the children about the apostrophe in a short group session, in which we presented them with examples of possessive and plural words and asked them to discuss whether particular words should have an apostrophe on them or not. We also formed a control group of children to whom we gave the same verbal material as we gave to the group whom we taught about apostrophes, but their task was to make judgements about the meaning of the words. Both groups saw the same sentences but their task differed. For example, one of the sentences was: "The market's fruit stall sells pears." The taught group had to say whether it was right to have the apostrophe and why. The control group had to decide whether the last word in this sentence should be spelled as "pairs" or "pears." The teaching was delivered by the researchers to the children in small groups.

A day later, we gave the children the same task as we had given them at the beginning of the study to see if the taught group was now any better than before at placing the apostrophe on possessive words. In this final test, the children whom we had taught about the apostrophe were a great deal better than they had been at the beginning of the study. The 10- and 11-year-olds used apostrophes more than they had before and put them much more frequently on the right words than on the wrong ones. The results for the 9-year-olds differed between the two experiments: in one experiment, they improved significantly in comparison with the control group but in the other one they did not. We don't know why there was this difference between the experiments but the success of the 9-year-olds in one of the two experiments can be seen as what is called "existence proof": it shows that 9-year-olds can improve on the use of the apostrophes through carefully designed instruction.

One more aspect of these teaching experiments that we want to report is that, in the second experiment, we included in the pre- and post-test two uses of the apostrophe: the possessive, already discussed, and the use of the apostrophe to show contraction, as in "I think I'm getting fatter." Our aim was to test the hypothesis that learning is specific to a rule, not just a matter of general familiarity. The children were only taught about the possessive, so they should only differ from the control children in the use of the apostrophe when it marks the meaning of possession. This hypothesis of specific learning was supported by our finding of a significant interaction between group, taught versus control, and type of task, use of apostrophe to indicate possession or contraction. The taught group performed significantly better than the control in the sentences where the apostrophe indicated possession but not in those where it indicated contraction. The latter use of apostrophes was actually easier for children in all age groups but they were not close to perfect performance and there was room for improvement.

Our success in this teaching experiment is not the only story of children's learning about apostrophes. Alexander McMillan, a teacher whose class had participated in our studies of the use of the past tense "-ed," developed a teaching programme about the apostrophe for his own pupils. McMillan (1999) created a programme which aimed to teach children about contractions, about forming plurals without apostrophes by adding "s," "es" or "ies" (the latter replacing the final "y"), and about possession. The participants in his studies were his students, whose mean age was 8 years and who had not been taught about the apostrophe before. He used nine lessons plus homework assignments for this teaching. The first three lessons were dedicated to teaching children about contractions, followed by two lessons where the children were taught about forming the plural, followed by two lessons on the possessive; lesson 8 focused on distinguishing between the two uses of the apostrophe (contraction and possession) and the final lesson consisted of forming noun phrases by combining owners with their possessions (e.g. given "shoes" and "tap dancer," the children had to form the phrase "the tap dancer's shoes").

In contrast to our results, McMillan's efforts were not rewarded: most of the children did not show much improvement from pre- to post-test. The overall improvement, including all three types of words (contractions, possessives and plurals), was modest—an improvement of 4%. Even though there was an improvement of 12% in the use of apostrophes to indicate possession, there was little change in the children's performance from pre- to post-test in the correct placement of the apostrophe to indicate contraction or in its omission with plurals that do not involve a possessive relation.

McMillan's teaching study differs from ours in three significant ways. First, he did not have a control group; so he could not know whether the modest improvement from pre- to post-test was significant. It is perfectly plausible that children in a control group would have shown some deterioration in performance from pre- to post-test in his tasks. At pre-test, the children were told that they would need to choose the correct spelling for the missing word in a sentence and were offered one choice without apostrophe and two choices with an apostrophe; for example, for the sentence "the trees swayed in the wind," they were to choose the correct form from three alternatives, *trees*, *trees'* or *tree's*. After being sensitized to the use of apostrophes by participating in this pre-test, and not receiving instruction on the use of apostrophes, the control group could well perform worse later on by over-using the apostrophe. McMillan does acknowledge the possibility that the children might have over-used the apostrophe after having taken his pre-test: "The children *were* presented with a test entitled Apostrophes. They *were* told that some sentences in the test did not need an apostrophe. The fact that the apostrophe was the area of focus and also the title of the test may have served to increase the rate of over-use" (1999, p. 383, emphasis in the original). This difference between McMillan's design and ours is instructive: the lack of a control group really does make it difficult to draw any conclusions from the results of intervention studies.

Second, none of the lessons involved a comparison between cases where the apostrophe is required with those where the apostrophe is not required. The only lesson that involved a contrast was lesson 8, where the children contrasted the two cases where the apostrophe *is* used. So in our view this means that, at each lesson, the children were only taught half of a rule. Putting the complete rule together was left to the children themselves. Perhaps only some children are able to put together the whole rule after learning half of the rule on one day and the other half on another day. We saw in Chapter 3, in the analysis of children's learning of the "k" versus "ck" ending, that it makes a difference for children's improvement if they are taught a rule by comparing the contrasting cases rather than one part of the rule at a time. It is thus possible that some children made good progress and others not: the modest average progress made by the children was a consequence of the way the instruction was designed. McMillan reports that six children made great progress, and the individual differences increased from pre- to post-test (as assessed by a change in the standard deviation). These results suggest that the form of instruction, which did not contrast the presence and absence of apostrophes, could explain the difference between his results and ours. His method worked for some children but not for others, whereas our method benefited the majority of the children. Unfortunately, this is only a discussion *a posteriori*; we cannot be certain of this.

Finally, the children in his study were younger than those in our study. It is possible that, for such young children, his intervention included too much that was new—they were taught about different forms of the plural in spelling and also about two uses of the apostrophe.

It is not possible to decide which of these different alternatives explains the discrepancy between our results in teaching children about the use of apostrophes to indicate possession and McMillan's results. However, there is an important lesson to be learned here: intervention studies work as "existence proof" that it is possible to teach children something more than as general evidence for any intervention. Evidence in the form of existence proof is important. Failure to obtain positive results from interventions cannot eliminate the information that we gain from carefully controlled intervention studies that do produce positive outcomes.

Summary

1 The possessive apostrophe is another morphemic spelling that transcends grapheme–phoneme relations. The two sequences "The girls charm" and "The girl's charm" have the same phonemes but entirely different meanings that are captured by the presence or absence of the possessive apostrophe.
2 Most children seem not to know about this function of the apostrophe before they are taught about it at the age of about 9 to 10 years, and they show hardly any such knowledge after they are given the relevant instruction.

3 Yet a laboratory study showed that it was possible to improve their understanding and use of the possessive apostrophe quickly and effectively. The rule may not be difficult to learn.
4 A parallel teaching study carried out in the classroom was not effective, for reasons which are not yet clear. We need to know more about what allows children to learn this morphemic spelling rule and what gets in the way of this learning.

The Difficult "-ion" and "-ian" Endings

There is much more evidence than this that most young children fail at first to use morphemic spelling rules even when they are writing highly familiar words that they are bound to have seen in print many times before. One striking example is how children learn the conventional spellings for the various derivational morphemes that signal that a word is an abstract noun or an agentive. We mentioned these endings at the beginning of this chapter.

In several different studies, which we summarized in an earlier book about teaching children to read and spell (Nunes & Bryant, 2006, Chapter 2), we ourselves confirmed the difficulty that young children have in learning about these particular grapheme–morpheme correspondences. We only sample here some of the information described in that earlier book. Figure 5.5 shows the frequency of correct uses of the suffixes "-ion" (e.g. "education") and "-ness" (e.g. "happiness") by a sample of over 700 children in eight different schools in Oxford and London. At about age 9, the children seem to approach 80% of correct spellings of these suffixes, even though they have a fixed form and a fixed function, which is to signal abstract nouns. This level of success is not at all impressive, given that there is no ambiguity in the spelling if you know about suffixes.

In another study, we contrasted the use of the endings "-ion" and "-ian." This comparison is important because words ending with these suffixes sound the same at the end. The suffix "-ion" is much more frequent than "-ian" in the English language—the MRC data base gives 2,859 words with "-ion" and 963 words with "-ian" but the frequencies of the words we used in our study do not differ much in children's books: our "-ian" words have a frequency of 33 in a million and the "-ion" words a frequency of 37. Figure 5.6 shows the percentage correct uses of "-ion" and "-ian" by 176 children in Years 4 or 5, attending 7 different schools in Oxford. They show a clear tendency to use "-ion"

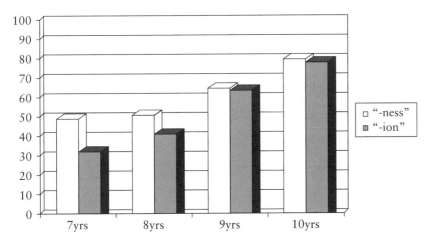

Figure 5.5 Percentage of correct spellings of the suffixes "-ion" and "ness" by children in eight different schools in Oxford and London (N > 700)

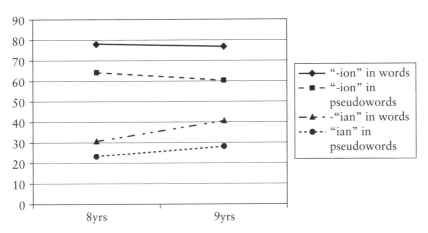

Figure 5.6 Percentage correct uses of "-ion" and "-ian" by 198 children in years 4 or 5 attending seven different schools in Oxford

more often than "-ian," which could result from the differences in frequency in the language or from the explicit teaching that children receive about "ion" as a possible letter-string at the end of words. This teaching, according to the teachers from the schools that participated in our study, does not focus on the connection between "ion" and the creation of an abstract noun, but only on the idea of a fixed letter-sequence used at the end of words. So, they learn that this is a possible spelling, but not when to use it.

Of those words that we used, the most frequent one in children's books is "magician" (according to the Children's Printed Word Database), but its higher frequency than that of the other words does not prevent it from being misspelled. In a longitudinal study with over 7,000 children (part of an epidemiological cohort study run by the University of Bristol), we found that children aged between 9 and 10 spelled "magician" more often with "-ion" than with "-ian": 2,212 spelled the ending of magician with "ion," 1,876 spelled it with "ian" and the remainder used other endings, such as "en," "un," "on," "an," etc.

All these examples simply reinforce our conclusion that, at least under the current conditions of instruction, young children do not easily use morpheme–grapheme correspondences, even when these seem to involve relatively simple rules.

Summary

Most children also take several years to learn to spell derivational endings like "-ion," "-ian" and "ness" which do not conform to grapheme–phoneme relations. Again grapheme–morpheme relations cause the majority of school children great and persistent difficulties.

When and How Do Children Start Using Morphemic Spelling Rules?

The claim that children represent morphemic structure in their spelling from the start

All the evidence that we have discussed so far suggests that children begin to understand and use the link between morphemes and spelling quite late in the long process of learning to read and write. The data suggest that most beginning readers are quite unaware that such a link exists (see also Notenboom & Reitsma, 2007). There is, however, another view on this chain of events. Rebecca Treiman and her colleagues have argued that children are aware of the impact of morphemes on spelling from an early age even at a time when they do not adopt the conventional spellings for inflections and derivational morphemes in their own language. Theirs is an interesting argument, but it seems unconvincing to us in the end.

Treiman and her co-workers reported two different research projects (Treiman & Cassar, 1996; Treiman, Cassar, & Zukowski, 1994) that led them to conclude an early rather than late effect of morphemes on children's spelling. We will concentrate on the first of these because it is the most relevant to the research that we have discussed already.

Treiman and Cassar's starting point was the fact that many two-morpheme English words end in a consonant cluster. A consonant cluster is a sequence of two or more consonants. Thus "build" is one word that ends with this kind of sequence and "killed" another. These two words end in exactly the same cluster, but there is a difference between them. In "build" this cluster is all part of the same morpheme, but in "killed" the /l/ sound at the beginning of the cluster is part of the stem morpheme "kill" and the /d/ sound at the end of the cluster is the (oral mark of the) inflectional morpheme.

Children find it hard to spell clusters properly, and their usual mistake is to leave one of the consonants out completely (Read, 1971; Treiman, 1993). When the cluster is at the end of the word, the vulnerable consonant is usually the first one in the cluster. So, a typical mistake would be for young children to write the words "build" as "bid" and "list" as "lit."

Treiman and Cassar's ingenious argument was that if children are aware that two-morpheme words consist of a stem plus a following inflection, this knowledge would lead them not to omit the first sound in the consonant cluster of a two morpheme word like "killed" because this is an essential part of the representation of the stem morpheme. They will, according to this argument, be more likely to include the /k/ sound in their spelling of "baked" than in their spelling of "connect," because their knowledge that "bake" is the stem of "baked" makes it easier for them to divide the cluster in "baked" into two sounds than the cluster in "connect."

In three different studies Treiman and Cassar asked young children to spell one- and two-morpheme words ending in consonant clusters, in order to test their prediction that children would be more likely to spell the first sound of the final consonant cluster in two- than in one-morpheme words. However, there was, in our view, something strange about their prediction. If some recognition that "baked" contains both a stem and an inflection allows them to separate the sounds in the final cluster, the result should be that they would be more likely to represent *both* consonants in the /kt/ cluster in "baked" than in an equivalent one-morpheme word like "connect." In other words, there should be more "kt" spellings of the cluster in "baked" than in "connect" and less "t"-only spellings. However, Treiman and Cassar did predict that children would omit the first consonant in the cluster more often in one- than in two-morpheme words, but they did not predict that the children would represent both sounds in the cluster more often in two- than in one-morpheme word, as surely they should have done if they were aware of the two morphemes. If their hypothesis is that young children know that a word like "baked" consists of two morphemes, it should follow that this leads them to represent both morphemes, which means that they should represent both sounds in the final cluster.

Let us look at what they found. In three studies these researchers asked children to spell one-morpheme words (e.g. "blind," "arrest" and "connect") and two-morpheme words (e.g. "tuned," "faced," "baked") which ended, in their oral form, in the same consonant clusters as each other, and recorded how the children spelled these clusters. They found that by far the commonest response was for the children to represent both sounds in the final cluster. This was true both of one- and of two-morpheme words and there was no sign at all of the children being better at representing both sounds in the two-morpheme than in the one-morpheme words. Thus there was no evidence at all to support the prediction which we think that Treiman and Cassar should have made, but didn't.

The next most common response made by the children was to omit the first and to represent only the second sound in the cluster. The children did make this omission less often in two-morpheme than in the one-morpheme words, as Treiman and Cassar claimed they would. However this difference was balanced by the fact that the children made the opposite mistake of representing the first sound in the cluster and omitting the second sound in the cluster more often in the two-morpheme than in the one-morpheme words. Thus, they were more likely to write "baked" as "bake" or "bak" than "connect" as "connec."

What are we to make of this curious last result? Treiman and Cassar claim that it supports their idea that the children recognized that there were two separate morphemes in the two-morpheme words. This seems to us to be a strange interpretation. If children see that there are two morphemes in "baked," they should, as we have remarked, be more likely to represent the sounds of both morphemes in their spelling. The fact that they wrote "bake" for "baked" more often than they wrote "connec" for "connect" could be due them having seen the word "bake" but no word like "connec" in print and were writing what they remembered seeing—i.e. using their word-specific knowledge. Thus these experimenters' claim that the 6-year-old children in these studies had already recognized the morphemic structure of two-morpheme words and that this structure had an impact on their spelling is most unconvincing.

Consistency in Spelling Stem Morphemes in English

There is evidence from three different languages—English, Portuguese and French—that children use knowledge of stems to spell other words that share the same stem but this evidence converges on showing a late rather than early use of morphological knowledge.

Our own work in English (Nunes, Bryant, & Bindman, 2006) was carried out with children in three age groups: the younger ones had the mean age of 7y6m and the older ones had the mean age of 9y6m. We asked the children to spell, on two different days, words and pseudowords that shared the same stem. The pseudowords were dinosaur names, and the children were presented with pictures of the dinosaurs which showed quite clearly the origin of their names. For example, *knotosaurus* had a knot in his neck, *halfosaurus*'s body was cut in half, and *combosaurus* had long hair and was combing it with a large comb. All the stems in the dinosaurs' names contained a silent letter—e.g. the "k" in "knotosaurus," the "l" in "halfosaurus" and the "b" in "combosaurus." Figure 5.7a shows a picture of halfosaurus and 5.7b shows a swordosaurus.

Our study aimed to explore whether the children who used the silent letters when they spelled the words would use these silent letters also when spelling the dinosaur name. We expected that the children who did use the silent letters would be the best spellers as they would be displaying strong word-specific knowledge. Would these children, at all age levels, be likely to use the same stem spelling for the dinosaurs' names? And what about the other children, who have less word-specific knowledge?: do they consistently generate the same spelling for these sequences of sounds, even if the spelling is not correct but is based on a phonological representation of the word?

We classified the children's stem spellings into three categories:

1 correct, and therefore including the silent letter;
2 phonologically acceptable but not correct, and thus the silent letter was absent;
3 not phonologically acceptable, that is, a spelling that could not be pronounced as the word that had been dictated; on few occasions, these contained the silent letter but in the wrong place.

Figure 5.7 A picture of halfosaurus (a) and a swordosaurus (b)

Table 5.2 Percentage of spellings in each year group where the word stem and the stem in the dinosaur name were the same (consistent spelling) by type of spelling produced for the word stem

Type of spelling used for the word stem	Year 3 (N = 51)	Year 4 (N = 50)	Year 5 (N = 46)
Correct	87	89	85
	(94)	(123)	(202)
Phonologically acceptable but incorrect	54	53	39
	(144)	(116)	(79)
Not acceptable phonologically	14	26	18
	(133)	(112)	(67)

Table 5.2 shows the number of spellings in each of these three categories, in brackets, for each year group. It is quite plain that the number of correct spellings increases significantly across year groups, with a concomitant reduction in the number of phonological spellings and spellings that are not phonologically acceptable. But the most interesting result in Table 5.2 is that if the children knew how to spell the stem, they were highly likely to use the same spelling when they wrote the dinosaur name. This indicates that word-specific knowledge and the use of morphological information develop hand-in-hand—but, of course, from this data set we cannot know whether one is causally related to the other. This is an idea that we explore later on in this chapter.

A second salient feature of Table 5.2 is that the connection between word-specific knowledge and consistency in the spelling of stems does not seem to depend on the children's age: even the younger children, in Year 3, showed high levels of consistency if they were able to spell the word's stem correctly. There were fewer younger children who could spell the stems correctly than older children but those who could spell the real words correctly also tended to use the same spelling for the stem in the dinosaur name. So it seems that the use of morphological information in the spelling of stems is connected to age, but perhaps this connection is due to the fact that they are both linked to the development of word-specific knowledge or general improvement in spelling. This hypothesis will need further examination.

Finally, it is also easy to see from Table 5.2 that phonologically accurate spellings are not a guarantee that the children will use the same spelling for the same stem the next day. The stem "sword," for example, can be spelled as "sord," "sored," "sward" or "sawred"—all four spellings are phonologically accurate and incorrect; the child might use one spelling one day and another the next day. One child actually told us that if she was not sure how to spell a word, she would spell it in different ways in the hope that one of the spellings would be correct.

Our study of children's consistency in the spelling of stems, which is only partially described here (for further details, see Nunes, Bryant, & Bindman, 2006), showed that children's consistency in the spelling of stems is related to their awareness of morphology: the children's awareness of morphology predicted their consistency in spelling stems at a later time, even after controlling for age and general intelligence. But this was not a one-way connection: children's consistency in spelling stems also predicted their later awareness of morphology, after using the same controls. So the pattern we saw in the responses presented in Table 5.2 was confirmed by further statistical analyses, and it can be concluded that the connection between awareness of morphology and spelling is a two-way connection.

For those who might be curious about the differences between the words, we have included here also Table 5.3, which presents the results for each of the eight stimulus pairs of real words and dinosaur names (we used ten pairs in the research but three contained vowel digraphs so we excluded them from Table 5.3).

Thus we have just discussed another example of morpheme–grapheme correspondences that is helpful for children to start using. Their ability to do so develops with age—but the connection with age is to some extent mediated by their progress on spelling more generally.

If this is the case, one would expect that children learning an orthography that is more consistent than English in terms of grapheme–phoneme correspondences will make progress in learning grapheme–morpheme correspondences at an earlier age than English children. We will turn to this later on, but now we wish to consider evidence of use of morphology in spelling from two other languages, Portuguese and French.

French- and Portuguese-speaking Children's Use of Morphological Information in Spelling

French spelling, like English spelling, contains many silent letters. But there is a difference between English and French, which can be explored to help us understand better how children use morphological information. In English, "comb" has a silent "b," and this "b" was still silent in the

Table 5.3 Percentage of children in each year group who used the same spelling for the stem in the word and in the dinosaur name for each pair of stimuli

Stimulus pair	Year 3 (N = 51)	Year 4 (N = 50)	Year 5 (N = 46)
Talk-talkosaurus			
Consistency if word stem correct	80	97	100
Consistency for phonological spellings	25	0	100
Consistency for non-phonological spellings	10	31	14
Comb-combosaurus			
Consistency if word stem correct	86	80	88
Consistency for phonological spellings	52	60	69
Consistency for non-phonological spellings	33	45	31
Iron-ironosaurus			
Consistency if word stem correct	87	100	74
Consistency for phonological spellings	26	33	33
Consistency for non-phonological spellings	10	0	14
Half-halfosaurus			
Consistency if word stem correct	90	96	100
Consistency for phonological spellings	50	17	0
Consistency for non-phonological spellings	16	27	0
Knot-knotosaurus			
Consistency if word stem correct	100	80	65
Consistency for phonological spellings	78	81	65
Consistency for non-phonological spellings	18	30	70
Sword-swordosaurus			
Consistency if word stem correct	75	90	78
Consistency for phonological spellings	61	53	33
Consistency for non-phonological spellings	4	14	6
Build-buildosaurus			
Consistency if word stem correct	71	46	80
Consistency for phonological spellings	62	50	57
Consistency for non-phonological spellings	11	24	33

pseudoword "combosaurus." In the French language there are many examples of stems which contain a silent letter at the end, like "comb," but this silent letter is typically pronounced when a suffix is added to it. For example, in spoken French the one-morpheme noun "regard" has a silent "d" at the end; it is written but not pronounced. However, the missing /d/ sound is pronounced in the two-morpheme word "regarder," which of course is derived from "regard." Exactly the same goes for "chant" and "chanter," and for "bavard" and "bavarder." In these words too the final consonant is pronounced in the derived verbs but not in the one-morpheme nouns. Yet, this consonant is represented in writing in the one-morpheme as well as in the two-morpheme words. So, here again we meet morphemic spellings which transcend grapheme–phoneme correspondences.

In an ingenious experiment with French-speaking Canadian children, Sénéchal and her colleagues (Sénéchal, 2000; Sénéchal, Basque, & Leclaire, 2006) asked 7- and 9-year-old children in their second and fourth year in school to spell stem words which end in a consonant in their written form even though this consonant is not pronounced. Some of these words, like "un regard" (a glance) " and "un bavard" (a chatterbox) have derived forms, such as "regarder" (to look at) and "bavarder" (to chat), in which the final consonants are pronounced. Others, like "tabac" and "choix" do not. If children can use morphological information in spelling and are able to connect the two-morpheme words with the one-morpheme stems, they should be able spell the silent consonants correctly at the end of "regard" and "bavard" more often than at the end of "tabac" and "choix." The two-morpheme derivations, "regarder" and "bavarder," would give them the necessary cue to include the silent final letter in the one-morpheme words.

This is, in fact, what happened. The children who took part in these studies spelled the "silent" consonant significantly more often in the first set of words than in the second. This was true of both 7- and 9-year-old children. The 9-year-olds used the silent final consonant in the spelling of words where they could use the clue from the derived two-morpheme word 52% of the time and the 7-year-olds only used the silent consonant in these words 18% of the time. So the 7-year-olds could use this morphological information but they were not impressively good at it.

These researchers also questioned the participants in their second study, who were only 9-year-olds, about the strategies that they used in order to spell the words. When the words with the final silent consonant had derived forms where the consonant was pronounced, 18% of all the children mentioned that they had thought of a related word; this was never the case when there was not a derived word in which the final consonant was pronounced. The percentage of children who reported using the morphological connection is not high, but according to the researchers this strategy had not been explicitly taught. It is also important to note that this strategy was only reported when it was appropriate. The researchers also analysed the probability that the children spelled the silent consonant correctly when the children reported using a morphological strategy, as described above, a phonological strategy, or retrieval (i.e. the children said they just knew the spelling). For this type of word, the children were more often correct when they reported a morphological strategy (80% correct), followed by retrieval (75% correct) followed by a phonological strategy (43% correct). So, they concluded that the children were using morphological relations between words to help their spelling. This seems quite reasonable, and Sénéchal's work is the best evidence that we have so far of children explicitly and systematically using morphological reasoning in their spelling.

Sénéchal's work shows that children use knowledge of morphology explicitly in spelling but we have argued before that not all knowledge that we use in spelling is explicit. So it is important to know whether it is possible that children use knowledge of morphology implicitly in spelling. At first glance this could seem like an untreatable problem: if the knowledge is implicit, how can we obtain unambiguous evidence for it? Fortunately, for quite some time now, psychologists have used a technique called priming, to study the use of implicit knowledge in word recognition, which we were able to adapt for investigating children's spelling. Priming is a technique that has been used in a variety of contexts and which is recognized as a procedure that elicits the effects of implicit processes in the recognition of objects, figures or words. These processes are considered implicit because people are not at all aware of using past memories in the recognition of the stimuli that they are asked to recognize (for a brief discussion, see Tulving, 2000). We explain first the technique when it is used in word recognition studies and then explain how we developed it for use in spelling.

When priming is used in word recognition, participants are shown words on a computer screen and asked to press a key as quickly as possible when they have recognized the word. In a priming study, you have a *target stimulus*—for example, "harmful"—and a morphologically related word, "harm," which is the *prime*. The effect of priming consists in the speeding of the recognition of the word "harmful" when it is preceded by the morphologically related prime, "harm." In order to know that the recognition was indeed faster, the word "harmful" is presented, either to the same people on another occasion or to other participants, without exposing them first to the prime. It is possible to know whether the prime had an effect by comparing the speed of word recognition in the primed condition with the baseline or control condition, when there was no priming. Because word recognition in adults takes place quickly, the processes that they use are generally implicit: they could not tell you that they read "harmful" faster after having read "harm" because the time difference is only measurable in milliseconds (i.e. thousandths of seconds). But these effects are reliable and have been demonstrated in many different experiments with adults reading different languages.

Priming studies of word recognition are usually not carried out with children because children's reaction times fluctuate too much, as they are still learning to read. Priming effects have been demonstrated with adults (Campbell, 1983) and children (Campbell, 1985) writing non-words to dictation, but in these studies they were not based on morphology. Some pseudowords could be spelled in two different ways, given their sounds and the English spelling system. For example, if you spelled, upon dictation, the pseudoword "prain" or "prane," either spelling would produce the right pronunciation. Campbell's priming studies have shown that the probability that both adults and children will use one or the other spelling can be changed if they hear the words "brain" or "crane" as a prime. Those participants who heard "brain" are more likely to spell the pseudoword as "prain" and those who heard "crane" are more likely to spell it as "prane." Even though the effect was stronger with adults than children, it was a robust effect, which was replicated across experiments.

In Campbell's studies, the priming was done by phonological similarity. We (Rosa & Nunes, in press) were able to adapt this technique to study morphological priming effects on children's spelling. The study was conducted with Portuguese children because European Portuguese has an interesting feature: often, when a suffix is added to a base word, the stress in the word changes, and the main vowel in the stem of the word becomes a schwa vowel, so that it is no longer pronounced clearly. For example, the word "tambor" (drum) in Portuguese can be made into a verb, "tamborilar," by adding a suffix; the stress is then changed to the last syllable, and the vowel "o," which was clearly pronounced in the word "tambor," is no longer clearly articulated. To give an English example, think of the words "magic" and "magician," where the same thing happens. There is no doubt that the first vowel in the word "magic" is /a/ but it is not so with the word "magician," whose first vowel is a schwa vowel, and is spelled by children quite often as "mugishen" or "migishen."

This change in stress and vowel pronunciation in European Portuguese allowed us to investigate whether it is possible to observe morphological priming effects in children's spelling. Children in their first four years in school make many vowel errors when spelling words like "tamborilar," and do not use the correct letter "o" in spelling. The question we wanted to answer was whether they would improve their spelling of this sort of vowel in this sort of word if they were exposed first to the stem word whose vowel is clearly pronounced. So we asked Portuguese children (a total of 805 children in grades one to four) in Lisbon to spell 24 words of this type, and 24 pseudowords, which were embedded in sentences. The classes of children were randomly assigned to one of three conditions of dictation. One group of children provided us with the *baseline*; the sentences that they heard were similar to those the other two groups heard, but the base-word (or pseudoword), from which the target stimulus was derived, was not included in the sentence. The second group heard the sentence, but one word in the sentence was replaced by the prime; they were an *oral-priming group*. The third group not only heard the sentence but had it also written on a page, where the target word (or pseudoword) was missing, and which they were asked to write; they were an *oral-plus-written priming group*. This experimental scheme is explained below by showing an example of the three conditions, where the target word was "tamborilar:"

1 *Baseline group*: heard the sentence "Ele está a tocar a pandeireta; ele está a tamborilar" (He is playing the tambourine; he is drumming) and was asked to spell the target word, "tamborilar."
2 *Oral-priming group*: heard the sentence "Ele está a tocar tambor; ele está a tamborilar" (He is playing the drum; he is drumming) which contained the prime, and was asked to spell the target word.
3 *Oral-plus-written priming group*: heard the same sentence as the previous group and spelled the same target word, which they had heard; the sentence "Ele está a tocar tambor; ele está a _____" was written on their answer sheet, where the target word was re-placed by a dash.

We used a similar model in the presentation of the pseudowords, which were constructed with a base form that had a clearly articulated vowel and a derived pseudoword, where the stress was on the suffix and the vowel in the stem was not pronounced clearly. In order for priming to be effective with pseudowords, the children would need to be using implicit knowledge of morphology as a linguistic structure, not implicit knowledge of relationships between the meanings of words. For example, the pair of pseudowords "candor" and "candorilar," created for the

study by analogy with "tambor" and "tamborilar," could not be previously associated with meanings, because they are made-up words. So,
if the children's spelling of the schwa vowel in "candorilar" improves
through priming, we can conclude that they know, at least implicitly,
that the pair of stimuli must be related, and that the stem in these two
stimuli should be spelled in the same way.

The results of this study were clear. First, even the children in grade
four (mean age 9y4m) were not performing at ceiling level on the spelling of the words: the rate of correct vowel spelling in grade four was
equal to 61%. Thus, at this age level there is plenty of room for improvement with priming. Second, there was a significant effect of priming
on vowel spelling in words, both for children in the oral priming and
in the oral-plus-written priming condition, but this was only observed
for children in grades three and four. Younger children did not improve
their vowel spelling significantly through priming. Finally, the effect on
pseudowords was weaker than the effect on words: only oral-plus-written
priming showed a significant effect and this was only observed with
children in fourth grade. Still, the effect was significant with pseudowords.
Actually, the children in the oral-plus-written priming condition spelled
the *pseudoword* vowels slightly better than the children in the no-
priming condition spelled the vowels in the *words*. The effect of implicit
morphological knowledge on spelling observed here is of great significance for our understanding of spelling development. The children could
not have previously made connections between the meanings of the
pseudowords. So, they could only be using their implicit knowledge of
morphology to parse the derived pseudoword into stem and suffix, and
then spell the schwa vowel in the target pseudoword in the same way
that it was spelled in the single-morpheme pseudoword. But nobody
had told them that these were single- and two-morpheme pseudowords:
this was implicitly and quickly identified by them themselves, as they
processed the information in the sentences and wrote the pseudowords.

The results of this study are consistent with the picture that we have
been painting here about children's use of morphological knowledge in
spelling: younger children do not seem to use morphological knowledge
in the same way that older children do.

Summary

1 Seven-year-old French-speaking children are to some extent able to
   connect two-morpheme words like "regarder" and "bavarder" with
   their one-morpheme stems, in a way that affects their spelling of the

endings of these stems. This shows some early knowledge of the relation between morphemes and spelling. However, there is also a striking growth in the strength of this effect between the ages of 7 and 9 years.

2 Nine-year-old Portuguese children also seem to be able to use the connection between stem and two-morpheme words in their spelling. Sometimes a particular vowel sound is pronounced in the stem word but not pronounced in the stem if it is part of a two-morpheme word. When the stem word is presented at the same time as the target two-morpheme word, 9-year-olds are more likely as a result to represent (correctly) the missing vowel sound in the target word.

The Case of Greek

All the research that we have presented so far on children's successes and failures with the relationship between morphemes and spelling has been about English, French and Portuguese. However, these orthographies are complicated ones, as we have seen. They contain a large number of conditional rules and these are not always well obeyed. Worse still, different kinds of spelling rules often clash. Morphemic spelling rules often flout grapheme–phoneme rules. Perhaps English-speaking children are slow to recognize and take advantage of morphemic spelling rules because of the complexity of written English and particularly because of the conflict between morphemic spelling rules and grapheme–phoneme rules.

This is a good reason to turn to other orthographies, and one obvious candidate is modern Greek. This is a much less complex orthography than English. Greek grapheme–phoneme relations are simpler than the English ones and once you know them you can read any word in the language and you will produce the right sound, since all Greek words conform to these relationships. There are no exceptions—no "pints," no "Gloucester," no "choix"—in Greek. Most Greek words can be deciphered on the basis of letter–sound correspondences and there are a few conditional rules to learn as well: for example, the Greek letter "α" (alpha) as a single vowel always represents the sound /a/ and the letter "υ" (ipsilon) the sound /i/, but the letter sequence "αυ" always signifies the sound /av/ if the sound that follows it is a vowel or a voiced consonant and /af/ if the sound that follows it is a voiceless consonant. Anyone who has mastered these correspondences and conditional rules will have no problem in reading Greek text.

It would be hard to think of any possible reason why children learning to be literate in Greek should attend to morphemes, if they only had to learn to read. But they also have to learn to spell and that does pose a problem. We have already mentioned that there are many more ways of spelling vowels in Greek than there are vowels. So, let us now look at this asymmetry in greater detail and consider the impact of morphemes on the spelling of these vowels.

The five vowel sounds in Greek are /a/ as in "cat", /ɔ/, as in "hot," /e/ as in "wet," /i/ as in "seat" and /u:/ as in "route." Three of these vowels can be spelled in more than one way:

1 "o" and "ω" both signify /ɔ/ as in "hot"
2 "ε" and "αι" both signify /e/ as in "wet"
3 "η," "ι," "u," "οι" "ει" all signify /i/ as in "seat."

Thus, anyone who tries to spell Greek words just on the basis of grapheme–phoneme relations will have a choice to make whenever she has to spell one of these three vowels. We must now consider how Greek readers and spellers resolve this choice. The answer depends on whether the vowel is in the stem or in an affix.

In stems there is no rule. Nothing tells the speller whether to use "o" or "ω" for the vowel /ɔ/ when it occurs in a word's stem. Sometimes "o" is the right spelling (e.g. τόπι (ball)) and sometimes "ω" (e.g. φωνή (voice)). The opening vowel in both these words sounds exactly the same and Greek children simply have to learn which spelling to use in which stem. Grapheme–phoneme correspondence will tell the speller what the choice is (e.g. between "o" and "ω") but she will only find out which is the correct choice through word-specific learning.

In contrast, word-specific knowledge need not, in principle, be the only way to go when people decide how to spell vowels in an affix morpheme. Here there is no choice. Particular affixes are always spelled the same way. For example, all inflections in this highly inflected language either contain a vowel or consist entirely of a vowel sound and the spelling of these inflections is invariable. For example, /ɔ/ at the end of a verb is the inflection first person singular present tense and it is always spelled as "ω" (γελῶ ("I laugh"), βγαίνω ("I go out")). The same sound at the end of a noun is an inflection, for the nominative in neuter, singular nouns is always spelled as "o" (e.g. μῆλο ("apple"), δῶρο ("present")).

We can make three comparisons here in our quest to find out how well and how quickly children learn the link between morphemes and spelling. One possible comparison is between spelling the three Greek vowel sounds for which there are alternative spellings in stems and inflections in real words. If children rely to any extent on morphemic spelling rules, they should be better at spelling these vowels in inflections than in stems. This is because they have the help both of morphemic rules and of word-specific knowledge when writing inflections. With stems, on the other hand, they have only word-specific knowledge to go on.

The second possible comparison is between how often children pick the correct spelling for the vowel sound in inflections in real words and in pseudowords—the acid test again. The comparison is actually a measure of the importance of word-specific knowledge: if the children do better with real word inflections than with pseudoword inflections, that means that sometimes they make the correct choice of spellings because of word-specific knowledge, and the extent of this difference will tell us how much children rely on this knowledge.

The third comparison is to look at the children's success with pseudowords alone, and to see how it changes as children grow older. If they have no idea about morphemic rules and rely entirely on word-specific learning, their choice of spellings in the pseudoword condition should be random. But if their scores are better than they would be by chance, we can draw the conclusion that they know about morphemic spelling rules. There is no other possible explanation for better-than-chance scores with the pseudoword inflections, since word-specific knowledge is quite irrelevant to the way in which children spell these entirely unfamiliar words.

We made these comparisons in a longitudinal study of Cretan children whom we saw on three separate occasions (Chliounaki & Bryant, 2007). The three sessions spanned a period of just under two years. The children were 6 years-old in the first of the three sessions, 7 years-old in the second and 8 years-old in the third and final session. In each of these sessions we asked them to spell a large set of real words and an equal number of pseudowords. Our main interest was in how often they chose the right spelling for the vowel sound in:

1   stems in real words;
2   inflections in real words;
3   inflections in pseudowords.

Notice that we did not have a score for the correct spelling of the vowel sound in stems in pseudowords, because there is no such thing. There is no way to decide, for example, whether the /ɔ/ sound in a pseudoword

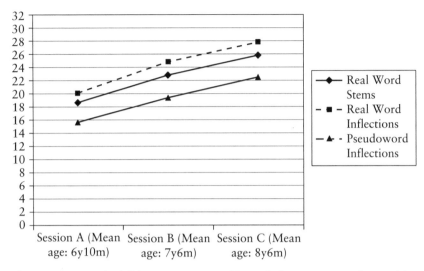

Figure 5.8 Greek children's correct spelling of the same vowel sound in stems and suffixes in words and pseudowords

stem should be spelled as "o" or "ω," but of course there is a definite correct and a definite incorrect spelling for this sound in pseudoword inflections.

Figure 5.8 shows three interesting results. First, as you can see, the children produced the correct spelling for the vowel sounds in inflections more often than in stems in all three sessions. This difference suggests that the children were to some extent relying on morphemic spelling rules, since they could use these with inflections but not with stems.

Second, the children, again consistently, spelled the vowel correctly more often in real word than in pseudoword inflections. This demonstrates their reliance on word-specific knowledge, since this knowledge can only help them with real and familiar words and not at all with pseudowords.

Finally, let us look at the scores for spelling vowels in pseudoword inflections, which is the acid test of their knowledge of the relevant morphemic spelling rules. In the first session, when the children were 6 years-old, their scores for pseudoword inflections were rather low but they were better than one would expect if the children had made their choices randomly. If their choices were random, one would expect an average score of around 12 correct choices out of 32 in the pseudoword task. In fact, in the first session when the children were 6 years-old, the average score for correct spelling choices was 15.7. This suggests that some of them were choosing randomly but that others were doing a great deal better than that.

So, using the binomial, we looked at how many children in the first session produced scores in this pseudoword task that were significantly above chance level. We found that 25 of the 90 children reached this level in the first session. This means that 27.8% of our sample systematically used morphemic spelling rules with pseudoword inflections in their first year at school. In the next session, nearly a year later, that percentage figure rose to 63.3% and in the final session when the children were 8 years-old to an impressive 77.8%. Thus, a substantial minority of these Greek children already knew quite a lot about morphemic spelling rules not long after they first arrived at school. There was also a sharp rise in the children's knowledge and use of morphemic rules over the next two years. By the age of 8 years, a substantial majority knew and used these rules well.

The Greek children's early start and rapid improvement were in sharp contrast to most of the results that we have reported for English children. This difference may well be due to the nature of the two orthographies. It may be quite easy for children to detect the connection between morphemes and spelling when everything else in the script is orderly and predictable, as it is in Greek. Other explanations seem much less plausible. The current practice in Greek schools is not to teach the children directly and explicitly about the links between morphemes and spelling. So, it is unlikely that the apparent difference between Greek and English children is anything to do with different kinds of teaching in Greece and in England. It seems much more likely that Greek children are relatively quick at discovering these links for themselves because the links stand out so clearly in this well-ordered orthography.

What processes are at work in Greek orthography to give Greek children this advantage? In Chapter 3, we argued that correct reading plays an important role in learning to spell. We showed that children learn the long-vowel spelling rules from their successful experiences with reading: during the period of acquisition of this rule, the children's reading scores actually predicted their spelling scores at a later age better than their spelling scores predicted their reading. Could this also be at work in Greek? Because of the asymmetry between spelling-to-sound and sound-to-spelling rules in Greek, Greek children can easily read words that they cannot spell correctly. They can have many successful reading experiences of these words, which are likely to lead to some learning of the words' spellings. So they can build a stock of word-specific knowledge even though they do not know the rules yet. This could well lead to rule learning later on.

Summary

1   Greek children, aged 6–8 years, spell the vowel sounds in inflections much more accurately in real words than in pseudowords. This is evidence for their reliance on word-specific knowledge.
2   However, they also spell these sounds more successfully in real word inflections than in real word stems. This is evidence that they are able to use morphemic spelling rules to some extent, since these rules apply to inflections but not to stems.
3   The number of 8-year-old children who consistently use morphemic spelling rules to spell inflections in pseudowords is relatively high: it reaches 77% by this age.

The Final "s" in Spanish (Andalusia)

Finally, we come to Spanish, which at first sight might seem to be a most unlikely language and orthography to mention in a chapter on morphemic spelling. Most Spanish words can be read and spelled entirely on the basis of phoneme–grapheme correspondences with no attention to morphemic factors at all. From the point of view of these correspondences it is a highly consistent orthography, and its structure seems not to reflect morphemes at all. Sometimes in Spanish, as in English, the pronunciation of the same stem differs across words. In English, as we have noted, the spelling of these words often reflects the fact that they share a stem and not the difference in pronunciation (e.g. "heal," "health"). This does not happen in Spanish. To take one example, cited by Defior, Alegria, Titos, and Martos (2008) "vaca" (cow) and "vaquería" (dairy) share the same stem but the spelling of the stems these two words reflects their different pronunciations, and not their common meaning.

However, differences in dialect do have the result that in some regions morphemes do have a possible role to play in spelling. One example comes from Andalusia. There are many words in Spanish that end in /s/ and this ending is always represented in Spanish spelling as "-s." Sometimes the /s/ sound, and therefore its spelling, represent an inflection or part of an inflection (e.g. for a plural noun or a 2nd person singular verb), and sometimes not, as in the word "pais" (country). However, Andalusians do not pronounce any of these finals /s/ sounds. Since they spell all these words in the conventional Spanish way, this means that they have many silent "-s" endings in their orthography, just as the French do. Andalusian children therefore have to learn to put an "-s" ending on many words which they do not pronounce in that way.

Defior et al. (2008) looked at how well 6-, 7- and 8-year-old Andalusian children spelled these silent "s"s in high- and low-frequency words which were of three kinds: plural nouns, 2nd person singular verbs and words in which the final "s did not represent a morpheme. These researchers found that with the low-frequency, and therefore relatively unfamiliar, words the children tended to put in the unpronounced "s" ending more in words in which it had a morphemic basis—in the plural nouns and the 2nd person singular verbs—than in words in which there was no particular morphemic reason for the final "-s." The difference in the spelling of the morphemic and the non-morphemic final "-s" was particularly marked in the oldest of the three groups.

This result is rather similar to the Greek children's greater success in spelling vowel sounds in inflections in real words than in their stems. Both the Greek and the Andalusian children, particularly the older Andalusian children, seem to be taking advantage of the morphemic structure of words to conquer a difficult spelling. Both groups get better at doing so as they grow older.

Over-generalization: A Clue about Children's Learning Morphemic Spelling Rules

The last three sections have provided consistent evidence for children learning morphemic spelling rules even though this is quite hard for them to do. It is time now to find out how they do this learning. Broadly speaking, there are two possible ways for children to learn spelling rules. They could learn these rules for themselves without any explicit help from other people or they could learn by being taught the rules.

In the Nunes et al. (1997a) longitudinal study of children's learning about the past tense inflection, we discovered an interesting pattern of spelling which indicated that some of the children might be in the process of constructing for themselves the rules about spelling this particular inflection. When children began to use the "-ed" ending with past verbs, they did so only sporadically and, almost without fail, correctly. We had asked them to spell 10 regular verbs; among the children who spelled most of them phonetically, some used the "-ed" once or twice. We put this correct use down to word-specific learning. But once the children started to use the "-ed" ending a bit more often—in our study, we defined this as using it at least three times in the 10 words—they displayed a pattern of spelling that had not yet been described in the literature. Many children, in fact, 71% of the children in the project, at one time or another put the "-ed" ending on irregular past verbs and 56% put the "-ed" ending on words that ended in /t/ or /d/ but were not past verbs—i.e. sometimes they used it correctly but at other times in the wrong places. This incorrect use could not be explained by word-specific learning. "Necsed" for "next," "sofed" for "soft," "heled" ("helled") for "held," and "exceped" for "except" were all fairly common examples of this kind of mistake, and they could not possibly have seen these letter sequences before.

The children in our study made the mistake somewhere in the middle of the process of learning about the past tense inflection. They were usually those who several months previously had spelled all /t/ and /d/ endings phonetically, and who were on the way to getting the spelling of past verbs entirely right.

Our evidence also suggested two definite developmental steps in these over-generalizations of the "-ed" ending. At first the children made the mistake with non-verbs ("necsed") as much as with irregular verbs ("lefed"). Later on they made it only with irregular verbs.

This seemed to be an important observation. It suggested to us that children start to make this mistake when they first realize that /d/ and /t/ endings are not always spelled phonetically, but are sometimes spelled as "ed." At first the rule underlying this particular alternative to phonetic spelling escapes them completely, and so they apply phonetic endings and the new (to them) "ed" spelling with no regard to the grammatical status of the word that they are writing. So, they make these over-generalizations with non-verbs as well as with irregular verbs. Later, however, there is a clear and crucial change when they no longer make the mistaken generalizations to non-verbs and but continue to make them with irregular verbs only. This is the first systematic sign that children finally realize something about the grammatical significance of the "ed" ending. Now they know that it is something to do with past verbs, and nothing to do with non-verbs like "next."

It also seems obvious to us that they do not make this change through any direct teaching, since no teacher would ever tell them to spell "held" as "heled." What, then, does prompt them to make the change? In our view, one of the main reasons for the change is that the children have actually started to use the "ed" ending and this increases the opportunities that they will have to learn about its significance. A lot of these will take the form of negative information: they are more likely to be told that the "ed" ending is for verbs if they produce spellings like "necsed" than if they do not. Another possibility is that the experience of noticing and then using the "ed" ending will cause them to pay more attention to the kinds of word that end in this way.

The importance of over-generalizations in children's learning about morphemes and spelling is also underlined by some research on French-speaking children. Quite independently, a group of researchers in France (Fayol, Thénevin, Jarousse, & Totereau, 1997) established much the same pattern of over-generalizations as we had, but this time with the plural inflection, and they reached a similar conclusion to ours about over-generalizing. Remember, however, that plural inflections on nouns, verbs and adjectives in French are, for the most part, silent which makes the task of learning about them quite a hard one.

Totereau, Thénevin and Fayol (1998) showed that at first French children spell plural noun and verb endings by sound—just as Nunes et al. (1997a) and Varnhagen et al. (1997) showed that English-speaking children do when at first they spell past tense verbs by sound. In the case of French, this means that initially children simply do not write the ending of plural words at all, just because these are not pronounced. For example, they omit the "s" ending from "filles" and the "nt" (or "ent") ending from "dorment" when trying to write the sentence "Les filles dorment" ("The girls sleep"). Totereau et al. also gave young French children a simple choice task. They showed them some pictures of single objects and others of several objects, and then asked them to choose which one was represented by a particular written word (e.g. "les maisons" ("the houses")). The children were at chance level in their choice of the appropriate picture. After a year at school many children can distinguish singular and plural nouns and verbs in reading, but not when they write. They do begin to use the "s" ending for plural nouns and adjectives in the following year but now they begin to make over-generalizations. They also put the "-s" ending at the end of verbs instead of the correct "-nt" ending.

Some time after this, they begin to use the "-nt" ending for verbs, but here again they over-generalize. Now they sometimes put "-nt" on the end of nouns as well, particularly when a noun (Totereau, Barouillet, & Fayol, 1998; Largy, Fayol, & Lemaire, 1996) or an adjective (Pacton,

2004) sounds the same as the verb. For instance, in French, as in English, the noun and verb for "dance" share the same-sounding stem ("la danse," "elle danse"), and a French child who is just beginning to use the "-nt" for plural verbs might well write "the dances" as "les dansent" instead of the correct "les danses."

These over-generalizations plainly show that French as well as English children do not at first understand the role of the spellings which indicate that words are plural. The over-generalizations also suggest that French children, like English children, develop their own hypotheses about these written endings which they test and modify. These wrong uses of the plural ending can be taken as definite signs that French-speaking children work out the connection between spelling and morphemes for themselves. In their case this is quite a striking conclusion, because as we have remarked already, French children are taught about the singular–plural distinction at school.

One interesting extra piece of information from the French research is that French children seem to be able to understand the spelling–morpheme connection in reading before they do so in spelling. We have already seen Totereau et al.'s (1998) discovery that French children appear to recognize and use plural endings in reading before they manage to do so in writing. Largy (2001) also showed that French children's spelling lags behind their reading by showing that many children who regularly omitted plural endings in their writing nonetheless could quite easily spot singular–plural disagreements which they were given to read (e.g. "la maisons" instead of the correct "la maison" or "les maisons"). Since reading leads the way, it is a reasonable speculation that children learn a great deal about how to represent this and other morphemic distinctions through their experience of seeing how such distinctions are made when they read.

However, there is a complication in the evidence on French children's over-generalizations, which is about the influence of the children's word-specific knowledge. Some of the over-generalizations made by French children are wrong spellings for the word that they are trying to write but the right spellings for other words. To take the last example of an over-generalization, which was "les dansent," the written word "dansent" is the wrong spelling for the plural noun but the right spelling for the 3rd person plural present tense verb "ils dansent" (they dance). The two words "danses" and "dansent" have different meanings but they are homophones. So, French children might write "dances" as "dansent" because they have often seen the spelling "dansent" before and have associated it with the sound of both words. Thus, word-specific knowledge could be a cause of some of the over-generalizations that French children make, and probably is because Totereau et al. report that these over-generalizations occur more often when the wrong spelling is actually the right spelling for a homophonous word ("danses"–"dansent") than when it is not ("maison"–"maisonent"). This is good evidence that word-specific knowledge plays an important part in many of the over-generalizations made by French children, as Pacton and Deacon (2008) clearly point out. Nevertheless the fact that the second kind of over-generalization does occur, albeit less often than the first, is good evidence that French children also make some over-generalizations for much the same reasons as English children too. No French word is spelled as "maisonent." Thus, when French children do spell "maisons" as "maisonent," they produce a spelling that does not exist and they must be doing so because they hold the wrong hypothesis about the French silent "-s" and "-ent" endings.

The results of a remarkable study of Dutch children's spellings (Notenboom & Reitsma, 2007) bolstered the idea that there can be two possible causes for over-generalizations, at any rate in Dutch and French. In Dutch, the spelling of the past tense ending for regular (or "weak," as they are sometimes called) past verbs is "-te" or "-de" (singular) and "-ten" or "-den" (plural). So, the root for the verb "werken" (to work) is "werk-," and so the past verb is spelled as "werkte" (singular) and "werkten" (plural).

When the root of the verb ends in "t" or "d," the addition of these past tense inflections creates a doublet in the middle of the word. For example, the root for the verb "wachten" (to wait) is "wacht-," and so the past verb is spelled as "wachtte" (singular) and "wachtten" (plural). It is the same with the "-de" ending. The root for the verb "landen" (to land) is "land-," and the past verb is spelled as "landde" and "landden."

In Dutch, as in English, doubling a consonant makes no difference at all to the pronunciation of the consonant sound. Not surprisingly, Dutch-speaking children, exactly like English-speaking children (see Chapter 2), are extremely reluctant at first to adopt doublet spellings for consonants in their own writing. Up to the age of roughly 9 or 10 years, according to Notenboom and Reitsma's data, many children systematically write the past verbs "wachtte(n)" and "landde(n)" as "wachte(n)" and "lande(n)."

However, when they start to spell these past endings with doublets correctly, they now begin to mis-spell some other words. They over-generalize the "tt" and "dd." Some children write "werktte" instead of the correct "werkte" (worked) and some write "wachtten" when they should write "wachten" (to wait). In fact these two examples are very like the French mis-spellings. The spellings "maisonent" and "werktte" just do not exist whereas the spellings "danses" and "danses" are incorrect spellings for the words that the children are trying to spell, but correct spellings for a homophonous word. Thus a child who wrongly writes "wachtten" instead of "wachten" (to wait) may be relying on word-specific knowledge. He has seen the written word "wachtten" before and has associated it with a particular sound, rather than with a particular meaning, and so he chooses the wrong spelling for "wachten."

Notenboom and Reitsma found that some children made both kinds of over-generalization—the kind that may have been based entirely on word-specific knowledge ("wachtten" for "wachten") and the kind that just cannot be explained in this way ("werktte" for "werkte"). Others only made the first kind ("wachtten" for "wachten"). The second of these two groups was much more numerous than the first. This echoes the results reported by Totereau et al. (1998). Word-specific knowledge does account for a lot of the over-generalizations of inflectional spelling in French and Dutch, but not for all of them. French and Dutch children, or at any rate some French and Dutch children, also make these over-generalizing mistakes because they are acting on hypotheses which are wrong and which they will soon learn to be wrong.

It is worth reminding ourselves at this point that the over-generalizations in English that we have been writing about so far could not be the product of word-specific knowledge. When English-speaking children over-generalize the past tense ending, they never produce spellings that happen to be the correct spellings for another word. "Sleped," "necsed," "direced" and "exceped" are not in the English dictionary and children have never seen these spellings anywhere before. They are creating these spellings for the first time with the help of an ingenious but incorrect hypothesis of their own.

Summary

1   When English-speaking children begin to use the "-ed" ending to represent the end sounds /t/ and /d/, many of them assign this ending to inappropriate as well as to appropriate words. They put the "-ed" ending on irregular, and therefore inappropriate, past verbs (e.g. they sometimes write "slept" as "sleped") and even on non-verbs

(e.g. they sometimes write "next" as "necsed") as well as on the appropriate regular verbs (e.g. "kissed").

2   These two inappropriate uses of the "-ed" ending decline over time at different rates. Children tend to stop putting the "-ed" ending on non-verbs, before they stop putting them on irregular verbs.

3   Our explanation for these striking and fascinating errors and their developmental course over time begins with the idea that, when children first adopt the "-ed" ending, they treat it as an alternative grapheme for /d/ and /t/ sounds at the end of words. Thus, they form a hypothesis which is about phoneme–grapheme and not about morpheme–grapheme relations. This initial hypothesis is at the wrong level.

4   The fact that some children eventually stop putting the ending on non-verbs but continue applying it to irregular past verbs ("sleped") as well as to regular past verbs ("necsed") suggests that they have changed their hypothesis. Since they now confine this spelling to past verbs endings, they must have adopted a morpheme–grapheme hypothesis.

5   This new hypothesis is for the most part correct, but it does not take into account the fact that irregular past verb endings are spelled phonetically even when they are pronounced as /t/ or /d/. There is evidence that later on some, though perhaps not all, children adjust the hypothesis to take irregular past verbs into account.

6   French-speaking and Dutch-speaking children also over-generalize morphemic spellings at roughly the same age as English-speaking children do. However, in both these languages, these incorrect spellings are often the correct spellings for homophonous words, e.g. the French words "(les) danses" and "(ils) dansent" sound exactly the same and French children quite often confuse their spellings. The basic reason for these mistakes may be that the children have learned to associate particular spellings with particular sounds (a form of word-specific learning) and not with their meanings.

7   However, in all three languages, children's over-generalizations also result in entirely new spellings, such as "necsed" in English, "werktte" in Dutch and "(les) maisonent" in French. All the English over-generalizations of the "-ed" ending necessarily, and some (but a minority) of the French and Dutch over-generalizations, are like this.

8   These new and therefore quite unfamiliar spellings are strong evidence for the idea that at first children form the wrong (phoneme–grapheme) hypothesis about spellings for morphemic endings before they form the right (morpheme–grapheme) hypothesis.

Word-specific Knowledge: An Alternative to Morphemic-spelling Rules but also a Crucial Basis for Learning These Rules

An essential part of our explanation for over-generalizations of conventional spellings for morphemes is that the children who make them form their own hypotheses about the relevant spellings—first, the wrong hypothesis and then the right one. Our idea, therefore, is that children eventually work out the morphological basis of these various spellings for themselves. The likelihood of children of having to discover morphemic spelling rules by themselves probably depends on what educational help the children receive about morphemic spellings.

We shall discuss the question of the effects of direct instruction on children's knowledge of morphemic spelling rules in Chapter 7. Here, we will just make the comment that in schools in England and Greece, whose spelling system we are about to discuss, there is hardly any direct teaching about morphemic spelling rules. This makes it highly probable that children in these two countries at least have to work these rules out for themselves.

If children actively work out, at least to some extent, the connection between morphemes and spelling, they probably depend on word-specific knowledge to do so. In some ways this is quite a surprising claim to make, because up to now we have dealt with word-specific knowledge as the antithesis of the knowledge of morpheme–spelling rules. This seems a reasonable position to take. After all, word-specific learning is specific. The child learns how particular words are spelled and that is all. Morphemic spelling rules, in contrast, are general and abstract; all regular past tense verbs end in "-ed," the "ion" ending denotes an abstract noun, and so on.

Nevertheless the argument that we are about to develop is that these two forms of knowledge are connected. We do not claim that they are the same, but that one leads, in part, to the other. It seems to us that, if children infer the rules for spelling morphemes for themselves, they must have information to do so, and this information must come from their knowledge of how specific words are written. From this they may infer the rules for these spellings. Therefore, the hypothesis that children discover spelling rules for themselves produces at least two predictions. According to the hypothesis, children get to know the spelling of familiar words first and then infer the relevant rules later on. So, the first prediction is that children should learn how to spell the inflections in familiar real words, which they can do on the basis of word-specific knowledge, before they can do the same with pseudowords since it is only possible to spell inflections in these words by knowing the relevant morphemic spelling rules. The hypothesis also predicts a strong longitudinal relation between the word-specific knowledge that children build up when they begin to read and write and their learning later on of morphemic spelling rules. Thus, the precise prediction is that children's success in spelling inflections in familiar real words should be strongly related to their later success in spelling inflections in pseudowords later on. The opposite longitudinal relation, from early success with pseudowords to success later on with real words, should be a relatively weak one.

One needs longitudinal evidence and for this we can return to the study by Chliounaki and Bryant (2007) which we began to describe in the previous section. There, we described how in three sessions spread over two years we measured the accuracy of Greek children's spellings of vowel sounds in stems and inflections in real words and in inflections in pseudowords. We reported a marked improvement in the children's success in all three of these tasks over the two years.

This overall improvement gave us the opportunity to look at possible causal connections between the two factors that interested us most, which were the children's word-specific knowledge and their growing understanding of morphemic spelling rules. We argued that the very great increase over time in the children's solutions to the pseudoword inflection task demonstrated that they had learned a lot about the morphemic spelling rules for these inflections. We also believed that the fact that they were consistently better at spelling real word inflections than pseudoword inflections was a sure sign of word-specific learning. The difference demonstrated that they learned the spelling for inflections in real words by becoming familiar with these specific words and not, at first, through learning morphemic spelling rules. These two conclusions led us to the hypothesis that children first learn how to spell a corpus of inflected real words word by word, and later work out the underlying morphemic spelling rules on the basis of this word-specific knowledge.

This hypothesis produced two clear predictions. One is that individual children learn about inflections in real words before they can spell them in pseudowords. The second is that, because, according to the hypothesis, knowledge about the spelling of real words is the basis for learning morphemic spelling rules, children's ability to spell real word inflections in one session should predict their spelling of pseudoword inflections in a later session, and not the other way round.

We tested the first prediction by examining the difference between individual Greek children's spelling real word and pseudoword inflections. We worked out how many of them managed to spell the vowel sounds in inflections significantly above chance level both in real word and in pseudoword inflections. Table 5.4 shows the results. Not surprisingly, more children succeeded with real words than with pseudowords However, the important result in Table 5.4 concerns the children who succeeded (i.e. were significantly above chance level in their choice of the right vowel spellings) with one kind of word but not with the other. Naturally, in each session, many children succeeded with real words but not with pseudoword inflections. The striking result is the near absence of the opposite discrepancy. Just one child in one session only succeeded with pseudowords but not with real word inflections. This pattern amounts to a strong suggestion that children generally succeed at spelling inflections in real words before they manage to do the same with pseudowords. This certainly supports the idea that children's accumulation of word-specific knowledge eventually makes it possible for them to infer morphemic spelling rules.

We tested the second prediction when we looked at the relations between our various scores over time. Figures 5.9 and 5.10 present one positive and one negative result, which together provide strong evidence for this causal idea. The positive result is to be found in Figure 5.9. It shows that the children's scores for spelling real word inflections are good predictors of their success in spelling pseudoword inflections in the

Table 5.4 Number of Greek children who spelled the vowel sounds in inflections significantly above chance level in real word and in pseudoword inflections

	SESSION		
	Session A	Session B	Session C
RW–PW–	35	10	3
RW+PW–	30	23	17
RW–PW+	0	1	0
RW+PW+	25	56	70
TOTAL N	90	90	90

Notes:

RW–PW– Children whose inflection spelling scores were not significantly above chance either in real words or in pseudowords.

RW+PW– Children whose inflection spelling scores were significantly above chance in real words but not in pseudowords.

RW–PW+ Children whose inflection spelling scores were significantly above chance in pseudowords but not in real words.

RW+PW+ Children whose inflection spelling scores were significantly above chance both in real words and in pseudowords.

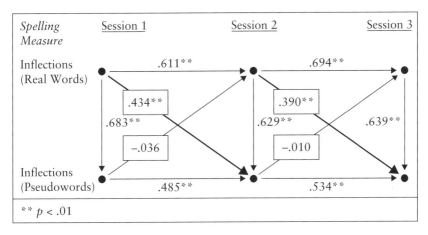

Figure 5.9 Correlations between Greek children's scores for spelling real word and pseudoword inflections across testing sessions

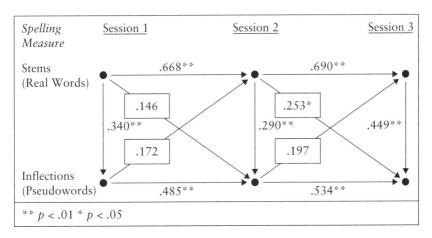

Figure 5.10 Correlations between Greek children's scores for spelling real word stems and pseudoword inflections across testing sessions

next session, but that their pseudoword spelling scores are not nearly so strongly related to their spelling of real word inflections later on. This is good support for the idea that children's word-specific knowledge, which they use in spelling real word inflections, is the basis for the inferences that they make later on about morphemes and spelling.

The negative result, which Figure 5.10 illustrates, was that the children's initial ability to spell the vowels in real word stems was only weakly related to their spelling of pseudoword inflections later on. This establishes that the connection that Figure 5.9 illustrated is specific to inflections. It is not just word-specific knowledge *per se* that leads to children learning about the rules for spelling inflections. It is children's knowledge of the spelling of inflections in specific words that eventually becomes the basis for their understanding the rules of spelling inflections. These two sets of longitudinal correlations strongly support the idea that children learn morphemic spelling rules by first assembling a bank of knowledge of the spelling of specific familiar words which are inflected and later by using this highly specific knowledge as the basis of inferences about the underlying rules for spelling inflections.

Summary

1   Greek children learn the spellings for inflectional morphemes in real words before they can spell the same inflections properly in pseudowords. This suggests that word-specific knowledge precedes knowledge of morphemic spelling rules.

2   This developmental sequence leads to a causal hypothesis, which is that children learn the morphemic spelling rules by inferring these rules from patterns of spelling that exist in the bank of word-specific knowledge that they have built up since beginning to learn to read and write.

3   Longitudinal correlations over time support this conclusion. Children's success in spelling real word inflections predicts their success in spelling pseudoword inflections later on and not vice versa.

Conclusion

When children begin to read and write, they tend to pay great attention to links between phonemes and graphemes but not to the equivalent links between morphemes and phonemes. To use Jaffré's terminology, their knowledge of phonographs is much more impressive than their knowledge of semiographs. The result is that they tend for a long time to make mistakes when morphemic rules contradict conventional grapheme–phoneme correspondences or go beyond them. Gradually, however, children accumulate a body of knowledge about the spelling of specific words, and make fewer spelling mistakes as a result. This knowledge, as the Greek longitudinal study shows, also becomes the basis for them inferring morphemic spelling rules, which they seem to construct largely for themselves.

However, this development is not a straightforward one. When children realize that the simple phoneme–grapheme connections that they have learned do not cover every aspect of spelling, they tend to form new, probably implicit, hypotheses about these connections. They conclude, for instance, that the /z/ ending is always spelled as "-s" when the /z/ is immediately preceded by a consonant. This idea very nearly always true, but it ignores morphology. They also conclude that "-ed" is a legitimate alternative spelling for /d/ and /t/ endings, which is true at the phoneme–grapheme level, but is only half the truth since it leaves out the morphemic reason for this alternative spelling. Thus, the children's first hypotheses remain at the phoneme–grapheme level at first, and this is why they often over-generalize spellings for morphemes, such as "ed" for the regular past in English and one reason why they over-generalize the "-s" and "-nt" plural endings in French.

Eventually, they change their hypotheses to include morphemes. Our evidence suggests that they do this through their word-specific knowledge. They make inferences about the relationships among familiar words whose spelling they have learned by rote, and discover that these relationships are morphemic ones.

Thus there is a delicate and intricate connection between children's word-specific knowledge and their growing understanding of morphemic spelling rules. Word-specific knowledge is an alternative to knowing about morphemic spelling rules. If you learn the word "kissed" by rote, you do not have to know any morphemic rule to spell its ending correctly. Word-specific learning also accounts for many of the mistakes that children make when they over-generalize morphemic spellings, at any rate, in French and Dutch. Yet, our research suggests the same word-specific knowledge also provides the essential information that a child needs to learn about morphemes and spelling. It is an ironic but fascinating relationship.

The conclusions summarized here raise some issues which will be discussed in subsequent chapters. The first of these is both theoretical and practical, and is about the role of teaching. If children now work these rules out for themselves, what is the role of teaching? Could teaching be effective? What sort of teaching is effective? The second issue is more theoretical. We have hypothesized that children acquire a body of word-specific knowledge from which they infer morphemic spelling rules. This hypothesis has implications for how memory must work: it means that somehow people can make implicit connections between items that are already in their memory. Is there a theory of memory to support this? We will turn to these points in Chapters 6 and 7.

Chapter 6

The Importance of Morphemes

It is clear now that children usually find morphemic spelling rules difficult for two main reasons. One is the clash between phonology and morphology. Most of the teaching that children are given about reading and writing in their first years at school deals with grapheme–phoneme correspondences. There is a solid rationale for this initial concentration on the connection between sounds and letters, but it has the baleful side-effect of getting seriously in the way of children's learning about the parallel connection between letters and morphemes. Morphemic spelling rules sometimes flout and sometimes go beyond the conventional grapheme–phoneme conventions, and teachers spend little or no time helping children come to terms with these apparent contradictions.

The second reason for children's evident difficulties with morphemic spelling rules is simply a lack of explicit teaching about them. Most English schools and most Greek, Portuguese and Brazilian schools, as well, provide very little in the way of systematic teaching about morphemes and spelling. Either by design or by oversight, the educational systems in these countries, and probably in many other countries too, leave children to work out most of these rules for themselves. This requires a great deal of quite sophisticated inferential reasoning by young school children who are treated in this way. They probably have to make these inferences using the bank of knowledge that they build up about the spelling of a myriad of words, as we pointed out in the previous chapter. By knowing and reflecting on the spelling of "confession" and "magician" and of "infection" and "musician," some children, at least, arrive at the conclusion that "-ian" is the way to spell "person words" and "-ion" should be used for the abstract nouns, even though these words all sound the same at the end—they all have a schwa vowel followed by the sound /n/.

Is there a reason to change current practice? Why not leave things as they are, teach children about grapheme–phoneme correspondences and leave it to them to figure out the story of the indirect connection between oral and written language, via syntax and morphology, for themselves?

In this chapter, we consider the reasons that have led us to believe that it is important to change things. The first part of the chapter examines the question of individual differences. Do all or at least most children actually figure out these rules for themselves? Do most adults know how to use the indirect connection between oral and written language? The second section looks beyond spelling and examines whether the indirect connection between oral and written language only impacts on spelling or whether there is more to it. It considers the consequences of knowing or not knowing about morphology. The third section examines the processes involved in learning about morphology and spelling. What predicts how well children learn about morphographs? We shall explore the measurement and the importance of children's awareness of morphology

Individual Differences in Spelling and Morphological Knowledge

The practice of leaving it to children to work the rules out for themselves is haphazard. When children have to provide their own solutions, you can be sure that some will do it better than others, and there is always the danger that some children will not manage it at all. The risk that these rules will simply bypass some children is exacerbated by the fact that children and adults might, in principle, be able to get by without having to learn morphemic spelling rules. It is possible, though not certain, that someone could become a proficient speller simply on the basis of word-specific knowledge. This hypothetical person would put the "ian" ending on "magician" and on "musician" without knowing that agents end in "ian": he/she would simply have learned the specific spellings for these two words.

In Chapter 5, we noted the intriguing irony that word-specific knowledge could be the basis on which children infer morphemic spelling rules or it could be an alternative to learning these rules. This dual relationship between word-specific knowledge and knowledge of morphemic spelling rules could also lead to individual differences among children. One child might infer the morphemic rules on the basis of his or her word-specific knowledge. Another might use this knowledge as a way of avoiding having to make these inferences at all.

This discussion raises two serious issues, both of which we will try to settle in this chapter. One is the issue of individual differences among children and eventually among adults in their knowledge and use of morphemic spelling rules. The work that we reviewed in the last chapter showed that some children at least learn some things about the connection between morphemes and spelling. The pseudoword tasks—the acid test—established that. For example, we found in our longitudinal study of Greek children that, by the age of 8 years when they had been at school for less than three years, 78% of them scored significantly above chance level in their spelling of inflections in pseudowords and therefore knew the relevant morphemic spelling rules. However, even this remarkable level of success is no guarantee that 100% of the children who took part in that study are bound eventually to learn these rules to the same extent, and of course we cannot assume that children learning other orthographies are as sensitive to morphemic rules as Greek children are.

It is also clear that the amount of knowledge that children have about these particular spelling rules increases with age. At any rate it is easier to find a child who really knows about the rules in a secondary than in a primary school. However, we still have to be able to say whether some children learn more extensively than others about the links between morphemes and spelling, and indeed whether only some children learn these rules and others do not. Average scores for different age groups tell us something about groups of children but not enough about individual differences.

The second issue is about teaching children or even adults explicitly and effectively about morphemic spelling rules. If there are, as we expect, large individual differences between people in how well they have worked out these rules for themselves and how well they use them, perhaps teaching will diminish these differences. These differences might be in people's ability or willingness to make the necessary inferences for themselves, or in the adequacy of people's banks of word-specific knowledge as a basis for these inferences. Explicit teaching should remove the need for individuals at a disadvantage in these areas to have to work out the connections between morphemes and graphemes. Thus teaching might remove a powerful source of these differences. But do these differences exist?

To answer this question one has to find a way of disentangling word-specific knowledge and knowledge about morphemes and spelling. The main tool that we have used to keep these two forms of knowledge apart is again the invaluable comparison between words and pseudo-words. Pseudoword tasks eliminate word-specific knowledge, as we have seen, and therefore give us a pure measure of any individual person's grasp of spelling rules. It is fair to say that any individual who passes such a test really does know the rule in question.

One must, however, be more cautious about someone who produces a dismally low score in a pseudowords task. The significance of this kind of performance is not so clear. Suppose that an individual's performance is no better than you would expect from someone who was acting randomly. What could one conclude? This is a negative result and, as is often the case with negative results, there is more than one possible way to account for it. One possibility is that the individual has no understanding of the rule in question. Another is that he does have some understanding, but it is too implicit to allow him to apply it to the entirely new word with which he is now faced; some level of awareness may be needed for individuals to use their knowledge in this new task. A third is that he actually does thoroughly understand the morphemic rule, but does not think it right to apply the rule to pseudowords, which he takes to be there as a measure of his grasp of grapheme–phoneme correspondences.

We must recognize this ambiguity, but that is not a reason for shunning pseudoword tasks as a measure of individual differences in people's knowledge about spelling rules. For one thing they will allow us to identify people who do well in these tasks and particularly those whose scores can be said to be significantly better than chance. These people definitely do know about the rule in question and it is useful to know how many of them there are and also what sort of person they tend to be. As for the people whose scores remain at chance level, we can at least be sure that their knowledge is different in some way to that of the individuals in the successful group. Either they simply do not know the rule, or they only know it in a way that is too implicit to be of any use with unfamiliar pseudowords, or they view pseudoword spelling tasks as a task where they show what they have been taught explicitly, i.e. a task where they demonstrate their knowledge of grapheme–phoneme correspondences. The reason for their failure will be unclear, unless the study throws up information that might help us remove some of this ambiguity.

After this long preamble we will now describe a series of studies on the extent to which individual children and adults know one of the most basic and simple of all the morphemic spelling rules. This is the rule that regular plural nouns and active third person singular verbs end in "s." One consequence of this rule is that it leads to a difference in the way that /z/ and /ks/ endings are spelled in one and in two morpheme words. The /z/ ending is usually spelled as "se" or "ze" or sometimes as "zz" in one morpheme words, but always as "s" in two-morpheme words: we write the /ks/ ending as "x" or "xe" in one-morpheme words but as "cks" or "kes" in two-morpheme words (see Chapter 5). How well do children and adults understand this rule?

Our attempt to answer this question begins with research by Nenagh Kemp (Kemp & Bryant, 2003) on adults' knowledge of the rule about the /z/ ending. We described the two studies, one with real words and the other with pseudowords, that Kemp did with school children on this question in Chapter 5. Kemp also gave a group of adults the same pseudoword spelling task that she had given to children in the second of these studies (see Chapter 5). This was a test of the adults' knowledge that the /z/ sound at the end of plural words is spelled as "s."

The adults who took part in this further study were divided into two groups: those who were doing, or at some time in their life had done, a university degree course ("the Tertiary group") and those whose education stopped at the time that they left school ("the Secondary group"). The crucial result here is how these two adult groups fared in the task which the children had found particularly difficult: the /z/ sound in the plural pseudowords in which that final sound is immediately preceded by a long vowel ("There are two *prees* in the garden"). The adults as a whole were right only 50% of the time—little better than the children in the previous study. The people in the Tertiary group (64% correct) were right more often than those in the Secondary group (43% correct) but both scores are remarkably low. They indicate that knowledge of this basic and simple morphemic spelling rule—that the ending of regular plural words is spelled as "s"—is by no means inevitable. We attribute the difference between the two groups to the fact that people who go to university undoubtedly spend more of their time reading and writing than people who do not. Yet, this difference is dwarfed by the extraordinarily low scores of both groups of adults.

There are two possible reasons for scores as low as these. One is that everyone participating knew a little but not very much about the rule for spelling plural endings, and therefore applied it imperfectly. The other is that some of the people knew the "s" ending rule and had no difficulty in applying it to /z/ ending words, while the rest did not: they could be acting randomly or could be systematically using the letter "z" for the sound /z/ because they were applying phoneme–grapheme rules.

If the first alternative is correct—i.e. if everyone knew a little about the plural rule—all the participants should produce moderately low scores. If the second is right, some should do very well and the rest should answer randomly or be systematically wrong. In fact, the pattern of the scores in this experiment seemed to fit the second alternative best, since some people had no difficulty with the task while others seemed to use "s" and "z" about half the time each. However, each participant was only given six items in this task and it is hard with such a small number of items to distinguish those who acted randomly, and thus used "s" and "z" about half the time, from those who did not, and were right most of the time.

So, Bryant and Mitchell (2007) went on to devise tasks which allowed them to make this distinction quite convincingly. These were again pseudoword tasks, but this time we settled on 30 items per task. Every item consisted of a sentence that contained one pseudoword, which was either a pseudo-noun or a pseudo-verb. These pseudo-nouns and verbs contained either one (just a stem) or two (a stem followed by an inflection) morphemes. The examples in Table 6.1 show how the participant had to make a choice in each item. The choice was between two spellings of the pseudoword. One spelling was appropriate for a one-morpheme word ("ze" for a /z/ ending and "x" for a /ks/ ending), and the other for a two-morpheme word ("s" for a /z/ ending and "x" for a /ks/ ending). With these tasks we could record how well each participant chose the right spellings for one- and two-morpheme nouns and verbs. Since the pseudowords were all quite unfamiliar, word-specific knowledge could not help participants make these choices. Thus, the tasks were a direct test of each participant's knowledge of the connection between morphemes and spelling.

The adults who took part in this study were young adults, most in their early twenties, who had reached a reasonable standard in their school education, but who had not been to university. We wanted to start with a non-university population of adults, because of the low scores that we had already seen in the Secondary group in the Kemp and Bryant (2003) study.

These adults very rarely made a mistake in the task with real words. They knew how these familiar words were spelled. Our aim in the pseudoword tasks was to find out how well they understood the rules that underlie these spellings.

Our analysis in these pseudoword tasks was designed to establish whether individual participants made their choices randomly, and therefore knew nothing about the rules, or whether they did better than that

Table 6.1 Examples of the choice spelling task with words and pseudowords

---

One-morpheme noun trials

	moys	
Mary only has one		
	moize	

---

	glox	
This curly		does not fit.
	glocks	

One-morpheme verb trials

	heeze	
Would you like to		on the lawn?
	hees	

---

	frecks	
We have a good time when we		at home
	frex	

Two-morpheme noun trials

	crees	
Are the three		ready yet?
	creeze	

---

	jicks	
We need ten more		than we thought.
	jix	

Two-morpheme verb trials

	droes	
Mary sometimes		her car.
	droze	

---

	brax	
He always		the door noisily.
	bracks	

---

and made the right choice all or most of the time. When there are 30 items and two choices per item, the average score for a group of people making their choices entirely randomly would be 15, but of course some individuals would score higher and others lower than that. The scores for a group acting randomly should form a classic bell-shaped curve, as in Figure 6.1a. In contrast, the scores for individuals who know the rules should all be much higher than that and bunched around the top possible scores. The statistics of the normal distribution allow us to say that anyone who makes the correct choice 21 times or more in a task with 30 two-choice items has a score that is significantly above chance level, and is therefore most unlikely to have chosen randomly. So one would expect individuals who know the rules to produce scores somewhere between 21 and 30 in each of our tasks, as in Figure 6.1b.

We found both patterns in all four of our tasks. Figure 6.2 presents the distribution of the individuals' scores in each task. It is quite easy to see that in each case there was a group of individuals whose scores formed a normal distribution around 15 and fell below the critical 21 mark, and another group whose scores ranged from 21 to 30. Each of the four distributions, therefore, suggested very strongly that this sample of adults formed two separate groups in each task, those who definitely knew the relevant spelling rule and those who seemed to respond randomly in the task.

This was what we had expected, but nevertheless we were startled at the relative size of each group. In each task, the group that definitely knew the rules was far smaller than the other. In the /z/ ending tasks, for example, 72% of the sample produced scores that fell below the critical 21 mark with nouns and as many as 80% with verbs. In both tasks the scores of these individuals formed a normal distribution around the chance level score of 15. We have to conclude that the individuals whose scores were lower than 21 correct in any task probably made their choices randomly in that task and, if they had any knowledge of the rule for the endings of one- and two-morpheme nouns or verbs, their knowledge was so implicit that it could not be used in the pseudoword task. There was a sharp contrast between this group and the relatively small number of individuals who managed to make the correct choice 21 times or more. Their scores fell outside that normal distribution. This minority of individuals almost certainly did know and use the relevant spelling rule.

The young adults as a whole did better in the two /ks/ tasks but the pattern was the same. Again, the majority produced scores that formed a normal distribution around chance level and were below the critical

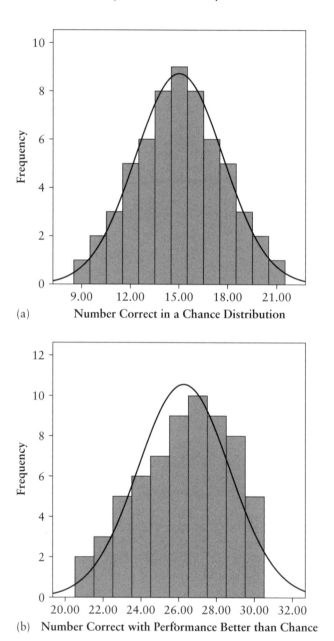

(a)

(b)

Figure 6.1 Theoretical normal distributions showing what happens if participants choose the alternatives randomly (a) or perform better than expected by chance (b)

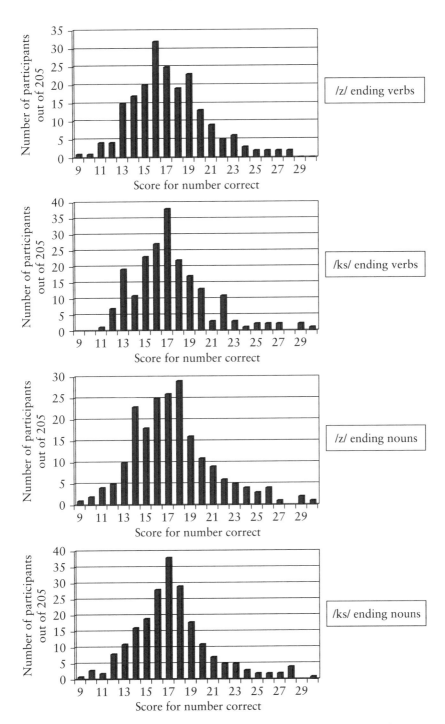

Figure 6.2 Frequency distributions of the scores observed in the four pseudoword spelling tasks

21 mark, and again the scores of a minority were higher than that and fell outside that normal distribution.

This striking and consistent pattern of results leads, we think, to an important conclusion. It is that a minority of individuals definitely understands the rules in question strongly enough to be able to apply them to entirely unfamiliar pseudowords.

The remaining individuals apparently acted randomly. It seems to us either that these particular individuals' understanding of the morphemic spelling rule was too implicit for them to be able to apply it to the pseudoword choice that we gave them or that they had no understanding of the rule at all. We cannot exclude the alternative possibility that the individuals who acted randomly treated the pseudoword task as a test of grapheme–phoneme knowledge, but it seems implausible to us. There are two reasons why this is not likely. First, if this group were treating the pseudoword task as a test of grapheme–phoneme knowledge, they would not produce random responses: they would produce systematic errors, and should be much more likely to use "z" for the two-morpheme words with /z/ sounding endings than to use "s." So they were not using the grapheme–phoneme rules to the exclusion of the two-morpheme rules. It is much more likely that they knew something about the fact that sometimes /z/-sounding endings are spelled with "s" but they did not know enough or in an explicit enough way to make the choice correctly more often than change. Perhaps their knowledge of this spelling ending was comparable to that displayed by the children who over-generalized the "ed" ending rule: they knew that both spellings could be appropriate but were not able to make the right choice systematically.

A second reason that makes it unlikely that this group was just using grapheme–phoneme rules most of the time is that many individuals who apparently acted randomly in one pseudoword task were significantly above chance level in another: if they had thought that pseudoword tasks were grapheme–phoneme tasks, they would have been unsuccessful in all four tasks. Yet, of the 80 participants whose scores were no better than chance in the /z/ verb task, only 31 produced significantly above chance scores in the /z/ plural nouns task. We also noted that 53% of the sample had scores in the significantly above chance range in one of the four tasks. All these people apparently knew that the pseudoword task is not just a measure of grapheme–phoneme knowledge, and yet they acted randomly in one or more of the four tasks.

So it seems that a strong and coherent knowledge of basic and simple morphemic spelling rules is not universal among adults, at any rate with the educational system that we have at the moment. When we leave it to individuals to infer the connection between morphemes and spelling, some succeed in doing so well: others do not. Some can use these rules with entirely new words: others cannot and probably have to get by with real words on the basis of their word-specific knowledge.

The split that we have just described provokes three further questions at least. The first is about when it happens. At what time in their life do some people work out these rules in a coherent enough form to be able to use them in the pseudoword task while others fail to do so? It is probably safe to assume that it happens some time during childhood, but we need a more precise answer than that. The second question is about the reasons for the split. The third question is about education. We need to know what we can do to remove the split. Is teaching the answer?

We have enough evidence from work done with school children to try to answer the first of these questions. In two further studies we gave the same four tasks to children in four primary schools and in one large secondary school. The children in the two samples came from a mix of social backgrounds, which was actually the same for the two main groups. The primary schools concerned were "feeder schools" for the one secondary school that we worked with in this project.

In each task, as Figure 6.3 shows, the primary and the secondary school children, like the young adults who did not attend university, were sharply divided into those who were and those who were not in the significantly above chance level range. Again the group with scores of less than 21 tended to form a normal distribution around the chance level score of 15, and again those with scores of 21 or more sharply diverged from this distribution.

Now that we have three samples of people of very different ages, we can ask what changes there are over time in the numbers who find out about the relevant spelling rules. Table 6.2 shows the percentages of people in each of the three samples (primary school, secondary school, young adults) who produced significantly above chance level scores. Table 6.2 shows definite differences across the different ages, but these do not form a straightforward increase with age. The most striking feature of these scores is that the secondary school children are the odd group out: the percentage of students producing significantly above chance level scores in each of the four tasks was higher in this sample than it was either with the younger children or with the young adults who were no longer in school. In fact, the percentages of individuals in the significantly above chance range were virtually the same in the two other groups, the primary children and the young adults. Yet, the

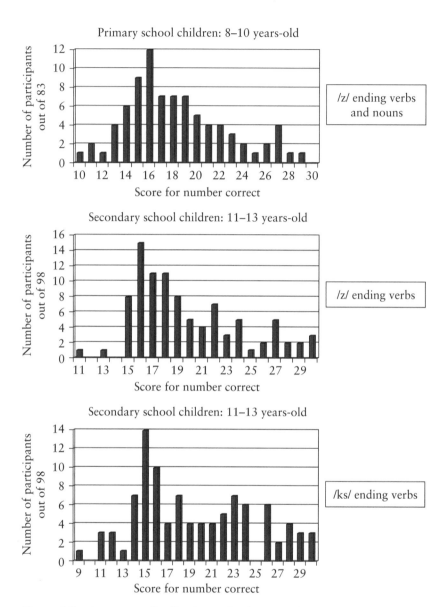

Figure 6.3 Frequency distributions of primary and secondary school children's scores in the pseudoword spelling tasks

Table 6.2 Percentages of people in each of the three samples (primary school, secondary school, young adults, not attending university) who produced significantly above chance level scores in the pseudoword spelling task

	/z/ nouns	/z/ verbs	/ks/ nouns	/ks/ verbs
Primary School (N = 72)	37.6	19.4	45.0	33.7
Secondary School (N = 98)	44.6	34.7	58.7	40.8
Young adults not in university (N = 100)	28.0	20.0	40.0	33.0

secondary school children, or at any rate some of them, had improved since the number of individuals in the significantly above chance level range was notably higher in this sample than among the younger children. What can account for this curious pattern?

One possible explanation is that many of the young adults had learned the spelling rules at school but then had forgotten them. This seems most unlikely to us. We know of no other evidence of any similar mass forgetting in research on reading and spelling, and it seems clear that most other orthographic rules and correspondences that people learn, such as the letter–sound correspondences and conditional rules like the split digraph, stay with them for life.

Another explanation, which seems much more convincing to us, is about the range of experiences and abilities in the three samples. We have already argued that children's success in inferring morphemic spelling rules for themselves depends greatly on the strength and extent of their word-specific knowledge of spelling. This bank of knowledge probably varies greatly between individuals in size and in organization. Some children will read a lot of books and magazines, and others will not. This variation may be a matter of the children's intrinsic interests or it may be determined by availability of things to read at home or by the amount of encouragement that parents give their children to read. Whatever the cause, these differences in reading experiences undoubtedly affect children's word-specific knowledge which, according to the argument that we have been developing, then determines how well they form inferences about morphemes and spelling. The children who form rich banks of word-specific knowledge are in a good position to make these inferences. As they grow older, more of them would be able to do well (to produce scores of 21 or more) in our morphemic spelling tests, which is why there are more children in this group at secondary school than there are at primary school.

We have one piece of evidence to support this idea. Emily Colchester (2006) did a follow-up study with primary school children in which she used a version of our choice task with /z/-ending pseudowords. She also gave them a version of the "title recognition test" which was devised by Keith Stanovich and his colleagues (1998). In this task the child is given a list of book titles, some of which are genuine titles of well-known children's books while others are made-up titles of books that do not exist. The child's task is to spot the genuine titles and to reject the spoof ones. The reasonable assumption behind this task is that, the more widely read a child is, the more familiar she will be with the titles of famous books. Therefore, children's success in spotting the genuine book titles should reflect their reading experiences.

Colchester found that the children whose scores were in the significantly above chance level range in the pseudoword task also did far better than the rest of the sample in the title recognition test. This result supports the idea that children's reading experiences determine how much they learn about morphemic spelling patterns, but it is only tentative support. We need a great deal more research, and particularly longitudinal research, to track the relationship between children's reading experiences and their knowledge of spelling rules.

There may also be a relationship between children's reading experiences on the one hand and the developmental paths that they take at school and also what they decide to do when they become adults, on the other hand. During the secondary school period, some children join the ranks of those who, according to our pseudoword measure, definitely do understand morphemic spelling rules, while others do not. The children who do eventually succeed in these tasks may do so because of the rich and varied experiences of reading; they may for the same reason decide to pursue their studies beyond school. These children would be unlikely to leave education at the age of 18 and would be more likely to decide to go to college or university. This could be the reason why the distribution of the young adults' scores was so like that of the primary school children: this sample may not have included people who would have begun to pass our pseudoword tasks while they were at secondary school.

This is an extremely tentative argument, but a fruitful one in the sense that it produces many clear and interesting predictions which could be tested in future research. Much of this research, as we have remarked already, would have to be longitudinal, but our hypothesis makes one prediction that can be tested by a simple comparison between two samples.

If the hypothesis is right, there should be a clear difference in the distribution of scores in the young adults who did not go on to university and in a sample of university students of the same age. John Dawson (2005) gave university students at a new university in the Midlands in the U.K. a version of our four pseudoword choice tasks but in a relatively difficult form. In each of the sentences that he read out to the participants the pseudoword occurred once only. Thus, when the target pseudoword was a plural noun or a third person singular present verb, the participants only heard that word and never the stem on its own (e.g. "Jim sometimes drux/drucks on the lawn").

Despite this added difficulty, the university students did relatively well in these demanding tasks. The proportion of the sample whose scores were in the successful 21+ correct range was consistently high: it varied from 88.5% (/ks/ noun task) to 82.2% (/z/ verbs). The number of people whose scores did not fall into this range was so small that it was impossible to determine whether these scores formed a normal distribution around chance.

This, of course, is quite different from the pattern of scores that we had found in the school and in the young adults samples, and we have further data that confirm this radical difference. Paul Mitchell (2004) had given exactly the same, relatively demanding, set of pseudoword tasks to another sample of adults who had completed secondary education and did not continue their education in university and so we were able to make a direct comparison between students and these adults. There were huge differences, as Table 6.3 shows. The proportion of the participants whose scores were significantly above chance was always

Table 6.3 Proportion of young adults not attending university and university students who scored above chance in the pseudoword spelling task

Group	N	Percentage significantly above chance level
Young adults mean age 21.7 years	205	17.0
Undergraduates Mean age 23.2 years	72	88.9

less than 20%: with the students this proportion was consistently above 80%.

Thus, we have found a striking split between the members of two sets of young adults. It concerns the strength of their knowledge about morphemic spelling rules. The vast majority of students and quite a small minority of adults who left school at 18 possess this knowledge in a strong form. They can apply this knowledge to words that they have never read or even heard before by taking into account the meaning that the surrounding sentence gives these words. Without any doubt these individuals have mastered the spelling rules in question.

What the remaining individuals in the two samples knew about morphemic spelling rules is not so clear, for reasons that we have already discussed. One can quite reasonably suggest that their knowledge about morphemes and spelling is weaker and more implicit, and certainly less effective for coping with novel words, than those whose scores are in the 21+ range, but we cannot yet say exactly why it is so.

One might even query whether this matters: why do we need bother about this knowledge since they hardly ever made mistakes in equivalent real word tasks? Both Dawson and Mitchell included real word tasks in their studies, and the participants made very few wrong choices in these tasks. Our answer is that the differences between two samples whose educational careers are also very different deserve a great deal of attention and some concern. There is currently much research to show that children who are good with morphological spelling rules have many advantages in literacy over those who are not. Morphological spelling rules are, in our view, not an isolated bit of knowledge: they are part of the connection between oral language and literacy. Spelling is literally the most visible part of this connection, but it is not the only aspect of literacy in which the indirect connection between oral and written language is manifest. If morphological knowledge is so important, perhaps the people who do not learn the underlying rules about morphemes and spelling are deprived of the kind of experience that makes this learning possible. In that case, we must ask what can be done about it—and the answer is, to analyse the effectiveness of interventions. But before we turn to interventions, we want to make the case for the more general significance of morphological knowledge.

Summary

1   We established in the previous chapter that in order to spell inflections correctly children can either use word-specific knowledge or

they can apply morphemic spelling rules. This raises the question whether there are individual differences in which route children and adults take to spell morphemes.

2 In a series of experiments we looked at the numbers of people who were significantly above chance level or not significantly above chance level in choosing the right spelling for morphemic endings in pseudowords. One cannot rely on word-specific knowledge to make the right choice in pseudoword tasks. These are tests of the participants' knowledge of morphemic spelling rules.

3 Two groups consistently emerged in each of these tasks; those significantly above chance and those not. This sharp division was found in primary and secondary school children, though the size of the significantly above chance level group was higher in the older than in the younger school children.

4 We found the same two groups in a sample of young adults who had been through secondary school, but had not gone to university. In this sample many less participants were significantly above chance level in their choices than were not. It was the other way round in a sample of university students, most of whom were significantly above chance.

5 This consistently sharp division suggests strong individual differences in the way that people cope with spelling morphemes. These are not just developmental differences. They deserve further study in children and in adults.

The Connection between Morphological Knowledge and Literacy

So much has already been written about the importance of the direct connection between oral and written language that we do not think it is necessary to review those arguments here. Many well-argued analyses of the literature (e.g. Adams, 1990; Bryant & Bradley, 1980; Ehri et al., 2001a, 2001b; National Reading Panel, 2000; Torgerson, Brooks, & Hall, 2006) have demonstrated the importance of children's awareness of phonology and of knowledge of phoneme–grapheme correspondences for reading and spelling. What about the indirect connection between oral and written language? How much do we know about its importance?

There are two aspects of the indirect connection between oral and written language: syntax and morphology. These are not entirely independent of each other. Inflectional morphemes—for example, "-s" for the plural, the "-ed" for past tense—are related to word classes, and this means that they are related to syntax. In English, only nouns take the mark of the plural: you don't use an "s" at the end of adjectives, even if you are qualifying two things, i.e. you don't say "nices girls," you say "nice girls." This is not a universal principle: in Portuguese, French and Greek, the mark for the plural is used with adjectives as well as with nouns.

Derivational morphology is also connected to syntax: we have exemplified this earlier on when we discussed the use of "-ion" to form one type of word, abstract nouns, and of "-ian" to form another type of word, agents. These word types are, of course, used in different sentence contexts. Derivational morphology is also connected to syntax in another way: we add different types of suffixes to form agents, depending on whether the stem is a verb or a noun. So, someone who reads is a "reader" and someone who directs movies is a "director": "-er" or "-or" are used with verbs; someone who plays music is a "musician" and someone who works in science is a "scientist": "-ian" and "-ist" are used with nouns.

In this section, we review briefly some of the evidence for the importance of children's awareness of morphology and syntax for literacy development. As you will see, assessments of children's knowledge of morphology are not independent of their knowledge of syntax. So, although we will speak of knowledge of morphology, their knowledge of syntax is always involved in performance in the same tasks. Similarly, we will speak of knowledge of syntax, but their knowledge of morphology will also be involved in the tasks. The distinction that we make depends on whether the measure primarily focuses on word affixes and stems, in which case we speak of morphological knowledge, or sentence structure, in which case we speak of syntactic knowledge.

How should children's knowledge of morphology and syntax be assessed in a society like England, where children do not receive instruction on morphology and syntax?

The first study that assessed children's knowledge of morphology was carried out by Jean Berko (1958). She reasoned that, as we learn our mother tongue, we encounter words that are morphologically related —we hear "dog" and "dogs"—and we make connections between the forms and meanings of these words. We also infer rules about how words are related to each other. Even at a young age, these experiences allow children to use implicit knowledge of these rules. In her pioneering study, Jean Berko showed children drawings of bird-like creatures that were not actual birds. She then told the children: "Here is a wug"—

also a word that they did not know, as it was a pseudoword (again the acid test). Next, she showed the children a picture with two wugs and said to the children: "Here comes another wug. Now there are two of them; there are two . . ." and she encouraged the children to complete the sentence. This was her test of the children's use of implicit morphological knowledge in speech: if the children could say "two wugs," they would show that they had some implicit knowledge of plural morphology.

Berko's original method is the basis for the development of many other measures of morphological knowledge, including the pseudoword spelling tasks that we described previously. Berko's study showed that morphological knowledge is not acquired in an all-or-nothing manner: the children could perform some of these transformations as if they knew the morphological rules but not others. The children that she assessed were either in kindergarten, aged 4–5 years, or in first grade, aged about 6–7 years. Both groups of children were competent in forming the plurals of some words but not of others. If all that they needed to do was to add an /s/ or a /z/ to some other sound like /g/ in "wug," they were right most of the time: 90% or above for the first graders in the different types of words and about 80% or above for the kindergartners. However, when the stem itself ended in /s/ or /z/, the children had much more difficulty: the plural of "nizz," which should be "nizzes," turned out to be very difficult: only 33% of the answers by first graders and 14% of those by kindergarteners were correct. So, even for the same meaning, if the morphological rule becomes more complex, the level of difficulty increases.

The simple plurals and the present progressive ("zibbing") were the easiest items. The children had great difficulty with some other morphological transformations; for example, forming an adjective from a noun was very difficult: only one child from all the 56 children she tested was able to provide the adjective "quirky" for a dog that is full of quirks and the comparative "quirkier" for one that is even fuller of quirks. Although "quirk" and "quirky" are not pseudowords, the children could not manage these transformations. They also found it very difficult to form an agent from a verb: whereas adults unanimously said that a man who "zibs" is a "zibber," only 11% of the children created this derived form; 16% created the form "zibbingman" or "zibman," using the idea of compounds; the rest could not provide any word that used the stem as part of their answer.

Berko also devised a compound-word task. She presented the children with 14 compound words, such as "fireplace," "football," "newspaper," "birthday" and "Thanksgiving," and asked them to define each word. She classified the children's answers into different categories: the category of interest here is the one that she called "etymological explanations," which consisted of using the elements in the compound to explain the meaning of the compound word. This was not an easy task, and only 13% of all the responses were classified as etymological. Even the word "Thanksgiving," about which children are explicitly taught in U.S. kindergartens, did not elicit a majority of etymological explanations: only 33% of the answers were of this type. The remaining 67% of the answers referred to a salient feature of Thanksgiving Day, such as "because you eat lots of turkey." Similarly, "birthday" was only defined as "a day" by 2% of the children, and none appears to have said anything about a connection to one's birth; their answers simply relied on associations with getting presents and eating cake. "Fireplace" was the word which elicited the largest number of responses that used the elements of the compound in the definition: 72% of the answers indicated that people put fire in a fireplace, but Berko remarks that this may have been due more to the fact that fire is a salient feature in a fireplace than to an etymological analysis of the word.

Berko contributed two methods for the assessment of children's morphological knowledge: sentence completion and word definition. The contrast between the children's performance in the two tasks is instructive: they could use implicit knowledge to generate answers and complete sentences, but they could not provide explicit explanations for the meanings of compound words. These discrepancies underscore the importance of exploring different methods in the assessment of children's knowledge of morphology and of attempting to form conclusions informed by a variety of methods.

The evidence for the importance of morphological knowledge that we review here will focus on three domains and will draw on different techniques for assessing morphological knowledge. The first section examines the connection between morphological knowledge and vocabulary learning; the second will focus on literacy learning; finally, the third section focuses on second language learning.

Morphological knowledge and remembering new words

In order to learn new words, children must do two things: (1) they must be able to remember the sequences of sounds that form the words; and (2) they must attribute meanings to these sequences of sounds.

Sue Gathercole and her colleagues have convincingly shown that children's phonological skills—more specifically, their phonological short-term memory—are strongly associated with their ability to learn new words (Gathercole, Service, Hitch, Adams, & Martin, 1999; Gathercole, Service, Hitch, & Martin, 1997; Gathercole, Willis, Emslie, & Baddeley, 1992). Their main assessment of phonological short-term memory consisted of asking the children to listen to some pseudowords and to repeat them. Since they called this a "non-word repetition task," we will use the term "non-word" in our description of their results, but, of course, the terms "non-word" and "pseudoword" are synonyms.

The children's performance on this task was correlated with one measure of their vocabulary which was taken at the same time and also with another measure of vocabulary that was given to the children about one year later.

The ability to remember sequences of sounds undoubtedly involves phonological skills, but it is unlikely that all sequences of sounds are remembered in the same way, irrespective of whether they are morphemes or not. If you are presented with non-words that cannot be easily analysed into morphemes—such as "hampent," "stopograttic," "woogalamic" or "dopelate"—you have to rely mostly on your phonological skills when trying to remember them. You might remember these sequences by their syllabic units, and the more syllables a non-word has, the more difficult it will be to remember it. However, if the non-words could be easily analysed into morphemes—such as "concentrationist," "unsausagish," "winteriser" or "computerist"—you could work with different units when attempting to remember them: "winteriser" can be remembered in three units (winter—ise—er) that are its constituent morphemes. So would "concentrationist," "computerist" and "unsausagish." In all these examples, there are fewer morphemes than syllables, and the task should be easier.

We tested the hypothesis that children do analyse non-words into morphemes, when they can, by comparing children's performance in a non-word repetition task where half of the words did not have a morphemic structure and the other half did. Our prediction was that, if children use the morphemic structure to remember the new sequences of sounds in non-words, they would perform significantly better in the non-words with a morphemic structure than in those without this structure. We composed a set of non-words matched in number of syllables to the non-words used by Gathercole and her colleagues but our non-words had a clear morphological structure. In order to ensure that there were definitely two types of non-words in our experiment, we presented our set of words and those used by Gathercole mixed and in random order to two adults, native speakers of English, whom we asked to say quickly what the morphemes that made up the non-words were. All the non-words that we created were easily identified as formed by morphemes and some of those used by Gathercole were also analysed into morphemes. So we excluded these latter words from our study. We then presented the two sets of words, again mixed and in random order, to 57 children, whose ages varied between 9 and 11 years, and asked them to repeat the non-words as accurately as possible. The children were given one point for each non-word repeated accurately.

The children's performance in the two sets of non-words was highly correlated: the correlation was 0.71, which is significant ($p < .001$), and this correlation remained as high and significant even after partialling out the effect of the children's age (see Chapter 3 for an explanation of why it is necessary to partial out the children's age): the partial correlation was 0.72. We then compared the children's performance in the two sets of non-words. Out of a possible score of 23, the children scored 18.7 correct in the non-words with a morphological structure and 17 correct in the non-words without a morphological structure. This difference was statistically significant ($t = 5.01$; df = 55; $p < .001$). So, we concluded that children used a morphological analysis when trying to remember a novel sequence of sounds. That must be why they found it relatively easy to repeat non-words that have an obvious morphological structure.

If this idea is correct, there should be a relation between children's morphological knowledge and their ability to use it to remember non-words with a morphological structure, but not with their ability to repeat non-words that do not have a morphological structure. We gave the children an assessment of their morphological knowledge—the sentence analogy task—and an assessment of their phonological awareness —a phoneme deletion task. We predicted that there would be a significant correlation between the children's performance in the sentence analogy task and their performance in the repetition of non-words with a morphological structure, after controlling for the children's age and their performance on the phoneme deletion task; the equivalent partial correlation with non-words that do not have a morphological structure was not expected to be significant.

In the sentence analogy task, the children hear a pair of sentences, each "spoken" by puppet: for example, the first puppet says "Tom helps Mary" and the second puppet says "Tom helped Mary"; then the first puppet says "Tom sees Mary" and the child is asked to produce the

sentence that the second puppet should now say. In the phoneme deletion task, the children are asked to say a word—for example, "meat,"
without the first sound /m/. We used a version of this task where the
children were asked to delete either the first or the last sound in the
words.

We then calculated the partial correlation between the children's
performance in the sentence analogy task and their performance in the
non-word repetition task, partialling out the effects of age and phoneme
deletion. The partial correlation between sentence analogy and the score
on the non-words with a morphological structure was low—it was
.27—but significant ($p < .05$); the partial correlation with the non-words
that did not have a morphological structure was not significant.

We concluded that children use their morphological knowledge in
remembering the sounds in a new word, whenever the word has a
morphological structure that they recognize. Thus, the better their
morphological knowledge, the greater will be their ability to remember
new words. So, the first part of the task in learning a new word—
remembering the sequence of sounds that make up the word—is influenced both by the children's phonological and morphological skills.

Morphological knowledge and learning new words

The second part of the children's task in learning new vocabulary is to
learn the meanings of the new words that they encounter. It is quite
clear to anyone that we do not explicitly teach children the meanings of
the majority of the new words that they hear: they have to infer these
meanings. How do they accomplish this amazing task?

Researchers working on children's first language acquisition have
suggested that children learn new vocabulary by implicitly understanding the constraints that morphemes and syntax impose on the possible
meaning of a word. Roger Brown (1957), a pioneer in the systematic
studies of first language acquisition, showed that children use both the
indefinite article "a"—syntactic information—and verb inflections—
morphological information—to infer the meanings of new words. He
presented young children with sentences that contained a non-word and
a picture: for example, he showed them a picture of a pair of hands
kneading a strange substance in an unfamiliar container and said to
some children "here you can see a sib" whereas to other children he
said "here you can see sibbing." He then asked the children to choose,
from a set of four pictures, the one that showed "a sib" or "sibbing,"
depending on what pseudoword the children had been exposed to. The

children who were told "a sib" chose a picture with the same container where the hand was doing something different and there was no substance similar to the one in the first picture; the children who were told "sibbing" chose a picture with a pair of hands doing the same action to a different substance in a different container. Brown concluded that the children had used the syntactic and morphological information to infer the meaning of the pseudowords.

Brown's work inspired many subsequent studies and a theory of vocabulary acquisition known as "syntactic bootstrapping hypothesis" (Gleitman, 1990; Gleitman & Gleitman, 1992), according to which children use their implicit knowledge of grammatical categories to narrow down the meaning of unfamiliar words.

Many experimental studies have provided support for this theory. We describe here one study in order to exemplify the methods typically used in these experiments. Katherine Wysocki and Joseph Jenkins (1987) tested whether children in grades 2 (aged about 8 years), 4 and 6 could use morphological information to infer the meaning of new words. The children whom they included in their study were average achievers in terms of their vocabulary scores in a standardized test. They chose a set of infrequent words, according to a frequency count for children's books, in order to be reasonably confident that the children would not already know these. Then they the formed two lists of words, A and B, which contained a set or words to be taught and a set of transfer words. Each of the transfer words had the same stem as one of the taught words. Half of the children learned list A, and for them list B formed a control set of words, whereas the other half of the children learned list B, and for them list A was a control set of words. This careful design allowed the researchers to be certain that, if the children performed better on the transfer words, it could only be due to their transferring information, on the basis of the common stems, from one task to the next.

The children were taught the definitions of the taught words in the classroom. Two weeks after the children had learned the definitions, they were post-tested on the taught, the transfer and the control words. These words were presented in sentences, and the children were asked to explain what the words meant. The prediction was that, if children can use morphological information to infer the meaning of new words, they would perform significantly better on the transfer than on the control words. The comparison between the taught and the control words was used as a first step in their analysis, to make sure that the teaching had been effective.

The children in all three grade levels performed better in the taught than in the control words—so teaching the children the definitions of words had been an effective way of getting them to know these words. There was also clear support for the children's use of morphological information in inferring the meaning of words: in all three grade levels, the children performed better in the transfer than in the control words. This result shows unambiguously that, from the age of about 8 years at least, children can use information contained in the stem to infer the meanings of new words.

It is beyond the scope of this chapter to review in detail all the work on children's ability to use morphology and syntax to infer the meaning of new words; some thorough reviews already exist (e.g. Anglin, 1993; Graves, 1986; Naigles, 1990; White, Power, & White, 1989) as well as some very interesting teaching studies (e.g. Jenkins, Matlock, & Slocum, 1989; Nunes & Bryant, 2006). The point that we wish to make here is that these studies hypothesized that morphology and syntax are part of the language-learning mechanisms used by children in inferring the meaning of new words, and provided experimental support for children's use of these mechanisms. Children can learn new words from reading texts that contain previously unknown words (Nagy, Herman, & Anderson, 1985) but some researchers (e.g. Schatz & Baldwin, 1986) have argued that syntax and context are not sufficient for word meanings to be inferred: the use of morphology to complement syntactical information is essential even in English, which is not a highly inflected language.

Further work extended these findings by showing that morphological knowledge may also explain individual differences in vocabulary: some children develop a larger vocabulary and a better understanding of the words that they know than other children, and one of the reasons for this difference between children is their awareness of morphology.

Studies of individual differences in morphological knowledge and its relationship to differences in vocabulary are based on correlational methods. Without attempting to provide a thorough review, we cite here a recent study that shows that morphological knowledge does explain individual differences in vocabulary, after controlling for the connections between morphological knowledge, phonological skills and vocabulary.

Catherine McBride-Chang and her collaborators (McBride-Chang, Wagner, Muse, Chow, & Shu, 2005) carried out a study with children in kindergarten and second grade, where they analysed the connection between morphological knowledge and vocabulary, controlling for the effects that phonological skills might have on vocabulary acquisition. They assessed the children's morphological awareness using two measures: one was morpheme identification, which tests whether the children can judge if two same-sounding stems are morphologically related or not, e.g. "blew" and "blue"; the second was a sentence completion task, similar to the Berko task, which taps the children's knowledge of morphological structure. The children's phonological skills were also assessed by two measures: phoneme deletion and non-word repetition, using non-words that do not have an obvious morphological structure. The children's vocabulary was assessed by an expressive measure of vocabulary, where the children are asked to identify pictured items.

They used the statistical technique called multiple regression analysis, which is similar to partial correlations as it also allows the researcher to investigate the connection between two variables after controlling for what both have in common with a third variable. McBride-Chang and her colleagues wanted to know whether the connection between morphological knowledge and vocabulary remains significant after controlling for the children's age, reading ability, and the measures of their phonological skills. Their results were quite clear: the correlation between the two measures of morphological knowledge and vocabulary remained significant after these strict controls.

Summary

1   There is clear evidence that children's knowledge of morphology is related to their vocabulary development. Differences in vocabulary knowledge are related to differences in children's morphological knowledge, after controlling for phonological skills. So, children's knowledge of morphology is important for their language development in general.

2   Experimental studies which investigated the connection between morphology and vocabulary showed that children use morphological information in carrying out both tasks necessary for learning a new word. When the new word has a clear morphological structure, children are better at remembering it than if it were a sequence of sounds without this structure. When inferring the meaning of a new word, they use morphological and syntactic information to do so.

Morphological knowledge and reading ability

If children use their morphological and syntactic knowledge to infer the meanings of new words that they hear, shouldn't they be able to use their morphological knowledge when they read? Different researchers have drawn the conclusion that this must be so, and tested its validity by using a variety of methods and different measures of reading to investigate the connection between morphology and reading. We will discuss first the importance of the indirect connection between oral and written language for word recognition and then for reading comprehension.

Word Recognition Studies

Different researchers have proposed that word recognition is not the product solely of decoding by using grapheme–phoneme correspondence, i.e. it is not the product only of the use of the direct connection between oral and written language. Word recognition is the result of the "orchestration" of different factors that produce fast and fluent reading (Berninger, 1989).

The most common form of this type of theory asserts that readers are able to access whole words by simple recognition, without having to analyse them, as well as through the grapheme–phoneme correspondences. This whole word recognition skill is known as "lexical recognition" or "sight vocabulary," and is assumed to work pretty much like word-specific knowledge does in spelling. Readers just know what the words are and form a more or less direct connection between the word and its meaning, without having to analyse them. This type of theory is called the "dual route model" of reading, because it recognizes that there are two ways of achieving word recognition. It has many illustrious proponents in the literature about adults' word reading (e.g. Butterworth, 1983; Coltheart, Rastle, Perry, Langdon, & Ziegler, 2001; Howard & Best, 1996; Job, Peressotti, & Cusinato, 1998; Morton, 1979; Paap & Noel, 1991; Patterson, Marshall, & Coltheart, 1985) and children's word reading too (e.g. Adams & Huggins, 1985; Alegria & Mousty, 1992; Berninger, Chen, & Abbott, 1988; Ehri, 2005; Manis, Seidenberg, Doi, McBride-Chang, & Peterson, 1996; Share, 1995; Stanovich, 1980). This is an important part of the word reading research, but we will not discuss the model here because our aim is to consider whether morphological knowledge plays a part in children's growing ability to read words.

Much research supports the view that adults also use morphemes in word recognition (e.g. Murrell & Morton, 1974; Schreuder & Baayan, 1995; Taft, 1985, 1988, 2003; Taft & Zhu, 1995): this would imply that children must learn to do so. But what is the evidence on children's use of morphology in word reading?

The idea that many factors participate in word recognition is not new: Goodman (1969) suggested that reading involves grapho-phonic, syntactic and semantic kinds of information, but surprisingly did not make explicit references to morphological processes in word reading, even though he used morphemes in the analysis of what sorts of miscues appeared in word recognition errors. Solid evidence for the importance of syntax and morphology in appropriate word recognition only appeared much later, as Goodman's work was actually about errors rather than accurate or fluent word reading.

Several researchers have investigated this issue and there is much evidence relevant to the role of morphology in word reading (e.g. Carlisle, 2000; Carlisle & Stone, 2003, 2005; Mahony, 1994; Mahony, Singson, & Mann, 2000; Reichle & Perfetti, 2003; Singson, Mahony, & Mann, 2000). Carlisle and Stone (2005) provide an excellent review of the different models that have been used to interpret the role that morphology plays in word recognition; we do not review these different models here and only seek to exemplify the nature of the evidence (for a discussion, see also Verhoeven & Perfetti, 2003).

One of the most comprehensive programmes of research on children's use of morphology in word recognition is that by Leong (1989, 1991, 1992, 2000; Leong & Parkinson, 1995). Leong (1989) used an interesting method to assess whether morphemes have an effect on children's word reading. In line with research methods adopted to investigate word recognition by adults, he used a lexical decision task, in which participants are shown for very brief periods (measured in thousandths of a second) some groups of letters: their task is to decide whether they are looking at a real word or not. The readers in these experiments only need to press a key if the stimulus is a word and a different key if it is not. This method is used, rather than pronouncing the word, for two reasons. First, the method produces fast responses, as the participant does not need to say anything, which makes the reaction time—i.e. the time between the appearance of the letters on the screen and the response of pressing the key—a sensitive measure of word recognition. Second, it is assumed that the factor that makes the lexical decision easier for the participant does so because it facilitates a form of processing printed words that the reader actually uses. For example, a researcher who wants to test whether morphology facilitates word recognition (e.g. Burani, Salmaso, & Caramazza, 1984; Caramazza, Miceli, Silveri, & Laudanna, 1985) will show the readers in the experiment a word, for example, "HARM," and later on another morphologically related word, for example, "HARMFUL." If a group of readers who see this sequence recognize "HARMFUL" more quickly than another group who did not see the word "HARM," a facilitating effect is shown. However, in order to show that this facilitating effect was due to morphological, and not to phonological or orthographic similarity, the researcher will also present readers with the sequence "HARM" and "HARMONY": these two words have the same amount of phonological and orthographic similarity as the pair "HARM" and "HARMFUL," but they do not have the same stem, so the facilitating effect should not happen. In a series of well-known studies, Caramazza and his colleagues have shown that this is the case for adult readers (e.g. Caramazza, Laudana, & Romani, 1988; Chialant & Caramazza, 1995): there are clear facilitating effects of morphology on word recognition.

Leong (1989) carried out a series of studies using reaction times in lexical decision tasks to test whether morphological analysis facilitates word recognition in children and also whether this facilitating effect is related to their increasing knowledge of morphology and reading ability. We describe his methods here in order to illustrate another approach to the analysis of how morphology influences literacy, without attempting to cover the studies in detail. He showed Canadian students in 4th, 5th and 6th grades (ages 10–12 years) the same words presented with a mixture of upper and lower case letters. When this mixture is random within the word, it usually makes reading more difficult: for example, reading "mAcHInE" is much more difficult than reading either "machine" or "MACHINE." However, if the mixture is not random, but rather coincides with the way the reader parses the words when attempting to recognize them, it has a facilitating effect. Leong showed the students two types of upper and lower case letter mixes: for example, "tractOR" and "tracTOR." In the first type of presentation, "tractOR," the word is analyzed into morphemes; in the second type of presentation, "tracTOR," the word is analyzed in sequences of sounds that can be pronounced, "trac" and "tor," but that do not coincide with the morpheme boundaries. Students' reaction times were indeed faster when the boundaries of the upper and lower case letter groups coincided with the morphemes, and this facilitating effect was larger for older students and also for those with higher reading ability within their grade level. In his subsequent work, he went on to show that morphology also had facilitating effects on judgements on whether words were spelled correctly or not (Leong, 2000) and to propose a model of how morphological skills affect word reading (Leong, 1991, 1992), alongside phonological skills and sentence comprehension. He tested this model in a longitudinal study of 10- to 12-year-olds, using a combination of tasks to assess morphological knowledge, which included his reaction time tasks and other tasks designed by Carlisle (1988), described a little later in this section. The details of his study are much too technical for presentation here. Suffice it to say that he provided strong evidence for participation of morphological knowledge in word reading, along with phonological knowledge and sentence comprehension, and argued that it is the orchestration of these three factors that explains fluent word recognition in normal readers of this age level.

Evidence for children's use of the indirect connection between oral and written language in word recognition has also been provided through experimental methods with pronunciation of the word as the outcome measure. These studies were about syntax rather than morphology. Rego and Bryant (1993) devised a new method to test this: they gave children in their first year of school (aged between 5 and 6 years) a word reading task, in which words are presented in isolation, and later presented to each child the very same words that the child did not read, this time in the context of a sentence. If children can use the context of the sentence to facilitate word recognition, they should now be able to read words that previously had baffled them. The sentences were generated in a way that they gave a context to the word but did not entirely specify the word: for example, one sentence was: "the girls went to the park and saw a big. . . ." There are different words that could fit at the end of this sentence; the word that the children had to read was "tree."

Rego and Bryant also gave the children three measures of the children's awareness of syntax. Two were sentence completion tasks: the children hear a sentence where a word is missing and have to provide a word to fill the gap. The child received a point if the word appropriately fitted into the sentence (these methods were based on work by Guthrie, 1973; Tunmer & Bowey, 1984; and Tunmer, 1989). The third was a sentence anagram task: the tester says words which could form a sentence but the order of the words is jumbled: e.g. "John the bike rides." The child is asked to produce the correct version of the sentence, and receives a point for each correct answer (this method was based on work by Tunmer, Herriman, & Nesdale, 1988). Rego and Bryant made two predictions. First, if knowledge of syntax does help children to decode words, the children should be able to read in the context of sentences some of the words that they could not read in isolation. Second, if this gain really is due to the children's knowledge of syntax, then there should be a significant correlation between syntactic knowledge and the gains made by the children when reading words in the context of sentences. Their study was longitudinal: the children were given the syntactic awareness tasks about six months before they were given the two forms of the word reading task and their gains in word reading from use of context were assessed.

Rego and Bryant found strong support for the existence of contextual facilitation: the mean number of words that the children were able to read significantly improved when the children read the word after hearing a sentence. The most significant result, though, was that this contextual facilitation of word reading was specifically correlated to how well the children had performed in the syntactic awareness tasks six months earlier. We used regression analyses to test whether syntactic awareness had a specific connection with facilitation of word reading by context (this is the same statistical technique presented in the previous section, in the description of the work about vocabulary by McBride-Chang and her colleagues). When the factors, such as the children's age, general intelligence, vocabulary and verbal memory, were partialled out, the correlation between each of the measures of syntactic awareness and the gains obtained from contextual facilitation remained significant. In contrast, the children's performance in tasks of phonological awareness did not pass this test: its partial correlation with the gains from reading the words in the context of a sentence was not significant. This means that the children were using the indirect, and not the direct, connection between oral and written language when their word reading performance improved by having the sentence context.

Later work by Nation and Snowling (1998) confirmed these results with poor readers: only poor readers with good syntactic awareness were able to profit from reading the sentences in context, which supports the idea that contextual facilitation of word recognition depends on the readers' ability to use the indirect connection between oral and written language.

A final word about the involvement of the indirect connection between oral and written language and word decoding is still necessary. There has been much debate in the literature concerning the separation of decoding from reading comprehension. Some early models of reading, known as "bottom-up," proposed that reading starts with lower level processes of assembling phonemes into sequences that form words; comprehension would be an entirely independent process, which only takes place after decoding is achieved. Current models of reading, such as "the simple view of reading," distinguish between decoding and reading comprehension, but distinguishing between two processes does not mean that they are entirely independent processes: they could still be influenced by similar linguistic processes. Hoover and Gough (1990) clearly assert that this independence is not assumed in their simple view of reading, and reject such radical bottom-up views:

> The bottom-up conception holds that reading is a serial process, with decoding preceding comprehension. On this view, decoding should take place before, and thus, independently of comprehension, and it should not be influenced by things taking place at any higher levels. Yet word recognition can be dramatically influenced by linguistic context (e.g. see Stanovich and West 1983), and this falsifies the strictly bottom-up model. (Hoover & Gough, 1990, p. 130)

Thus the evidence that we discussed does not challenge the simple view of reading, even though it provides evidence that decoding is influenced by morphological and syntactical knowledge, which might also influence reading comprehension. Nevertheless, some researchers (Adlof, Catts, & Little, 2006) have suggested that this simple view should be made a little more complex by the addition of a fluency factor, which has been connected to morphological knowledge and which influences reading comprehension. This is the topic of the next section.

Summary

1   There is considerable evidence showing that fluent and skilled word reading is not based exclusively on the direct connection between oral and written language. The indirect connection, which operates through syntax and morphology, also plays a role in word reading.

2   Some could argue that the effects of syntactic knowledge observed by Rego and Bryant (1993) and by Nation and Snowling (1998) resulted from the participation of beginning and non-fluent readers in these studies; they claim that this effect would disappear if the readers had attained an efficient level of decoding, which no longer requires the participation of the indirect connection between oral and written language.

3   However, the participants in Mahony's (1994) study were high school and college students and those in Leong's studies were young adolescents; these are all readers who had attained fluent reading. The strength of the evidence provided by Leong's work lies in the fact that word recognition was measured by a variety of methods, including tasks that required very fast word recognition and others that involved pronunciation of the words.

Reading Comprehension

The participation of the indirect connection between oral and written language in processes that lead to word decoding is clearly important in literacy, and shows that syntactic and morphological effects on literacy go beyond spelling. This section analyses whether the indirect connection is also important for reading comprehension.

Joanne Carlisle (1995) was among the first researchers to test this hypothesis. She worked with a sentence completion task where the children are asked to produce a derived word that adequately completes a sentence. As in Berko's work, the word that the children have to produce is constrained both by morphology and syntax. The children hear a word—for example, "farm"—and they are asked to use this word to complete a sentence, where a derived form should appear—"my uncle is a . . ." Carlisle used different pairs of base and derived words. In some pairs, such as "farm"–"farmer," it was easy to note the connection between the two forms because the stems sounded the same; she termed these "transparent." In others, the connection between the two forms was less transparent, because the stems differed: for example, the cue word given before the sentence was "explode" and the children were asked to complete the sentence "we heard a terrible . . ." Note that, in both cases, the measure of the children's morphological awareness cannot be independent of their syntactic knowledge: the children need to use their syntactic knowledge to figure out what kind of word fits into the sentence.

Carlisle tested 184 children on this task when they were in their first year in school. She also tested their phonological awareness, by using a phoneme deletion task. Later on, when they were in second grade, she tested their word reading and reading comprehension skills. Her hypothesis was that children's morphological awareness assessed in first grade would show a higher correlation than their phonological awareness with reading comprehension, assessed in second grade. In contrast, their phonological awareness would show a higher correlation with word reading than morphological awareness. Her first prediction was supported by her findings: the correlation between morphological awareness and reading comprehension was .55 and that between phonological awareness and reading comprehension was .41. This result suggests that morphological knowledge matters to reading comprehension, and that it matters more than phonological awareness does. This is a finding that has been replicated by other authors since (Jarmulowicz, Hay,

Taran, & Ethington, 2008). Surprisingly, her second hypothesis was not supported by her findings: the correlations between phonological awareness and word reading, and between morphological awareness and word reading were actually the same, and equal to .50. She was puzzled by this finding but further research, described in the next paragraphs, helps explain why morphological awareness might influence word reading.

Bill Nagy, Virginia Berninger and Robert Abbott (2006) explored the connections between morphological knowledge and reading comprehension using a larger variety of literacy measures. Their theory was that morphological awareness promotes children's reading comprehension in at least two ways.

The first, and quite direct, connection between morphological awareness and reading is that morphological awareness contributes to the children's understanding of English orthography, and thus to their fluent reading. These researchers had already shown that morphological awareness is related to reading fluency (Berninger, Abbott, Billingsley, & Nagy, 2001) and expected it to be related also to reading comprehension. As we have argued in the previous chapters, the spelling of some words is a representation of morphology which flouts letter–sound correspondences. Children who realize this will understand the orthography better and should also be able to read more fluently; furthermore, by making the connections between morphemes and meaning, they should be able to read with comprehension.

The second connection between morphological knowledge and reading comprehension is indirect, mediated by the children's reading vocabulary. Morphological knowledge helps children learn new, morphologically complex words, through the processes illustrated earlier on in the previous section. Previous work by Nagy and his colleagues showed that most longer words in English are composed of more than one morpheme (Nagy & Anderson, 1984); if children encounter these words in print for the first time, they will need to use their morphological knowledge to infer the words' meanings and, in some cases, also their pronunciation. This hypothesis about a connection between morphological awareness and reading vocabulary makes good sense: if we hear a new, morphologically complex word—for example, "paintless"—and we can make connections betweens its parts, "paint" and "less" and the meaning that each one of them has, we are more likely to learn this word than if we had to learn it simply as a sequence of sounds, with no connection to anything else. If we were only using phonological information, we could easily be in doubt about how to read the end of the word: should the "-ess" at the end be stressed, as it is in words such as "princess" and "address," or not, like in "happiness" or "blindness"? By making the connection between "painless" and other words with the same suffix, such as "shameless," of "homeless," we will conclude that the "-ess" is not stressed, and we will add it to our reading vocabulary. Thus our morphological knowledge should contribute to our word reading skill, at least when we need to read multi-morpheme words with a pronunciation not entirely predictable from phonological rules.

To test these hypotheses, Nagy and his colleagues (2006) asked a large number of students (about 600) selected from four different grade levels—from fourth grade (approximate average age 10 years) to ninth grade—to answer three measures of morphological knowledge, which they combined into a single measure later, through the appropriate statistical techniques. They also gave the children measures of phonological awareness and a variety of measures of literacy outcomes. The literacy measures included reading comprehension, spelling, reading vocabulary and decoding of inflected words and pseudowords. The reading comprehension and spelling measures were standardized measures. In their measure of reading vocabulary, the children were asked to read single words and identify a phrase that explained the words' meaning. In the task of reading inflected words and pseudowords, stem pronunciation and stress were important for word identification: for example, the pseudoword "betongue" can only be read correctly by children who identify "tongue" as the stem; otherwise, their pronunciation of the stem in "betongue" will not be appropriate.

The first step of their analysis consisted in showing that morphological knowledge makes a contribution to reading, which is independent of the children's phonological skills. They did this by using a sophisticated statistical technique called structural equation modelling, which, similarly to partial correlation, allows us to test whether two variables correlate significantly after partialling out what both variables have in common with a third one. We do not describe their procedures here in detail; suffice it to say their aim was to test their theory of how morphological knowledge and reading are connected.

In their preliminary analyses, Nagy and his colleagues found that, after controlling for phonological skills, the children's morphological knowledge contributed significantly to reading comprehension, reading vocabulary, and decoding of suffixed words and pseudowords. This was true for all the grade levels that were included in their study.

The next step in their study was to test whether their hypothesis about the different ways in which morphological knowledge and reading comprehension are connected could be supported by the same type of analysis. Nagy and his colleagues hypothesized that the children's awareness of morphology would make a significant contribution to reading comprehension in two ways. One was by means of an indirect connection, via their reading vocabulary. The second connection should work directly, as a consequence of the children's understanding of the orthography. A simplified visual representation of their model is presented in Figure 6.4.

The test of this model requires that three correlations should be significant: (1) the partial correlation between morphological knowledge and reading vocabulary, when overlaps with age and phonological skills have been controlled for; (2) the partial correlation between morphological knowledge and reading comprehension, after controlling for what these two variables have in common with phonological skills; and (3) the correlation between reading vocabulary and reading comprehension, after partialling out what these two have in common with morphological knowledge. Their results supported the hypothesis that there are two forms of connection between children's knowledge of morphology and reading comprehension. However, these different connections did not appear in all the grade levels that they tested. In fourth and fifth grade, the correlation between morphological awareness and reading vocabulary was so high—it was equal to .85—that it was not possible to show an independent connection between reading vocabulary and reading comprehension after partialling out the overlap between morphological awareness and reading vocabulary. This negative result does not mean that there is no connection between reading vocabulary and reading comprehension at this time in children's development. It only means that it cannot be demonstrated independently of the connection that morphological awareness has with reading vocabulary. In the later

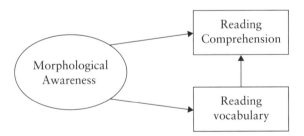

Figure 6.4 A visual representation of the direct connection between morphological knowledge and reading comprehension and of the indirect connection, via reading vocabulary

grades, the existence of the two forms of connection between morphological awareness and reading comprehension could be demonstrated.

Hélène Deacon and John Kirby (2004) obtained similar results regarding the importance of morphological awareness for reading comprehension with approximately 100 Canadian school children, using a different measure of morphological awareness, the sentence analogy task, described earlier in this chapter. Their study was also longitudinal and they used a statistical technique called multiple regression which, like partial correlations, allows for controlling for the overlaps between variables before investigating the correlations between the variables of interest in the study. When the children were in their second year in school, they assessed the children's morphological and phonological awareness as well as their general intelligence. Later, when the children were in grades 3, 4 and 5, they were assessed in word reading, pseudoword reading, and reading comprehension. Deacon and Kirby found that, after controlling for the overlaps with verbal ability and phonological awareness, the children's morphological awareness still predicted their reading comprehension in the three subsequent grades. These results are impressive indeed: sentence analogy was a significant predictor of reading comprehension three years after the children had been assessed on this task, and after controlling for the overlaps with phonological awareness. There is, to our knowledge, no other longitudinal study that covers such a long term and provides such clear results.

These studies throw some light on the processes by which morphological knowledge is related to reading comprehension and also show that individual differences in morphological knowledge explain, at least in part, individual differences in reading comprehension. Because the latter two studies used stringent controls for individual differences in phonological skills, they show that morphological knowledge is important independent of its connection with the children's phonological skills. Similar work in French (Casalis & Louis-Alexandre, 2000) shows that the importance of morphological knowledge for reading comprehension is not restricted to children learning to read in English.

These studies focus on the children's first language. The next section of this chapter considers whether morphological awareness is also important for learning a second language.

Summary

1   Learners—both children and adults—show different levels of knowledge of morphological rules in their native language, when they are

tested either in written form (section 1 of this chapter) or in oral form (section 2).

2   The extent of people's morphological knowledge determines:
    1   how well they analyse pseudowords into stems and affixes as they hear them and use this analysis in spelling;
    2   how successfully they analyse new words that they hear into stem and affixes and use this information both to remember the sounds in the words and to make an inference about their meanings;
    3   how much use they can make of stem and affix information in order to learn new words when they first encounter them in texts;
    4   how much they use morphological information in word reading, in order to read more fluently and with better comprehension.

Transfer of Morphological Skills across Languages

Learning a second language today is an important part of the school curriculum and it is also a progressively more important skill for employment. Monolingual European citizens are at a disadvantage for employment in jobs directly related to the European Union and their mobility is undoubtedly restricted across European countries in comparison to that of bilingual citizens. In view of the growing importance of second language learning today, educators and policy-makers should be asking the question: is there anything that can be done in the teaching of the children's first language that would make them better learners of a second language?

There is much research on transfer of skills across languages in bilingual children. The research shows that there is definitely transfer across languages, both of phonological and morphological awareness (for reviews of transfer across languages, see Bindman, 2004; Defior, 2004; Siegel, 2004). However, the situation of the monolingual learner who is taught a second language in school is different from that of bilingual learners, and it is the case of the monolingual learner learning a second language only in the classroom that we consider briefly here.

Much research has focused on interference effects from the native language (L1) when we learn a second language (L2): for example, English and French both have a simple past (e.g. "I studied this book") and a past form composed with an auxiliary ("I have studied this book") but their meanings differ in English and French. French speakers use the "passé composé"—that is, the form with an auxiliary—with the same meaning as the simple past, the latter being less frequent in colloquial speech. In English these two forms have a different meaning: the past form with the auxiliary verb is the "perfect past." This similarity in syntax but difference in meaning results in a variety of mistaken uses of the perfect past in English by Francophone learners and in French by English learners (Collins, 2002; Payre-Ficout & Chevrot, 2004). Analyses of L1 interference on L2 have a long tradition but this is not our concern here. We mention the question of interference just to acknowledge it. However, L2 researchers do not seem to have asked whether there is anything in children's competence in their native language that can help them learn a second language—in particular, whether they will be better learners of L2 morphology if they are more aware of morphology in their own language.

Learning to use morphology in fluent speech and in comprehension in a second language is very difficult. Robert DeKeyser (2005), in a recent analysis of the difficulty of learning a second language, concluded: "Morphology in L2 is hard: Basic word-order is typically nonproblematic past the initial stages of acquisition, but even the most basic morphology is often lacking from the speech of untutored immigrants and of classroom learners who are not able to monitor themselves effectively" (p. 6). DeKeyser further argues that there is agreement that learners need to have their attention drawn to morphology because morphology is a weak cue in the initial stages of learning and, if it becomes stronger over time, this only happens in a very slow and gradual fashion.

His conclusions emphasize explicit tutoring and conscious monitoring of morphology in L2. There is, in fact, recent and strong evidence for the importance of awareness in learning L2 morphology (see, for example, Ellis, 2006; Mackey, 2006). Is it possible that awareness of morphology in the learners' first language would prepare them for learning a second language, at least when both languages are inflected?

This is certainly a plausible hypothesis and would be in line with theory in second language learning. In the context of the education of bilingual children, James Cummins (1979) argued that children's knowledge of their first language would be a major factor in their learning of the second language. According to his threshold hypothesis, children must attain a certain level of competence in their first language in order to benefit from the positive cognitive effects of bilingualism. From this original thesis to the idea that awareness of morphology in the first language, rather than implicit knowledge of morphology, is an important factor in second language learning may be a large step, but this is certainly a sensible hypothesis to investigate. Yet, as far as we know, very little research has been done on this topic. This is surprising because studies of children learning to read in L2 in immersion programmes have shown that the same measures that predict reading development in L1 predict reading development in L2, but they are most often given in L2 to the children learning to read in L2 (see, for example, da Fontoura & Siegel, 1995; Droop & Verhoeven, 1998; Geva, 1995; Geva & Siegel, 2000; Geva & Zadeh, 2006).

We have been able to carry out an exploratory study to analyse this hypothesis. In collaboration with Portuguese colleagues who are teachers of English as a second language and researchers, we (Castro, Nunes, & Strecht-Ribeiro, 2004) analysed whether Portuguese children's awareness of morphology in Portuguese was a predictor of their English learning after one year of instruction. All the children were monolingual Portuguese students in the age range 9 to 12 years. They were all starting their school learning of English at the time of the study.

At the beginning of the year, the children were given a series of assessments: an assessment of their verbal ability (the Weschler Intelligence Scale for children, translated and adapted to Portuguese), the British Picture Vocabulary Test administered in English, and three measures of morphological awareness in Portuguese: a task similar to the Berko test, where the children were asked to complete phrases and were required to inflect a pseudoword; a Portuguese adaptation of the sentence analogy and the word analogy tasks (developed by Nunes, Bryant, & Bindman, 1997a, and adapted by Rosa, 2004). The sentence analogy task was described earlier on. The word analogy task is similar in presentation: one puppet "says" a word and a second puppet "says" another one, with the same stem and a morphological change; the first puppet then "says" a third word and the child is asked to provide the correct word to help the second puppet. The child's production is considered correct if it has the same stem and the analogous morphological change. This is not always the same phonological change: for example, when the first pair of words is "magic": "magician" and the second pair is "science": "scientist," the same type of morphological transformation does not involve similar phonological transformations.

The children received English instruction for one school year, during two periods of 50 minutes each week. The same book and instruction method were used with all the children.

At the end of the school year, the children were given individually an oral assessment in English. In order to stimulate their oral production, the researcher used a magazine which contained pictures of different rooms. The children were asked which room they liked most and then asked to describe the room. After this initial period of free production, they were asked the same questions about the room, so that comparable structures would be required for their answers. The researcher scored the children's production by considering the variety of their vocabulary, the variety of sentence structures used, and the morphological correctness of the sentences (e.g. appropriate singular and plural agreement).

Although the children's level of production was limited, there was sufficient variation in their scores to allow for a multiple regression analysis. The aim of this analysis was to examine whether the children's scores on morphological awareness tasks given in Portuguese at the beginning of the year would correlate significantly with their English production at the end of the year, after controlling for their age, general verbal ability and their previous knowledge of English words (assessed by the British Picture Vocabulary Test). Because most of the children were not able to identify a single picture from its English name before they started learning English in school, this score was not considered in the analysis. The variations in the children's age were not significantly correlated with their English scores at the end of the year but their verbal ability, measured in Portuguese, was significantly related to their English scores (it explained 34% of the variance in the children's English scores). After controlling for the children's age and verbal ability, the partial correlations between each of the three measures of morphological awareness and the children's English scores were still significant. The pseudoword inflection task and the sentence analogy task each explained 15% extra variance in the children's English scores, after controlling for age and verbal ability; the word analogy task explained 5% extra variance.

The stringent controls used in the analysis, the fact that all the students were being taught by the same method, and the use of a longitudinal approach—i.e. the children's awareness of morphology in L1, Portuguese, was measured at the beginning of the year and the children's learning of L2, English, at the end of the year—are the strengths of this study. So, it is reasonable to conclude that there is evidence that children's awareness of morphology in their native language is related to their L2 learning.

Two further studies also support the hypothesis that children's awareness of morphology in their first language might help them learn a second language better. Miriam Bindman (2004) examined the connection between English children's awareness of morphology in English and their ability to solve morphological awareness tasks in Hebrew. Hebrew, like many other languages, preserves the spelling of the root morpheme (or stem), even when its pronunciation changes. This root is represented by consonants, as consonant and vowels as written separately (for more details, see Ravid, 2001; Ravid & Schiff, 2006). Two words that sound similar but have different consonants for their root spellings cannot be related in meaning. Bindman took advantage of this feature in order to assess whether the proficiency shown by learners of Hebrew in using this principle when judging the relatedness of words was specifically related to their morphological awareness. About half of the participants in her study were learning Hebrew as a modern language and received approximately 2 hours of daily instruction; the other half were studying biblical Hebrew texts for 3 hours a week and also had a weekly lesson of modern Hebrew. Both groups had little exposure to spoken Hebrew outside the classroom.

The children were given the sentence analogy and word analogy tasks designed by Nunes, Bryant, and Bindman (1997a) in English as a measure of the L1 morphological awareness; these have been described previously in this chapter. There were two measures of Hebrew knowledge: a sentence completion task and a judgement of relatedness task. In the sentence completion task, the children heard a sentence and were asked to provide a word that completed it. In the judgement of relatedness task (the Root Morphemes Task, as described by Bindman), the children were presented with a printed Hebrew word, the target word, and with four other printed words also in Hebrew, the choice words. This judgement of relatedness depended on the children's understanding of morphological aspects of Hebrew spelling. All of the incorrect choices showed a connection with the target word: one was always a homophone, a second shared vowels with the target, a third shared a prefix or suffix, and a fourth shared consonants (sometimes two consonants and sometimes all three consonants in the root but these were in the wrong order). Because Hebrew is a highly inflected language, and because the consonants and vowels are written separately, the related words may actually be less similar visually than some of the unrelated words.

Bindman found that there was a strong correlation between the children's performance in the L2 tasks, sentence completion and judgement of relatedness, and their performance in the L1 tasks, sentence and word analogy. Using regression analyses, she was also able to show that this connection between the children's awareness of morphology in L1 and their performance in the L2 tasks was specific, and not a result of general verbal ability: after controlling for the overlaps between age and English vocabulary (used as a measure of general verbal ability), the correlation between the L1 morphological awareness tasks and the children's performance in the Hebrew tasks was still significant.

Finally, a third study, by Hélène Deacon and her colleagues (Deacon, Wade-Woolley, & Kirby, 2007), also supports the idea that children who have better awareness of their first language become better learners of a second language. The participants in their study were all from English homes and came from diverse socioeconomic backgrounds. They were enrolled in French immersion classes, mostly from kindergarten on, although some started the French programme in their first year in school. At the start of the study, when the children's mean age was about 6 years 4 months, their knowledge of French vocabulary was similar to that of a 3-year-old French Canadian: thus, they were learning some French but their knowledge of English was considerably stronger, as their vocabulary levels were age-appropriate (in fact, slightly above average).

The researchers gave the children the sentence analogy task in English at the beginning of each of their first three years in school; we will focus here on the results of the longitudinal prediction of the French measures from the English sentence analogy task given in Grade 1. The French measures were vocabulary, given only in Grade 1, French sentence analogy and French word reading; the latter two tasks were given at each grade level. The researchers were interested particularly in the reading measures and so some of the analyses which would be of interest to us here were not presented. For example, we would want to know whether the English morphological awareness task predicted the children's French vocabulary performance after controlling for general intelligence and phonological awareness. We argued previously that being able to identify morphemes helps you learn new words in your first language. If morphological awareness is more than the specific knowledge of particular stems and affixes in your own language, and is a general ability that can be applied in L2 also, one would expect that morphological awareness measured in English is related to the children's ability to learn French words. Deacon and her colleagues report a moderate and significant correlation, equal to .51, between English morphological awareness and French vocabulary knowledge. However, they did not control for the overlaps between general intelligence and age, on one hand, and the two variables of interest, morphological awareness in English and French vocabulary, so we do not know whether this connection really is a specific one.

The English sentence analogy task correlated significantly with all the six measures given in French (morphological awareness in grades 1 through 3, and word reading in grades 1 through 3): the correlations varied between .26 and .48. The highest correlations were between

English morphological awareness and French word reading in all three grade levels.

The researchers then ran a series of regression analyses in which they wanted to see whether English morphological awareness predicted French word reading, after controlling for the overlaps with the children's general intelligence (measured by a non-verbal task), English vocabulary, phonological awareness, and French morphological awareness. These three analyses showed that the children's English morphological awareness (measured by sentence analogy in Grade 1) still made a significant contribution to the prediction of the children's French word reading in all three grades. This result is indeed very strong: after controlling for overlaps with so many possible factors, the children's awareness of morphology in L1 still predicts their L2 word reading.

Thus, the small body of evidence available to date suggests that children's awareness of morphology in their own language is a good predictor of their learning of L2 in the classroom. These conclusions are presented tentatively: we would like to see training studies which increase the children's awareness of morphology in their own language and assess whether this increased awareness does make them better learners of L2.

Summary

1   Learning a second language in the classroom is difficult, and morphology is one of the most difficult aspects of second language learning. We reviewed studies that show that children's awareness of morphology in their first language is related to how well they learn vocabulary, morphological relations and word reading in a second language.

2   The possibility of using morphological knowledge from L1 in L2 has the fascinating implication that morphological skills work in a general way. When you learn that words are formed by morphemes in your language, you can use this insight in another language: this is a very abstract form of knowledge because it shows that children are not just learning the specific affixes that exist in their own language and stripping them from words but rather are learning a process for doing the same when the affixes and stems are new.

3   There is, to our knowledge, no intervention study that assesses whether improving children's awareness of morphology in their own language, as they learn to read and spell, could have a positive

effect on their L2 learning. If research shows that this is so, the task of learning L2 in the classroom could be made easier for many students.

The Reciprocal Influences between Morphological Awareness and Learning to Spell

In Chapter 5, we argued that children infer morphological rules from knowing a set of words that is large enough to illustrate these rules. Their word-specific knowledge gives them a basis from which to make inferences. We also argued, at the beginning of this chapter, that it is unlikely that all children infer morphological rules with the same ease, even if their word-specific knowledge is at similar levels. The young adults who participated in our spelling studies were all at ceiling level in spelling real words with morphographs: they differed only when we asked them to spell pseudowords, and some seemed to have such implicit knowledge of morphology that they could not use it in order to analyse pseudowords and spell them systematically correctly. This means that word-specific knowledge does not tell the whole story of how children learn.

A possible explanation for individual differences in children's ability to infer morphological rules from their word-specific knowledge is the differences in their level of morphological awareness: entirely implicit knowledge of morphology may not be sufficient for this difficult task. We have presented in this chapter many different measures of morphological knowledge but have not distinguished between implicit knowledge and awareness of morphology. How can we tell apart tasks that measure implicit knowledge from those that tap awareness of morphology?

In our view, when people use morphology simply to speak and understand their native language, this does not demonstrate that they are aware of morphology. Children speak correctly and discriminate words that differ by a single phoneme without being aware of phonemes. Traditionally, children are only credited with phoneme awareness if they are able to manipulate the sounds in words intentionally: earlier on we described the phoneme deletion task, where children are asked to delete either the first or the last phoneme in words. This is an example of intentional manipulation of phonemes. The same conception can be used to help us distinguish between implicit knowledge of morphology and awareness of morphology: using morphology in speaking and understanding sentences is evidence of morphological knowledge, but this knowledge may be entirely implicit. Carlisle's (1995) definition of morphological awareness is quite clear: in order to credit children with awareness of morphology, they should be required to manipulate morphemes intentionally.

According to this criterion, some tasks seem to require morphological awareness without doubt: in the sentence analogy and word analogy tasks described earlier on, the children have to manipulate morphology intentionally. Another task that seems to involve awareness of morphology is the judgement task where children are asked whether two words that have a same-sounding stem are morphologically related. In order to correctly answer that "teacher" comes from "teach" but "dollar" doesn't come from "doll," the children must consider more than the sounds of the words, and look for a similarity in meaning. A fourth example of a task that involves awareness of morphology is Berko's definition of compounds. The nature of other tasks is less clear: Berko's pseudoword inflection task could possibly be carried out with entirely implicit knowledge of morphology, because language is being used here just to speak—completing the sentence sensibly is a matter of language comprehension and production. Because these tasks require different levels of awareness, they can lead to different results when researchers attempt to explain the connection between children's awareness of morphology and their learning of morphological rules. We must keep this in mind when we consider different studies.

The hypothesis that there is a connection between children's awareness of morphology and their use of morphology in spelling has been investigated for over ten years now. The initial studies focused on children's awareness of morphology and their performance in standardized spelling tests, which were general measures of spelling, not specific measures of children's use of morphographs (e.g. Derwing, Smith, & Wiebe, 1995; Fowler & Liberman, 1995).

We (Nunes, Bryant, & Bindman, 1997a) carried out the first study where the spelling performance was measured only with respect to the use of morphographs. This study focused on children's learning of the "-ed" ending. As described in Chapter 5, we gave the children three types of words to spell: (1) regular past verbs, which are spelled with "-ed" even though the "ed" is never pronounced; (2) irregular past verbs, which are spelled phonologically, not with "ed"; and (3) non-verbs that have a /d/ or /t/ sound at the end, so they sound like the other two types of words but are never spelled with "ed." The study involved a large sample (more than 350 children) and the children were seen three times over the period of just over one year. Children from three grade levels participated—the younger ones were in their second year in school and had a mean age of 6y6m, the middle group was in the third year in school and had a mean age of 7y5m and the older group was in the fourth year in school and had a mean age of 8y6m. These age levels were ideal for our study as most of the children in the second year in school have already mastered basic letter–sound correspondences: in our study: only 16% of the children did not spell systematically correctly the ends of at least half of the words that should be spelled correctly. So this is a good time to check how well they can cope with the morphograph "-ed."

Our hypothesis was that, when English children start to learn to read, they focus their attention on letter–sound correspondences. This may be so either because letter–sound correspondences are the most salient aspect of the connection between oral and written language in alphabetic orthographies or because they are specifically taught to do so. Their attention to morphemes is at this time either completely lacking or very faint. So, they would spell initially past regular verbs mostly by using phonetic transcriptions. We found that 21% of all the children in our sample did so. However, as children progress in school and encounter regular past verbs in writing, they start to acquire some word-specific knowledge of regular past verbs: so they may spell a few correctly, but certainly do not spell them systematically correctly. Once children note that some words that end in /d/ or /t/ sounds are spelled with "ed" at the end, they start to use this ending, but at this time they do not know where this ending really belongs. This is where awareness of morphology becomes important: in order to know where to use and where not to use the "ed" ending, they need to use their knowledge of morphology so that they can infer a rule. As it turned out, they do not seem to make this inference in one step: they first realize that the "ed" ending belongs with verbs, without distinguishing between regular and irregular verbs, and then later they make this finer distinction too.

If the acquisition of the morphological spelling really proceeds in this way, the children's awareness of morphology at an earlier age should predict their correct use of the "ed" spelling at a later age. So we used a statistical technique that by now has become familiar in the test of these hypotheses—multiple regression analysis. We tested whether the children's performance in morphological awareness tasks at the beginning of the study predicted their correct use of the "ed" spelling at a later age after controlling for their age, their general verbal ability, and also for how well they could use the "ed" ending at the earlier time. The children's use of the "ed" ending at the beginning of the study is a measure of their word-specific knowledge: so if children's morphological awareness predicts their correct use of the "ed" spelling at a later age, after controlling for their word-specific knowledge, this means that children with the same word-specific knowledge differ in their ability to infer the spelling rules due to differences in their morphological awareness. Our measures of knowledge of morphology were sentence analogy, word analogy and a version of the Berko pseudoword inflection task, which we created for this study.

In line with what we expected, we found that sentence analogy and word analogy continued to be significantly correlated with the children's correct use of "ed" in spelling, after the controls we have just mentioned had been taken into account. This predictive value of morphological awareness could be found when the children were tested on spelling 13 months after they had answered the word and sentence analogy tests. The pseudoword inflection test did not withstand this stringent test, and did not show a significant correlation with the appropriate use of the "ed" spelling after the controls had been taken into account. However, this measure may tap implicit knowledge rather than awareness of morphemes, and implicit knowledge might not be sufficient for inferring the appropriate morphological rule regarding when to use and when not to use the "ed" ending.

This initial study was entirely based on real words and, as we have argued before, real words can be spelled correctly using morphological knowledge but also using word-specific knowledge. We also carried out a predictive study where the same children were asked to spell pseudo-verbs (Nunes, Bryant, & Bindman, 1997b). A large number of the children (80%) who participated in the first study were located again about one year later and invited to participate in this second study, which was also longitudinal. They were given a phonological awareness task about 12 months after the initial session and a pseudo-verb spelling task about 20 months after the first testing session. So by the time the children were asked to spell the pseudo-verbs, they were already in their 4th, 5th and 6th year in school, and most of them were already using the "ed" at the end of the regular verbs systematically, but not exclusively.

The pseudo-verb spelling task included verbs created by analogy to real verbs, but their stems differed in the initial consonants. For example, by analogy to "yell"–"yelled," we created the pseudo-verb "crell"–"crelled," and by analogy to the real verb "leave"–"left," we created the pseudo-verb "neave"–"neft." How could the children tell whether the pseudo-verbs were regular or irregular? The answer is in their stems: the general rule (to which there are very few exceptions) is that if the verb stem sounds the same in the present and in the past, the past form is spelled with the "-ed" suffix; if the verb stem sounds different in the present and in the past, the past form is irregular and is spelled phonetically. In order for the children to have sufficient information to know whether the stems sound the same or not in the present and in the past, we read short texts to them, and asked them to spell only the pseudo-verb, which we presented as the target word before the text, then inserted in the text, and then repeated once again after the text had been read. The text contained two uses of the stem, either in the present, the present continuous, the future or the infinitive—but these all have same-sounding stems. One example of each type of past pseudo-verb is presented here to illustrate the method.

> *Regular pseudo-verb*: Target pseudo-verb: crelled. Harry is crelling his book. Maybe he will crell mine tomorrow. He crelled another one this morning. Crelled.
> *Irregular pseudo-verb*: Target pseudo-verb: neft. Our neighbours are going to neave their dog this morning. We wanted to neave our dog two weeks ago, but in the end we neft him yesterday. Neft.

The regular and irregular pseudo-verbs were presented to the children mixed and in random order. The children were just told that we wanted them to try to spell these invented words as well as they could.

We were interested in finding out two things. First, do the children use the same processes in spelling regular verbs and regular pseudo-verbs? Do they also use the same processes to spell irregular verbs and pseudo-verbs? If this were the case, there should be a correlation between the spellings for the real and the pseudo-verbs. Second, does the children's awareness of morphology predict their spelling of pseudo-verbs, as it does their spelling of real verbs?

In order to answer the first question, we calculated the partial correlation between the spelling of the real verbs and the spelling of pseudo-verbs, after controlling for the children's age and verbal ability. These partial correlations were both significant: the partial correlation between spelling regular real and pseudo-verbs was .77 and the partial correlation between spelling irregular real and pseudo-verbs was .28. So it can be concluded that the processes that children use to spell regular real and pseudo-verbs are very similar and that the processes that the children use to spell irregular real and pseudo-verbs is partially the same, but not as similar as the processes involved in spelling the regular items. The difference between these two correlations is probably due to the fact that, because the children were already making the inference that past verbs are spelled with "ed," but had not learned to restrict their rule to *regular* past verbs, they were over-using the "ed" rule with these novel words: with the real verbs, they could also use their word-specific knowledge in helping them to restrict the use of the "ed" to the appropriate cases. This interpretation is in agreement with the percentage of correct spellings for the regular and irregular pseudo-verbs: the percentage of correct for the regular pseudo-verbs were 60, 70 and 80, respectively, for the children in the 4th, 5th and 6th years in school; the corresponding percentages for irregular pseudo-verbs were 27, 30 and 38. This low level of performance on endings that should be spelled phonetically supports the idea that the children were using, indeed over-using, the "ed" ending at this time in their development. They use the same processes to generate the spelling of regular real and pseudo-verbs but they do not do very well with irregular pseudo-verbs, in comparison with real irregular verbs, because they cannot use word-specific knowledge.

Our second question was whether the children's spelling of the regular pseudo-verbs would be predicted from their morphological awareness, after controlling for their age, verbal ability, and phonological awareness. The multiple regression analysis showed that this was the case: the correlation between the word analogy task and the children's spelling of the "ed" ending in pseudo-verbs was significant after these controls were taken into account. Although this was a positive result, we feel that it must be interpreted with caution, because all the correlations were relatively weak, even though significant.

Many other studies have confirmed the results of our longitudinal study and extended the idea that morphology is not only important for spelling but also to children's writing (Green, McCutchen, Schwiebert, Quinlan, Eva-Wood, & Juelis, 2003). There is little doubt today that morphological awareness is a predictor of children's ability to spell words that contain morphographs, and that this connection operates independently of the children's general verbal ability. This has been found not only in English but also in other languages (see, for example, results for Hebrew: Levin, Ravid, & Rapaport, 1999; for Dutch: Rispens, McBride-Chang, & Reitsma, 2007; for Danish: Arnback & Elbro, 2000; for Greek: Bryant, Nunes, & Aidinis, 1999). However, we think that the connection between morphological awareness and spelling is not a one-way street: our hypothesis is that learning to read and spell also has an effect on the children's awareness of morphology.

It is quite easy to think why learning to spell might affect children's awareness of morphology. When we hear, for example, the words "emotion" and "magician," they sound the same at the end: yet their spelling differs. As we learn about spelling, we could well reflect on why these words are spelled differently. Olson (1996) suggests that writing objectifies language: we can analyse written language at our leisure whereas oral language is ephemeral. When we spell, phonemes and morphemes become objects to be represented: so it is reasonable to expect that becoming literate affects our awareness of the sounds as well as of the morphemes of our language.

The hypothesis that becoming literate affects the way we think about language is not new. Evidence that becoming literate improves the learners' awareness of sounds, even in the absence of systematic school instruction, was provided in the pioneering work by Sylvia Scribner and Michael Cole (1981) and has been confirmed since by other researchers: becoming literate in an alphabetic script increases one's awareness of phonemes more than becoming literate in non-alphabetic scripts, which do not represent phonemes in the same way (Mann, 1986; Read, Zhang, Nie, & Ding, 1986). There is much less evidence for the effect of spelling on awareness of morphemes but the evidence that is available is actually quite convincing.

We (Nunes, Bryant, & Bindman, 2006) carried out two studies investigating the consequences of learning to spell for children's awareness of morphemes, using different measures of awareness of morphology and of children's ability to spell with semiographs. In the first study, we used as measures of the children's awareness of morphology the sentence analogy and word analogy tasks; the children's ability to spell with the "ed" ending was our measure of their use of semiographs. This study is the mirror image of the previous one. Our aim now was to see whether the children's progress in spelling could predict their growth in morphological awareness. The same technique as we used before, multiple regression analysis, was used here, but the order in which the children did the assessments was the reverse. They did the spelling assessments on the first occasion in the longitudinal study and the word analogy and sentence analogy tasks about one year later. After controlling of the children's age and verbal ability, the children's spelling ability was still a significant predictor of their awareness of morphology. This shows that the children's awareness of morphology helps them infer the rules for the correct use of the "ed" ending and that, at the same time, the more they learn about spelling, the more aware they become of morphology.

In order to be more confident in these results, we replicated this longitudinal design using a second set of measures. Our spelling measure was the consistency in the use of stems whose spelling is not completely predicted from the way they sound. We used both word–word pairs and word–pseudoword pairs. In Chapter 5, we explained the measure of word–pseudoword pairs, which used dinosaur names. The stems used in the dinosaur names had silent letters—e.g. "knot"–"knotosaurus"—so that the spelling of the stem was not predictable from the way they sounded. We used a similar method for creating the word–word pairs, and chose stems that had some unpredictability in their spelling from the way they sounded—for example, "naughty"–"naughtiness," "treasure"–"treasures"; and "know"–"knowledge." The children wrote one word from the pair on one day and the second word from the pair on a different day, so that they could not check how they had spelled the stem and copy it when they wrote the second word in the pair.

Thus, we had two measures of constancy in the spelling of stem, one using word–word and one using word–pseudoword pairs. Our measure of morphological awareness was a pseudoword definition task. In this task, we tell the children that we are going to present them with made-up words, but that these made-up words make sense. Their job is to figure out what the words might mean and to explain them to us. All the pseudowords are composed of a real stem and a real affix, so that they actually can be interpreted, even though they are invented. We gave the children a point if their pseudoword definition used information from both morphemes. For example, the children would get a point if they indicated that "chickener" is someone who looks after (feeds, keeps) chickens; "uncomb" is to comb your hair and then mess it up, or "shoutist" is a person who shouts a lot. Incidentally, one child was convinced that shoutist is a real word and that it refers to the person who shouts the orders for the army's exercises.

Our spelling measures were new and so we first assessed their validity by analysing their partial correlation with the use of the "ed" ending. After partialling out the overlaps that the three measures had with the children's age and verbal ability, the partial correlations were still significant: the use of "ed" showed a partial correlation with consistency in spelling pairs of words equal to .28 and with consistency in the word–pseudoword pairs of .50. So we could be confident that our spelling measures did assess children's use of morphological information in spelling.

We then tested the hypothesis that the children's spelling predicted their morphological awareness after an interval of about 13 months, and after controlling for the children's age and general verbal ability. We used three multiple regression analyses, each one with a measure of spelling and the predictor; all three analyses tested whether the spelling measures predicted the children's ability to define pseudowords. In the analyses where the use of "ed" and the consistency in spelling the word-pseudoword pairs were the predictors, the results were significant; in the analyses where the spelling measure was the word–word consistency pairs, the results just missed the expected significance level (this is normally $p < .05$ and the result for this analysis was $p = .07$). Taken together, the results of these two studies do support the idea that children's progress in spelling is related to improvements in their morphological awareness. So this is a two-way connection: children need some awareness of morphology to infer spelling rules and, as they learn more about spelling, this reinforces their awareness of morphology.

Our studies do not stand alone in showing this reciprocal influence between awareness of morphology and spelling. Levin, Ravid, and Rapaport (1999) found similar mutual influences in a study of Israeli children learning to read and write Hebrew.

Conclusion

This chapter focused on why learning about morphemes matters and the vicissitudes of this learning without systematic instruction. We started out by saying that children and adults may attain good spelling performance without developing a strong awareness of morphology, which would allow them to cope with spelling morphographs in entirely new words. As the entirely new words that the participants in these studies had to spell were pseudowords, one might think that perhaps this does not matter. But the subsequent review of research showed that awareness of morphemes does matter for a large variety of tasks that are meaningful in today's literate societies. We suggest that leaving the task of discovering morphology entirely to children is a questionable educational approach. Research has shown that this is a powerful linguistic skill, with consequences for vocabulary learning, reading comprehension, and there are indications that it is also important for second language learning. Such a transferable skill should not ignored by education planners and policy-makers, but it seems that morphological knowledge is now an "invisible skill." Invisible skills are left to learners to acquire for themselves, informally, and this is the situation of the learners whose morphological knowledge was analysed in this chapter. The children who took part in all the studies reported here did not receive instruction on morphology: they had to infer this knowledge from their reading and spelling experiences. What might happen if children do receive instruction? What sort of instruction should they receive? These are the questions that we turn to in Chapter 7.

Chapter 7

Teaching Children about Morphemes

It is important that we always remember that research on children's reading is done in particular educational contexts. The children who take part in the research are being taught to read, and what they do in the tasks that researchers give them, is bound to be affected by what they have been taught. Researchers, therefore, are destined to study not just the nature of children's learning, but the effects of the instruction that they have been given at school, which varies not just from country to country but also from school to school and even from teacher to teacher within the same school.

This note of caution is certainly needed in the case of research on morphemes and spelling, because the educational context of such studies is rather a restricted one. All the research that we presented in the last chapter was done with children and adults who had been given hardly any explicit instruction about the link between morphemes and spelling at school. Thus, all the problems that children have in learning the conventional spellings for morphemes, and all the patchiness that we have reported in what children and adults know and do not know about the rules underlying these spellings, might very well stem from this simple fact. These difficulties might disappear, or at least be minimized, if teachers were to teach their pupils systematically about morphemes and spelling.

Alternatively, teaching might make no difference. We cannot assume that children who are given explicit teaching of this sort would soon understand the way that morphemic spelling rules work. There is an empirical question here. We need studies about whether it is possible to teach children the link between morphemes and spelling in an interesting and effective way. Until quite recently, however, there was no systematic evidence on this question. Teaching children about morphemes and spelling was a topic as neglected in research as it was in the classroom.

Since the turn of the century, however, several psychologists have begun to study what children can learn about spelling rules based on morphemes in teaching experiments or, as they are often called, intervention experiments. We have already written a detailed description of our own contribution to this necessary research in a fairly recent book called *Improving Literacy through Teaching Morphemes* (Nunes & Bryant, 2006). In this chapter we shall summarize some of the studies presented in that book and some other intervention research, and we shall try to place it in the context of the theoretical framework that we have been developing in this book.

Comparisons between Teaching Phonology and Morphology

Initial intervention studies with normally developing children

The first intervention studies that dealt with morphemes were comparisons of the effects of teaching children about morphology and phonology (Lyster, 2002; Nunes, Bryant, & Olsson, 2003). There was a good reason for starting in this way. Most of the research that psychologists had done on reading instruction in the final 20 years of the last century had been about phonology. These intervention studies had been remarkably successful. They showed that teaching children about sounds in words and about grapheme–phoneme relations radically improves their reading and spelling, and thus had provided us with some of the most convincing evidence that we have on the importance of phonology in learning to read. Of course, they had strong educational implications as well.

It made sense therefore when researchers started to work on teaching children about another aspect of language—morphology—to include interventions on phonology as well. The aim of such studies was always to disentangle the effects of the two kinds of teaching, and to establish whether it was as worthwhile to teach children about morphemes as about sounds. We shall describe two studies with normally developing children which took this form. In the following section we will describe a similar study that we did with with children who had fallen behind their peers in reading and spelling.

We did a study of 7- and 8-year-olds in English schools (Nunes, Bryant, & Olsson, 2003). The study took the usual form for an intervention experiment. It consisted of a sequence of three parts. The first was a pre-test in which we assessed the children's knowledge of morphological and phonological spelling rules and their general level of ability in reading and spelling. We included standardized tests of reading and spelling in these tests, as well as specific tasks that we devised ourselves to measure children's use of the phonological and morphological spelling rules that we taught during the intervention period. The second period which lasted for 12 weeks was the time when we carried out the intervention, and the final third period was a post-test when we repeated the measures that we had used in the pre-test. The purpose of the study was to compare the effects of different kinds of intervention on the progress that the children made between the pre- and the post-test.

We divided the children into five intervention groups and we taught them in four of these groups in different ways during the intervention period. These four intervention groups each consisted of 55 children. We taught the first of these intervention groups about phonological spelling rules, such as the split digraph, entirely orally and with the help of no written material at all during the intervention (Phonology Alone). We taught children in a second group (Phonology with Writing) the same rules but we asked the children to write words that conformed to the rules that we were teaching. So, for instance, we gave the children in both these groups a phonological game in which we asked them to pick rhyming words. In one item we told the children that we were thinking of a word that began with "f" and rhymed with either "hat" or "hate." The children in the Phonology with Writing group were also shown two cards, one with the rime "-at" and the other with the rime "-ate" written on it, and then we asked them to write their answer to the question. However, the children in the Phonology Alone group did not see these cards; nor did they have to write their answer. They answered orally.

We taught the children in the third and fourth groups about morphological spelling rules: we introduced the third group to these rules purely orally (Morphology Alone) and we asked the children in the fourth group to write examples of these rules (Morphology with Writing). One of the games that we gave the children in these two groups was about agentive endings, like "-ian" at the end of "mathematician" and "-er" at the end of teacher. We asked these children to complete sentences like "A person who does magic is a ?" We read out these incomplete sentences and we also presented them in writing to the children in the Morphology with Writing group and we invited these children to write the missing word at the end of the sentence, but we read out only the sentence to the Morphology Alone children and only asked them to tell us their answer.

Finally, we included a large Control group as the fifth group. There were 237 children in this group and they went through no especial intervention. We simply gave them the pre- and post-tests, so that we could use their scores as a baseline to measure the effects of the teaching that we gave the children in the other four groups.

The results of this study were simple and encouraging. We found significant improvements in all four intervention groups in our standardized reading test. The children in these groups made more progress in reading, as measured by this test, than the children in the control group did. In fact, there were no significant differences in the post-tests between the four intervention groups. Thus, teaching morphological rules improved children's reading as much as teaching phonological rules did.

When we looked at the effects of the intervention on the specific phonological and morphological rules that we had taught them, we found definite signs that teaching morphology had worked. The two morphology intervention groups did better than the other groups in our post-test measures of spelling according to morphemic rules. However, the two phonology intervention groups did not show any clear signs of having learned about the conditional phonological rules that we taught them better than the other groups had.

To summarize: the study showed that morphological teaching can have an effect. It can improve children's reading as well as phonological intervention does, and it can help them to learn about morphemic spelling rules, which otherwise they would find hard to understand.

The second intervention study that we shall describe also supported the general conclusion that morphological spelling rules are teachable, and that this sort of teaching can make at least as valuable a contribution to children's education as teaching them about phonology. Solveig Lyster, a Norwegian psychologist, set up an intervention with a large group of 6-year-old children and their pre-school teachers in their last year before school (at the time of this project children in Norway did not go to school until after their 7th birthday). She divided the children into three groups, a Phonological group, a Morphological group and a Control group.

The design of the study followed the familiar pre-test, intervention period, post-test sequence. The pre-tests were mainly about children's awareness of phonology: they included, for example, rhyme and phoneme tasks. Lyster also introduced two tasks about compound words like "fire-engine," but she gave no measures of children's awareness of other types of morphemes, and only assessed their awareness of stems used in compound words.

The intervention lasted for 17 weeks with one session per week. The children in the Phonology groups were taught about sounds in words with the help of various rhyme and phoneme tasks during these intervention sessions. The teaching given to the Morphology group was about the relationship between prefixes and suffixes on the meaning of word and the grammar of sentences. The Control group children were visited by the experimenters but not taught anything special or unusual.

The children were given some reading tasks before arriving at school and at the time they got there, and then 3–4 months later they had to take a battery of reading tasks that were measures of their use of phonological and orthographic rules and their awareness of syntax. Again there seems to have been no direct measure of their understanding of the use of prefixes and suffixes in spelling.

Again the intervention was successful, in that the children in the two intervention groups did significantly better in the post-tests than the children in the control group, but there was very little sign of any specific effects of intervention. For example, Morphology group children as well as the Phonology group children did better in the post-test phonology tasks than the children in the Control group. There was some sign that the Morphology training made children particularly aware of syntax. Perhaps if there had been more direct measures of children's use of morphemes in reading and spelling, the project would have shown other specific effects of teaching pre-school children morphology.

To summarize: to us the most important result of this second study was the effectiveness of the Morphology intervention. It helped the children over a surprisingly wide front. Putting the Nunes et al. and the Lyster study together, we can be reasonably confident that children will lose no ground in learning to read and to spell and will probably gain a great deal by being taught about morphemes.

Intervention with children who had fallen behind in reading and spelling

The next study that we describe here is a study of the effects of phonological and morphological interventions with poor readers. In general, the study of the nature and difficulties of poor readers has made great progress. This progress includes issues related to the definition of dyslexia and classification of subtypes (e.g. Fletcher, Francis, Rourke, Shaywitz, S.E., & Shaywitz, B.A. (1992); Fletcher et al., 1997; Stanovich, Siegel, Gottardo, Chiappe, & Sidhu, 1997), the development of poor readers' skills (Snowling, 1980; Snowling, Goulandris, & Defty, 1996), analyses of the gene-behaviour connection (Grigorenko, 2001; Grigorenko et al., 1997; Hohnen & Stevenson, 1995; Pennington, 1999; Pennington, Gilger, Pauls, Smith, S.A., Smith, S., & DeFries, 1991), irregular brain activity in children at risk for reading problems (Simos, et al., 2002) and a better understanding of causes (e.g. Bradley & Bryant, 1978, 1980; Mody, 2003; Olofsson & Lundberg, 1985; Olson, Wise, Conners, Rack, & Fulker, 1989; Stanovich, Cunningham, & Cramer, 1984; Torgesen, J.K., 1999; Torgesen & Wagner, 1992; Treiman & Baron, 1983; Tunmer & Nesdale, 1985). All this impressive research has led to the definite identification of children's difficulties with phonological awareness and learning phoneme–grapheme correspondences as a cause in many children's reading problems.

Effective interventions for poor readers based on strengthening of children's awareness of the phonemes in their language and learning of phoneme–grapheme correspondences have been developed, implemented and evaluated by so many different research teams in different parts of the world that no extensive coverage of references can be provided, but only a sample is included here (e.g. Alexander, Andersen, Heilman, Voeller, & Torgesen, 1991; Blachman, Tangel, Ball, Black, & McGraw, 1999; Byrne & Fielding-Barnsley, 1993; Foorman, Francis, Fletcher, Schatsschneider, & Mehta, 1998; Hatcher, 2000; Hatcher, & Hulme, 1999; Hatcher, Hulme, & Ellis, 1994; Lovett et al., 1988, 1989, 1990, 1994). There is little doubt today that these programmes are effective as early interventions for children at risk and, later on, for poor readers.

However, not all children respond well to these phonological interventions (Foorman, 2003; Torgesen, 2000; Vellutino, Scanlon, & Sipay, 1997) and many researchers have sought to find other ways of improving the educational prospects of children at risk for reading problems. We can distinguish two approaches in this further research: one is to continue to offer children with reading problems phonological intervention for longer periods and the other is to attempt to combine phonological interventions with other forms of intervention.

Researchers who have pursued the path of providing phonological teaching for longer periods argued that this form of intervention works differently for different children. For some, phonological intervention works like inoculation: early intervention prevents reading failure. For others, it works like insulin: continued intervention is necessary for the maintenance of the effectiveness of the treatment (Coyne, Kame'enui, Simmons, & Harn, 2004). There certainly is evidence that the continuation of phonological interventions through first grade with children who did not seem to respond to treatment in kindergarten increases the proportion of children for whom phonological intervention is effective (e.g. Vellutino, Scanlon, Small, & Fanuele, 2006), but there are children who still need help.

There is currently great interest in which type of poor readers do not respond to phonological intervention (Otaiba & Fuchs, 2006) and what sort of additional help could be offered to them (see, for example, Berninger, et al. (2003); Denton, Fletcher, Anthony, & Francis, 2006; Foorman, Seals, Anthony, & Pollard-Durodala, 2003; Hagvet, 2003; Torgesen, 2004; 2005; Torgesen, Rashotte, & Alexander, 2001; Tunmer, 2008). We shall not review all the alternatives that have emerged in the literature. Some of these have involved combinations of interventions, for example, phonological and reading comprehension teaching. These combinations are important in providing good interventions for poor readers but they do not necessarily help us understand the processes by which children are achieving improvement. Teaching fluency or reading comprehension, for example, is teaching the outcomes directly: both fluency and comprehension are themselves related to more basic processes. A more analytical approach to intervention factors is required in order to understand the underlying processes.

In our view, an obvious candidate for investigation at this more analytical level is an intervention designed to promote the poor readers' syntactic and morphological ability. The question is whether this type of intervention works. Our past research showed that children who go on to become poor readers definitely do less well on phonological tasks at the start of school, but their syntactic and morphological awareness seems largely unimpaired at that time (Bryant, Nunes, & Bindman, 1998). Some research (Egan & Pring, 2004; Shankweiler, et al. 1995; Tsesmeli, & Seymour, 2006) has shown that older poor readers show worse performance in morphological and syntactic awareness tasks than an age-matched group of normal readers. However, this difference could be the result of the poor readers' diminished experience with print and not one of the causes of their backwardness in reading. In all these studies, the poor readers' scores in the morphology and syntax tasks did not differ from a group of children matched by reading level. We argued in Chapter 5 that children infer morphological rules from knowing a large enough set of words that illustrate the rules. Their word-specific knowledge gives them a basis from which to make inferences. If left to discover these rules on their own, poor readers, who will have a reduced bank of word-specific knowledge, are bound to end up with difficulties in the use of morphographs in reading and spelling at a later point. However, if they are not left to discover these rules on their own, could morphological intervention help them? Would this be an opportunity to teach to their strengths, assuming that their late difficulties with morphology were not inherent to their cognitive functioning but a result of lack of exposure to print?

As far as we know, we have carried out the only study of this possibility. Our aim was to investigate the effectiveness of teaching morphological rules to children who had already fallen behind in reading and spelling. Because morphological knowledge has been shown to contribute to word recognition and spelling, a morphological intervention might help them develop these skills even in the absence of phonological intervention, at least during the time when we worked with them. We also wanted to know whether a phonological intervention aimed at improving poor readers' use of conditional phonological rules (see Chapters 2 and 3) would be just as effective. Previous research has shown that poor readers have significantly more difficulty with conditional phonological rules than children of the same reading age (Nunes & Aidinis, 1999). Thus our question was to see whether it is possible to build on poor readers' strengths in morphological knowledge and use their strengths to overcome their difficulties in word reading and spelling.

We invited 12 schools in the Oxford and London areas to participate in this study and assessed the reading and spelling of all the children in their fourth to sixth year in school; the children were in the age range 8.5–11.9 years. We identified 59 children as very poor readers: their IQ was in the normal range and they showed an average delay in word reading and spelling of at least 18 months (the average delay for the group was 28.6 months). The children were randomly assigned, within each school, to one of three groups: control, phonological training in association with writing, and morphological training in association with writing.

Table 7.1 shows the results at pre-test for the three groups. The scores in this table are standardized scores, and so the mean for children with normal reading levels is 100. Table 7.1 clearly shows that the participants in this study were considerably behind in reading and spelling.

The training encompassed activities similar to those used in the study that we carried out with normal readers, reported earlier on in this

Table 7.1 Pre-test standardized reading and spelling scores for the phonological intervention, morphological intervention and control groups

	Control (n = 15)	Phonological intervention (n = 22)	Morphological intervention (n = 22)
Standardized reading score	78.0 (8.0)	77.9 (6.9)	77.1 (8.1)
Standardized spelling score	77.0 (6.2)	77.7 (4.1)	74.3 (4.9)

chapter. The children participated in approximately 20 weekly sessions of 45 minutes each, though some children completed fewer sessions because they were occasionally absent from school. The post-test was administered about one week after the programme had been completed: the pre- and post-tests were separated by approximately 7 months.

The pre- and post-test measures included a standardized test of word decoding and word spelling, and a measure of children's ability to spell with suffixes which assesses children's use of suffixes in spelling. When we compared the children's success in reading in the pre-test and post-test, we found that the control group made approximately the progress expected during the period in terms of the increase in their reading age: their improvement in reading age was 6.7 months. The morphological training group made an advance of 11.7 months in reading age and the phonological training group of 13.1 months in reading age in the same period. Statistical comparisons showed that the difference between the phonological training group and the control group was statistically significant but the difference between the morphological training group and the control group was not statistically significant.

The differences between the groups were not significant for word spelling, although both intervention groups made more progress in spelling than the control group. However, there was a significant and specific effect of the morphological intervention in the suffix spelling test: the children who received the morphological intervention showed significantly greater gains at post-test than the control group and the children in the phonological intervention group also did much better than the control group but the difference was not significant.

These results demonstrate that phonological intervention can help older poor readers: in this study, the intervention was tailored to where their difficulties lay at the time: these were with conditional rules and not with simple phoneme–grapheme correspondences. Although the poor readers who were given this intervention did not make significantly more progress than the children in the control group in spelling, they did benefit in word recognition and they made almost twice the progress that would be expected of children reading normally for their age during the time they received the intervention: their mean reading age increased by 13 months over this 7-month period.

The effects of the morphological intervention are less clear. Poor readers can certainly learn about morphology through instruction: they made significantly more progress in suffix spelling than the control group. They also made more progress in word reading than the controls, but this difference was not significant. However, they did not differ significantly from the children who received the phonological intervention: their level of progress was more similar to the latter group's than to the control group's.

This intermediary performance by the morphological group, between the control group and the phonological intervention group, must be interpreted with caution. We provided the children with a relatively modest level of input: approximately 15 hours of instruction over about 7 months. It is quite possible that morphological interventions would require much longer periods to work well with poor readers. All the children had received much phonics instruction in their regular classrooms: phonics activities are part of their reading and spelling instruction, and so our phonological training programme was an addition to what they already had. In contrast, English schools do not include morphemes in their reading instruction, with the exception of very few prefixes ("re-" and "un-," for example) and suffixes ("-ed" was the only one which appeared occasionally in the literacy activities for some children at this time). Thus, the children were being taught about morphology only during our sessions whereas the phonology group's learning was being reinforced in their regular classroom activities.

Summary

1 Poor readers can use their morphological skills to improve their reading but this does not compensate for their difficulties with phonology.
2 This suggests that effective interventions should combine both forms of teaching.

Teaching Both Phonology and Morphology to Poor Readers

We argued that comparisons of the separate effects of teaching phonology and morphology are important both when the children are normal readers and when they have reading difficulties: such intervention studies are essential to test causal hypothesis in reading and spelling, along with longitudinal studies (Bradley & Bryant, 1980). It is particularly important to see whether poor readers can profit from morphological interventions: if it were to be shown that phonological interventions are sufficient and that poor readers just cannot learn about morphology, we would have little reason to try to combine phonological and morphological interventions. But now that we know that poor readers can learn about morphology through teaching, there is good reason to study the effectiveness of interventions that combine phonological and morphological teaching.

We know of only one study that has done this, but unfortunately this study only included a group that received the combined treatment, and did not compare the improvement in this group with parallel groups receiving only one of the two types of intervention. However, it is still worth reporting this study because of the large and sustained effects that this combined treatment showed. Tijms, Hoeks, Paulussen-Hoogeboom, and Smolenaars (2003) worked with an intervention based on phonological and morphological analyses of Dutch. The participants in their study had been referred to a dyslexia treatment centre and were selected according to the following criterion: their reading or spelling was at least one standard deviation below the mean for their age, their IQ was in the normal range, they had no additional sensory or neurological impairments, and their difficulties could not be explained by socioeconomic or linguistic background. The age range of the poor readers was from 10 to 15 years.

Tijms and his colleagues were mostly interested in the long-term effects of this combined treatment: most research follows poor readers for short periods after treatment and some have queried whether treatments offered to poor readers cannot be effective (e.g. Foorman, Francis, Shaywitz, Shaywitz, & Fletcher, 1997; Wagner, Torgesen & Rashotte, 1994). Tijms and colleagues used a different design in their analysis of intervention effects: instead of using a control group and random assignment of participants to the groups, they compared the intervention group with the norms for their age levels. Before the intervention, the group differed significantly from the age norms. As the treatment proceeded, during 6 months, there were steady increases in performance at reading words, reading text and spelling. These improvements ranged from nearly halving the distance between the scores of the participants and the norm for reading words to a reduction of this distance by more than three-quarters for spelling. At the end of treatment the performance levels showed further improvement. Although this is not completely clear in the paper, it seems that not all participants benefited significantly from the treatment, but those who did maintained their gains over a 4-year period.

The only disappointing result for the researchers was that the effects on spelling declined over time, even though word reading and comprehension did not. They noted that this is disappointing because employment in The Netherlands will require text reading and spelling skills from most people, and thus their participants were showing a decline in an important skill.

Summary

1   The studies that we described so far show a general effect of morphology interventions on children's reading and a more specific effect on spelling.
2   These suggest that teaching on morphology is well worth including as a basic part of literacy instruction.

A Detailed Analysis of the Effects of Teaching Morphemes

Having settled that it is quite possible to teach children about morphemes and spelling in general, we can now ask whether this is true of even the most difficult of morphemic spellings. One obvious candidate is the spelling of endings with the sound /ən/, like "education," "mathematician" and "hasten." These three words all end in exactly the same sound but, for morphemic reasons, they are spelled quite differently, as we remarked in Chapter 5. However, these particular morphemic rules are never taught, nor even mentioned, in the classroom.

This probably makes it different from other rules that we have been dealing with, like the plural "-s" ending and the past tense "-ed" ending. These are well known, and teachers do give instruction about them in the classroom from time to time. However, they almost certainly do not teach anything about the distinction between "-ion" and "-ian" endings, because the rules for these two spellings are not generally known. We can find no evidence at all that teachers make children aware of the fact that nouns with "-ion" endings are almost invariably abstract nouns and with "-ian" endings very nearly always refer to people and are often agentive endings or indicate a group membership (e.g. Brazilian, Italian). When we questioned teachers (Nunes and Bryant, 2006), we found that they could not produce this simple explanation for when to use "-ion" and "-ian," and they were certainly glad to find out about it because of the huge and persistent difficulties that children have with spelling these two endings, which we documented in Chapter 5.

So, we took the "-ion" vs "-ian" distinction as a test case in the study of teaching morphemic spelling rules. We wanted to know whether it is possible to teach these untaught but enormously valuable spelling rules and we decided that we needed evidence not just from "laboratory" studies ourselves, but also from classroom studies in which the teaching was done by school teachers to their own pupils and it was up to the teachers to decide how to put the information across.

From the Laboratory to the Classroom

Beginning with laboratory-type studies

We began with "laboratory studies," though in truth these studies were all done in schools. However, we ourselves, the researchers taught the children outside the classroom, either on their own or in very small groups. In our later "classroom studies" (see the next section) the teachers taught the children and did so in much the same way as they taught them anything else.

In the first of the laboratory studies that we shall describe here, we tackled the basic question whether it is possible to teach children explicitly about morphemic spelling rules. We concentrated on one rule which is quite a simple one but is never taught at schools. This is a rule about a distinction that young children, and some adults too, find an extremely difficult one. Our idea was that teaching children about the underlying rule should do a great deal to remove this difficulty.

The distinction that we chose was between the "-ion" and "-ian" endings. Many words ending in the sound which is represented as /ən/ are spelled either as "-ion" or as "-ian." "Education," "institution" and "hesitation" are examples of the first spelling, and "logician," "magician" and "statistician" of the second. The endings of the words in these two groups all sound the same, of course, but their spelling is different for a reason, which we have explained above: the "-ion" words are abstract nouns, which are all derived from verbs: the "-ian" words are derived from nouns and they refer to people. These people are usually agents: "magicians" do "magic" and "mathematicians" do "mathematics" or belong to a national group: "Egyptians" come from Egypt.

We thought that there might be a direct connection between the fact that children are not taught this simple rule at school, and their very frequent mis-spelling of the "-ion" and "-ian" endings. To test this idea we designed and carried out an intervention study on spelling these endings. The study had an additional purpose, which was to compare explicit and implicit methods of teaching children this particular spelling rule. By "explicit methods" we mean of course explaining the rule to the children. By implicit we mean presenting the material in a way that would encourage the children to work the rule out for themselves. Since children depend a great deal on implicit knowledge to read and spell words, it is quite possible that implicit methods of teaching might work as well as or even better than explicit methods.

Two hundred $9^1/_2$ -year-old children took part in our study. All of them took a pre-test which was designed to measure how well they spelled words and pseudowords with "-ion" endings. The test consisted of a set of written sentences, which were incomplete because one word was missing in each sentence. We ourselves dictated the whole of each sentence and we asked the children to write in the missing word. In some sentences this word was a real word and in others a pseudoword. All the real words and most of the pseudowords that the children had to write ended in the /ən/ sound. These /ən/ ending words were either abstract nouns or they referred to people. Here are some examples, with the target words in italics:

I hate *injections*.
The *discussion* went on and on.
The *electrician* fixed the light.
The *magician* performed a magic show.
If you often tekate, that shows that you like *tekation*.
Someone who does lagic is a *lagician*.

After this pre-test the children went to two "intervention" sessions in which we taught them something about spelling. These sessions each lasted for about 20 minutes. The children came to these sessions in pairs, and each time they played some games that we had constructed for them. We divided the children into four groups (three experimental groups and a control group). The children in the three experimental groups played spelling games in the two sessions. The games were the same for all three groups (we shall describe them later) but we presented them in different ways to the children in the three groups.

One group was the Explicit group: whenever the children in this group produced a spelling or made a judgement about spelling we told them whether they were right or wrong, and we discussed with them the "-ion/-ian" rule. At the end of each game we gave these children a list of the words that had cropped up in each game, and we organized this list into two separate parts. One part contained all the "-ion"-ending words that they had just seen, and the other all the "-ian" words. Again we discussed with them the reason why the ending was spelled quite differently in the two sets of words.

We gave the children in the next group, the Implicit group, the same games with the same words and we treated the children in this group in the same way as the children in the Explicit group, except that we left out the explicit discussion of the rule. We told them nothing about the underlying rule. So, the children in the Implicit group were told whether their spelling decisions were right or not and what the right spelling was if they made the wrong decision. Although we ourselves did not tell them anything about the rule, we asked them to try to figure out why the spellings were right or wrong, and gave them time to discuss it between themselves. At the end, just like the other group, they saw the two separate sets of words, but we never told them why the words in the two sets ended in different ways.

The third group was called the Mixed group, because they went through a mixture of these two procedures. In the first part of each of the games that they played, we treated them as we had the Implicit group, and in the second we changed to the Explicit procedure. So, halfway through each game we started to discuss with them the reasons why their answers were right or wrong.

The fourth group was a Control group. These children also went to two intervention sessions, but during these sessions we taught them about a completely different aspect of literacy. They were encouraged to analyse texts and make inferences about them, in order to improve their reading comprehension. Thus the children in this group acted as a control for the other three groups.

Now we can turn to the spelling games that we played with the children in the three experimental groups. There were two of these and we presented both on a laptop computer. The two games were the Analogy game and the Corrections game, and each one was presented in a different teaching session.

In the Analogy game, using sound as well as visual presentation, we showed the pairs of children four puppets, two beside each other in the top half, and the other two in the bottom half of the screen. Under each puppet was a word box, and the game started with the puppet in the top left part of the screen saying a word (e.g. "magic"). After the puppet produced this word, the same word, but now written, appeared in the word box below it. Then the puppet to the right spoke another word that was derived from the first and had a /ən/ ending ("magician"). Again the written version of this last word appeared in this puppet's word box immediately after he had spoken it. The third puppet, on the bottom-left, then spoke another stem word, in this case "music" and this too was followed by the written version of the word appearing just under the puppet. Finally, the fourth puppet pronounced a word derived from this new one ("musician") but this was followed immediately by a question mark appearing in the box below. We asked the two children to write the fourth puppet's word for us. They discussed the spelling between themselves and came up with a joint solution, and then we told them whether they were right or not, and showed them the correct spelling.

What we did next depended on whether we were using Implicit or Explicit methods. When we were using the Implicit method, we asked them to think about the spellings and try to figure out the reason for the differences between the words in the pairs. With the Explicit method, however, we joined in the discussion. We asked them whether they could find a similarity in the meaning of the words ending in "-ian." Some pairs of children did, others did not, and if they did not realize that they were both about people who do something, we made this explicit. We then asked them to think about the words ending in "-ion." As these are abstract nouns, they found it very difficult to come up with a definition, and we often had to help them. Some specific terms did emerge: "things you feel"—i.e. feelings—and "things that happen to you"—i.e. events—are examples of explanations that the children produced. At the end of the game we showed the children a list of all the two-morpheme words (e.g. "musician," "protection") that we had used during the game. This list contained a set of "-ion"-ending and a set of "-ian"-ending words. We reminded the children in the Explicit and the Mixed groups, but not those in the Implicit group, that these two sets of words had different sorts of meanings and discussed with them how this difference in meaning was connected to a difference in spelling.

In the Correction Game, on the second day of teaching, we showed children written sentences (again on the screen of a laptop computer) and asked them whether a particular word in each sentence was spelled correctly or not. The word that we asked them to judge was always a two-morpheme word with either an "-ion" or an "-ian" ending. This word was always presented in childish hand-writing, while the other words in the sentence were all typed (see Figure 7.1). The two children discussed each target word and made a joint decision about its spelling. If they judged the spelling as wrong, we asked them to write the word in the right way. Then we told the children what the correct spelling was, and, if they were in the Explicit group, we also discussed the reason for the "-ion" or the "-ian" ending, whichever it was. We ended the game in exactly the same way as the Analogy game, by showing the children a list of all the two-morpheme words that they had judged in the game. Again we separated the words with "-ion" and "-ian" endings in these lists, and again we discussed the reason for this difference with the children in the Explicit and the Mixed groups only.

We wanted to measure the effect of the concentrated experiences that the children in the three experimental groups went through in the Analogy and the Correction games. So, we gave two post-tests to the children in these groups, and also to the children in the Control group who had not played these games. The post-tests were identical to the pre-test: the children had to spell the same words and pseudowords on

Confeshon

The gang made a _____ to the police.

musician

The _____ was wonderful.

Christion

Joe was a _____ .

Figure 7.1 The Correction Game: the pairs of children were asked to judge whether the spelling of the handwritten word and to correct its spelling when they thought that it was wrong

all three occasions. The children took one of the post-tests soon after the second intervention session and the other two months later. Half of the words in these tests had been included in the training and the other half had not.

The children's performance in the post-tests provided us with clear evidence that our instruction did work and also that our explicit instruction worked best. Figure 7.2 shows how well the children spelled the two-morpheme real words in the three tests (pre-test, immediate and delayed post-tests). The children in all three experimental groups spelled the words a great deal better in the immediate post-test than they had in the pre-test, and their scores in this post-test were much higher than those of the children in the Control group. This shows that the instruction about morphemes and spelling that we gave to the experimental groups but not to the Control group did have an effect.

We also compared the scores of the three experimental groups in the post-tests. The children in the Explicit group improved a great deal

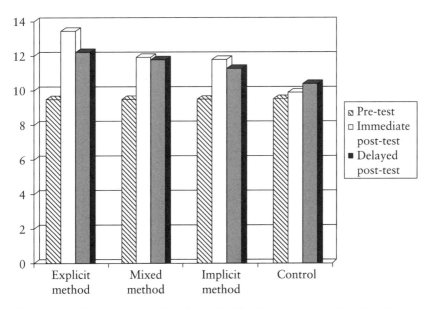

Figure 7.2 The mean number (out of 16) of correctly spelled "-ion" and "-ian" endings in real words in study 1

Note: The scores in this figure are the adjusted scores from an analysis of co-variance of the scores in the two post-tests, in which the pre-test scores were the covariate. In the immediate post-test the scores of all three Taught groups were significantly higher than those of the Control group.

more sharply than the other two experimental groups did between the pre-test and the immediate post-test. In the short term, at least, it seems that children respond extremely well to explicit and open teaching about the link between morphemes and spelling. However, the Implicit and the Mixed group also improved from pre- to post-test and their scores in the immediate post-test were also higher than those of the Control group. This tells us that the children responded to the teaching that was designed to help them work out the rules for themselves. Thus, both methods had an effect, and the tangible impact of the Implicit method, though the smaller of the two, was surprising and impressive. Two months later there was a general levelling out of the scores of the three experimental groups, but the children in the Explicit group continued to outperform the control group children.

We also looked at children's spelling of pseudowords. We had not used pseudowords at all during in the intervention, and so they provided an especially stringent test of the effectiveness of our teaching about morphemes. The results were also positive in this case, as Figure 7.3 shows. All three experimental groups spelled the pseudowords in the immediate post-test a great deal better than the Control group did and this difference lasted quite well over the next two months.

Summary

1   Our first attempt to teach the spelling distinction between "ion" and "ian" established that it is possible to show children the rule and to encourage them to use it.
2   We also showed that one can do this explicitly or with methods that are implicit and encourage implicit learning.
3   On the whole, the explicit method made the greater impact, at any rate in the short term, but the success of both methods was remarkable and encouraging.

Classroom intervention—the first step

Our next move was into the classroom. Some teachers in a particular school in London were interested in our work on morphemes, and they also wanted to do their own research on possible new teaching methods. So, we agreed with them on a joint project on teaching the "-ion/-ian" distinction. They would carry out a version of the interventions that we have just described in their classrooms, and we would measure the

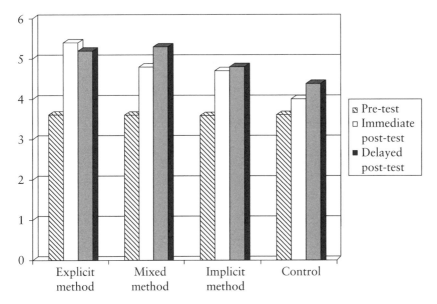

Figure 7.3 The mean number (out of 8) of correctly spelled "-ion" and "-ian" endings in pseudowords in study 1

Note: The scores in this figure are the adjusted scores from an analysis of covariance of the scores in the two post-tests, in which the pre-test scores were the covariate. In the immediate post-test the scores of all three Taught groups were significantly higher than those of the Control group. In the delayed post-test the Explicit and Mixed groups scored significantly better than the Control group.

effect of the intervention by giving their children the same pre-tests and post-tests as before.

The children in this study were again 9-year-olds. The teachers randomly assigned them to two groups—a taught group and a control group. The teachers gave the children in the taught group classroom versions of our Analogy and Correction games in two lessons only. They talked to the children about the spelling rule that underlies the distinction between the two endings, as we had done with the Explicit group in our earlier study. They did not teach the control group children about morphemes but taught them about making inferences when reading, to improve reading comprehension, as we had done with the control group children in our study. This instruction was also in two lessons only, lasting the same amount of time as the instruction offered to the group that learned about morphemes.

We ourselves administered the pre-test just before the classroom teaching began and an immediate post-test soon after it stopped. We also gave the children a delayed post-test after a 2-month interval. We had no idea which group each child belonged to when we gave these tests, which were given to the children in their classrooms, where the intervention and comparison groups were actually mixed.

The pattern of the results of these tests was much the same as it was in our earlier study. The Explicit instruction had a strong immediate impact, so that in the immediate post-test the taught group spelled the "-ion" and "-ian" endings in real words (Figure 7.4) and in pseudowords (Figure 7.5) much better than the Control group managed to do. The taught group were still ahead of the control group two months later, but the difference was a great deal smaller with both kinds of word and it was not statistically significant.

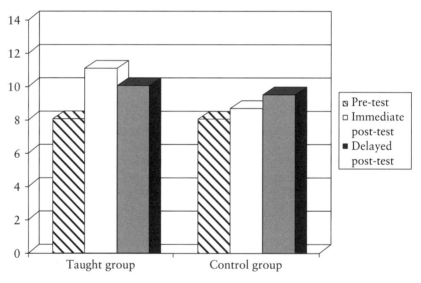

Figure 7.4 The mean number (out of 16) of correctly spelled "-ion" and "-ian" endings in real words in study 2

Note: The scores in this figure are the adjusted scores from an analysis of co-variance of the scores in the two post-tests, in which the pre-test scores were the covariate. There was an overall difference between the Taught and the Control groups in the two tests. The difference between the Taught and Control groups was significant in the immediate post-test (with an effect size of 0.16 of a standard deviation, which is small but quite good, considering that only two teaching sessions were used) but not in the delayed post-test.

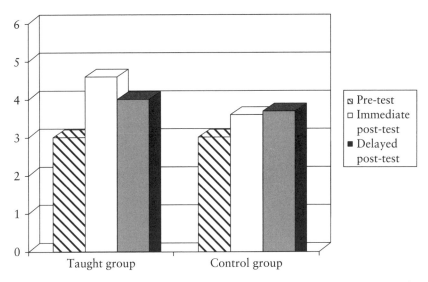

Figure 7.5 The mean number (out of 8) of correctly spelled "-ion" and "-ian" endings in pseudowords in study 2

Note: The scores in this figure are the adjusted scores from an analysis of co-variance of the scores in the two post-tests, in which the pre-test scores were the covariate. The overall difference between groups fell just short of significance. In a separate analysis of covariance of the immediate post-test the scores of the Taught group were significantly higher than those of the Control group, with an effect size of 0.42 of a standard deviation.

So, the second study showed that it is possible to teach children an entirely unfamiliar rule in the classroom as well as in the laboratory, and that this can be done in two lessons only. It also raises the question about how to make sure that children remember the new rule. It is not surprising that the children tended to forget something that they thought about in only two lessons, which had taken place two months before. There might be a relation between the amount of teaching that the children are given in the classroom and how well they remember the rules over time. It is easy to test this idea.

Classroom interventions organized by the teachers

The intervention experiments that psychologists carry out serve two very different purposes. One of the aims of these studies is absolutely straightforward. It is to test a psychological hypothesis. In our own experiments that we have just described; that hypothesis was that children will learn about morphemic spelling rules rapidly and efficiently when they are given explicit instruction about those rules, and, as we have seen, the hypothesis turned out to be largely right. The second purpose of psychologists' interventions is to establish a teaching method that will work in the classroom as well as in the laboratory. Psychologists need not take this step in their intervention work, but since their interventions usually involve some form of teaching, these experiments usually give them some opportunity to test ideas about teaching practices as well.

Of course, the danger here is that the psychologists' interventions are so unlike the classroom: what goes on in the quiet and well-ordered setting of the psychologist's laboratory with one or two children at a time might be quite irrelevant to the complexities of a classroom with as many as 30 children. In the last experiment that we described, the teachers themselves did the teaching and, though they used the material that we had prepared in the previous project, they themselves decided how to use this material in their own ways. So, this experiment was very "classroom-like" and its success encouraged us to think that our intervention methods would work well in school settings.

This encouraged us to take a next step towards the classroom. We felt that we needed to check two further concerns. One was whether our methods would transfer as well to the classroom when several morphemic spelling rules were being taught. The classroom project that we have just described was about the "-ion"/"-ian" distinction and nothing else. Our next step was a project in which teachers were to teach children several different morphemic spelling rules.

Our second question was whether the intervention would work when we had absolutely no control over how it was administered. We reasoned that if, in the future, we were to send our materials to schools in the form of a teaching programme, different schools would vary greatly in the way that they set about delivering this programme. For this reason, we felt that only a programme that was impervious to these variations would be a worthwhile and effective one.

We devised two programmes, one which we called Morpheme with spelling and the other Morpheme only. We organized these two programmes into seven sessions and we put the material for each of these sessions on a CD which we then sent to the teachers who were going to carry out the interventions, with a few written instructions about how to use the material. These teachers taught classes of 9-year-old children.

This procedure of simply sending the CD and not monitoring the teaching itself was the main new step in this particular intervention study. It seemed to us that if we were eventually to have an effect on the way that children are taught to read, our job would be to provide material and ideas about how to use this material. We would have no control over exactly how this material would be put across. That was not going to be our business, nor was it any part of our expertise; this is the teachers' expertise. So, we would simply be in the position of sending our material, and advice how to use it, to the teachers and then leaving them to get on with it. That, therefore, was what we decided to do in the project as well.

Our only requirement was that we could give all the children who took part in the project a pre-test before and a post-test after the intervention in order to assess their spelling of common affix morphemes. Otherwise the teachers could deal with the material as they liked. They could determine the intervals between sessions, they could even break up or combine sessions and they could decide on their own way of administering the various games and tasks that we had designed.

We devised two sets of material to give to the teachers, one for the Morphology Alone programme and one for the Morphology with spelling programme. The two programmes were very similar. Both consisted of the same series of games, all of which used visual material in PowerPoint. The games in both programmes emphasized syntax, since we felt that we needed to teach children a great deal about parts of speech, and a wide variety of derivational and inflectional affixes. In the games about parts of speech, we gave children sentences with a missing word and several choices for that missing word. Thus one sentence, with appropriate pictures, said "We saw a _____ in the town centre" and the alternatives for the missing word appeared on the screen—e.g. "car," "computer," "sing," "buses," etc. Two of these choices were possible, and the other two for different reasons were not.

Other games were about affixes. For example, the children saw pictures of a "bicycle" and a "tricycle" and were asked to explain what in the two words described the most important difference between them: they were asked about words like "uniform" and "binoculars" in order for them to reflect on and discuss the significance of these two words' prefixes. Finally, the material included made-up words like "biheaded" and "bitailed" and the children were asked to produce drawings showing a "biheaded monster" and a "bitailed horse." Another example was the affix "en," which is both a prefix, as in "enlarge," and a suffix as in "lengthen." Children easily see the connection between "en" at the beginning and at the end of a word, but that connection is always quite new and interesting to them.

Much of the material in these games was designed to engage children's imagination by using pseudowords. For example, the game includes a picture of two strange-looking men each holding a box and the caption reads: "They are montists. They look after ------------ which they keep in their little black boxes."

The two programmes were rich and varied, and we cannot list all the activities in the seven sessions in each programme in this chapter. But here is a list of the some of the exercises in them:

1　The participants decided whether "-ist" or "-ian" was the best ending to put on a particular word to make it an agentive, and whether "ness" or "-ion" was the best ending to convert a word into an abstract noun.
2　The children discussed which of "un," "dis" or "in" converted particular words into their opposite.
3　They discussed which kind of stems took particular affixes: e.g. verbs take "er" for agentives and nouns are converted into adjectives by a "y" ending (e.g. "bumpy").
4　They compared the effects of making adjectives by adding "less" and "ful" to words.

Thus far we have described the common parts of the two programmes, Morphology alone and Morphology with spelling. In fact, the two programmes were not very different, but in the first the teachers emphasized the way that spoken words are constructed from morphemes, while in the second they concentrated more on the spelling of the morphemes. In both programmes we asked the children to write the words involved and therefore the morphemes. However, in the Morphology only programme the teachers mainly discussed the morphemes as building blocks for words, while in the Morphology with spelling they also emphasized the stable correspondences between affix morphemes and their spellings.

The two programmes were strikingly successful. All three groups—Morphology alone, Morphology with spelling and the Control group—improved in their spelling from pre- to post-test. However, the two intervention groups, Morphology alone, and Morphology with spelling, improved much more than the children in the Control group did. The Morphology with spelling group did slightly better than the Morphology alone group, which was no surprise since the tests themselves were about spelling, but the difference was not statistically significant. The most important point made by these results is that, once again, explicit instruction about morphemes worked. It improved children's spelling by telling them about rules which they had not been able to learn in any useful way for themselves. Explicit instruction about morphemes and spelling is effective. Children enjoy it. They know more about their language as a result and they spell better than they did before.

The effects of the programme were not restricted to spelling. In the pre- and post-tests we also gave the children vocabulary tests. In one of these, the children chose the correct word (from a set of three) to complete a sentence. In the other, we gave the children a pseudoword, composed of a real stem and a real affix, but in a non-existing combination (see Chapter 5 for a description of this task). The comparisons between the Control and Intervention groups in these tasks showed that the children in both Intervention groups made significantly more progress from pre- to post-test than those in the Control group.

Summary

1   In this last intervention project we administered the pre-test and post-test and we provided the intervention material to the teachers on a CD. We left it to the teachers to decide how and when and how often to teach their pupils with our teaching tasks. We ourselves had no contact with the children during the intervention period.

2   Our pre- and post-tests were designed: (1) to measure children's use of morphemic spelling rules; and (2) to assess their vocabulary and their understanding of the morphemic structure of spoken words.

3   We also broadened the teaching material to include a wide variety of inflectional and derivational affixes and several new games with morphemes.

4   There were two intervention groups and a control group in this project. One intervention group was taught just about the morphemic structure of words and the other was taught about this structure and also its relation to spelling (i.e. to morphemic spelling rules).

5   The results of this ambitious project were positive. The children in the two intervention groups improved more than the control group in their use of morphemic spelling rules. The improvement in these two groups' vocabulary scores was also greater than the control group's.

6   The children in intervention groups enjoyed the intervention sessions and apparently found them interesting too.

Epilogue

This chapter is easy to summarize. The quite consistent message that we get from the studies that we have reviewed is that it is possible and practicable to teach children about morphemes and spelling in an interesting, enjoyable and intellectually respectable way. Children learn well and quickly from this sort of teaching, they benefit from it and they evidently enjoy it as well.

What justification, therefore, can there be for the common practice of leaving virtually all the learning about morphemes to children's own necessarily haphazard inferences? Why is it that we concentrate so much on telling them explicitly about grapheme–phoneme correspondences and yet we want them to work out grapheme-morpheme correspondences for themselves? Surely we can protect them from a great deal of quite unnecessary difficulty by teaching them about morphemes. Now that it is clear how well this teaching works, not to teach our children morphemic spelling rules would be worse than neglect: it would be negligence.

Chapter 8

A Framework for Understanding How Children Learn to Read and Spell English Words

In a recent critical analysis of theories of reading, Sadoski and Paivio (2007) argued that theories of reading and spelling must attempt to show how they are connected to theories of cognition. This seems right to us. It would not be sensible to propose that there are learning and memory processes that work only for the purpose of learning to read and spell and have no connection with how children remember and learn other things. Our aim in this chapter is to outline a cognitive framework for understanding the development of children's word reading and spelling and for designing instruction.

The basic idea behind this framework is that, in order to understand how children learn to read and spell words, we need to consider the *object* to be learned, the constraints and possibilities of learning brought to the learning situation by the *learner*, and the *context* in which learning takes place. This triad of requirements provides the structure for the final chapter in this book. We will consider, in turn, how each of these three factors influences children's reading and spelling. Our aim is to provide a broad discussion, by summarizing points that we have made before and by exploring others.

What Sort of an Object is a Written Language?

Writing, we argued in Chapter 1, represents oral language in two ways. First, it is a notation for oral language: it allows us to encode, record, transport, and reproduce oral language in a systematic way. English orthography does this by using many resources; the most commonly recognized resource is the use of letter–sound correspondences. However, because English orthography uses a borrowed alphabet that does not contain enough letters to represent all its different phonemes, these letters have been used imaginatively and flexibly in the development of English orthography in ways that go well beyond one-to-one correspondence between single letters and single phonemes. For example, combinations of letters, such as "ai" or "sh," typically represent one phoneme only. This is why psychologists use the term grapheme–phoneme correspondence rather than letter–sound correspondence to describe how the alphabetic code works in written English.

However, the effects of using digraphs to represent single phonemes go well beyond a mere change in the grapheme unit. In the English orthography, the presence of a digraph sometimes determines the pronunciation of another letter. This is the case with doublets: when a suffix (that starts with a vowel) is added to a stem that has a short vowel followed by a consonant, the consonant is doubled (e.g. "hop"–"hopping") and this preserves the pronunciation of the vowel as short. Doublets thus become part of the complex set of rules for spelling and pronunciation that we discussed in detail in Chapter 2. These doublets involve conditional rules: if a vowel comes just before a doublet, it must be read as short; if you want to represent a long vowel in spelling, do not use a doublet after it. The difference between digraphs and doublets is that in the digraph we can still think in terms of grapheme–phoneme correspondences but doublets affect the pronunciation of a different letter.

Split digraphs, such as A+Consonant+E ("a-e") may be an intermediary case: the final "e" affects the pronunciation of the vowel that appears before the consonant and so this may be a conditional rule; but the number of split digraphs is limited, if we ignore the consonant that appears between the two vowels. They are "a-e," "i-e," "o-e" and "u-e."

In short, the direct notational connection between oral and written language, which involves the representation of the sounds of oral language through letters, seems to operate though two types of rules: *grapheme–phoneme correspondences* and *conditional rules.*

However, English orthography is not limited to representing what we hear in oral English: there is a second connection between oral and written language which is indirect and which works through the meanings encoded in syntax and morphology. This second connection has a significant, though less often acknowledged, impact on writing. Writing uses spaces not to represent pauses in oral language but to represent words, which are elements defined by syntax and morphology, not by phonology. We might pronounce the same words differently in different sentences in spoken language but we spell them in the same way, irrespective of the context. For example, we say /I hato run/ but spell this as "I had to run" (though some children do use the spelling "hat" for "had" in this context; see Nunes & Bryant, 2006).

In English, morphemes also retain their spelling even if their pronunciation varies, as they often do in suffixes: we pronounce the plural inflection as /z/ in "trees" but we still spell it with "s" and we spell the past tense with the "-ed" ending even if it sounds like a /t/, as in "kissed." English orthography also makes spelling distinctions that are not marked in oral language: we spell the endings of "confession" and "magician" differently, although they sound exactly the same, for morphological reasons. Another example of a distinction in writing that does not appear in speech is the use of apostrophes: English orthography uses apostrophes to mark possession but there is no difference between the spoken phrases "the boys' drink" and "the boys drink." Finally, when we read words, we often need to use different syllable boundaries in pronunciation if a letter sequence is part of the same morpheme or not: we pronounce the "sh" as a digraph in "washed" but we split this letter sequence when we read "misheard." *Thus English orthography involves the use of a second type of conditional rule, based on morphemes, and consequently the use of a different type of unit, not described by phonology.*

To use Jaffré's (1997) terminology, phonograms (letter–sound units) and semiograms (morpheme–spelling units) are analytical units: they make it possible for us to break words up into smaller portions. However, on occasion, English also demands word-specific knowledge by making distinctions in spelling between one-morpheme words, such as "meat" and "meet," which sound the same but have different meanings, and by using spellings that cannot be predicted from phonograms or semiograms. We saw in Chapter 3 that children had great difficulty in spelling the word "said," which is the fifth most frequent word in children's story books (surpassed in frequency only by "a," "the," "and" and "to"): its spelling would be "sed" if we used phonograms and "sayed" if we used semiograms consistently. Other words, such as "sword" and "knife," which contain silent letters, also seem to demand the use of word-specific knowledge. *So, a third type of knowledge must be part of English orthography: this involves learning a connection between a whole word and its meaning. Analytical resources do not suffice for word identification in reading or correct spelling.*

Three types of unit, therefore, simultaneously affect the generation of word spellings and reading in English: grapheme–phoneme correspondences, morpheme–spelling correspondences, and whole word representation. These three units are linked to different functional rules in writing: phonograms help in the pronunciation but have no direct connection to meaning, semiograms support word analysis and help us interpret the meaning of the word, and whole words can be directly connected to word meaning.

This might seem complex enough to create difficulties for children, but the sets of rules in English spelling don't end here. English orthography is not entirely determined by functional rules and word-specific knowledge: there are also matters of form. For example, some spellings, such as "ck" or doublets, can be used at the end but not at the beginning of words. Others, such as "ai" cannot be used at the end of words. *Therefore, along with functional rules in spelling children must also learn form rules*, even if these rules have no consequence for word reading (we would read "car" and "ckar" in the same way, if we came across the latter spelling).

English orthography, therefore, is not a simple object. How do children learn about it? It is an empirical question whether children learn all these aspects of English orthography—or the majority of them, at any rate—and how their learning is affected by the learning environment. They could in principle manage almost all, if not all, of this by some form of word-specific learning, and make direct connections between words or groups of words and their meaning (in the case of the apostrophe, for example, the connection would have to be between a group of words). So we turn now to a discussion of the constraints and resources that the children themselves bring to the task of learning to read and write.

Children as Learners of English Orthography

The fact that rules definitely exist for spelling words in English and in other languages as well does not mean that children do learn them. The question is still very much an open one, or at any rate was an open question when we started doing some of the research that we have described in this book. One possibility was that children learn to read and spell words like "boil," "bake" and "baked" through word-specific learning: they simply remember how each of these particular words is spelled. The alternative, which interested us greatly, was that children read and spell these words correctly by finding out about the digraph "oi" in the first case, the split digraph "a-e" in the second, and the "-ed" spelling for the past tense inflection in regular words in the third.

At the time, we were faced with only two virtual certainties. One was that children do learn quite quickly, though somewhat haphazardly, about one-to-one letter–sound correspondences and that they apply this learning with a will. The work of Read (1986) and Treiman (1993) on creative or invented spelling provides us with clear evidence for this learning. The conclusions reached by these two authors mesh well with the ample evidence, gathered since the early 1980s, that children's phonological skills play an essential part in the progress that they make with reading and writing in their early years in school. In particular, there is a very strong relationship between their ability to break words up into phonemes and their eventual success in reading and writing. Add to this the consistent evidence that teaching children about letter–sound relationships has a beneficial effect on their reading and writing and also that many dyslexic children display a marked insensitivity to phonological segments, and you can see that there is an almost cast-iron case that children, or at any rate children who learn to read and write reasonably well, depend to some extent on learning about letter–sound rules to be able to do so.

The second virtual certainty that we faced when we began this book was the importance of word-specific knowledge. People need this kind of knowledge to spell words that sound exactly the same but have different meanings (our example of "meet" and "meat"), and words with sounds that can be spelled in more than one way ("beef" not "beaf," and "leaf" not "leef"). However, it is important to realize that children may rely on word-specific knowledge for other reasons quite apart from the need to resolve these ambiguities. Word-specific knowledge may not just be knowledge about ambiguous or downright irregular spellings. There is no reason at all why children and adults should not also build up and use a large bank of word-specific knowledge that includes words like "boil," "bake" and "baked" whose spellings are definitely not ambiguous or irregular, but conform well to widely known spelling rules. In other words, although these rules undoubtedly exist, children and adults may by-pass them completely and rely on word-specific knowledge instead.

The impressive evidence for the importance of letter–sound rules in children's reading and spelling combined with the obvious need for word-specific knowledge in many orthographies must have been the reason why several current theoretical accounts of children's reading and spelling confine themselves to these two factors and ignore generative spelling rules, such as morphemic spelling rules, altogether. David Share's well-known "self-teaching" hypothesis (Share, 1996, 1999) is that children learn first about grapheme–phoneme correspondences and then use these phonologically-based rules to help them build up a very large bank of word-specific knowledge. Although the phonological side of this two-sided theory could include more complex grapheme–phoneme links such as English digraphs and even split digraphs, there is no place at all in Share's hypothesis for morphemic spelling rules.

Our own conclusions are different from his. We believe that we have established in at least three languages (English, Portuguese and Greek) that many children do learn about and can use morphemic spelling rules and conditional phonological spelling rules, such as the split digraph, as well. The main evidence for this claim is the success of many children in pseudoword tasks which they can only carry out by applying conditional or morphemic spelling rules and, to a lesser extent, children's ability to generalize from the experience of learning one specific instance of a spelling rule to other specific instances as well. This kind of evidence establishes that, somewhere between children's learning of basic letter–sound rules and their eventual vast but little understood bank of word-specific knowledge, there is an important place for rule-learning as well. All theories of children's reading and writing, in our view, should attend to and account for this kind of learning as well.

This view is a controversial one. There have been several attempts to show that people's apparent use of morphemic spelling rules can be explained in terms of learning at a lower and much less abstract level. This was the main theme of a recent and interesting review article by Pacton and Deacon (in press). They took as an example the evidence presented by Pacton, Fayol and Perruchet (2005) about children writing the "-ette" ending which is one way of representing the diminutive in French. These authors had reported that French children used this ending in a pseudoword task more often with obviously diminutive words ("A little vitar (a pseudoword) is a /vitaret/) than with words that apparently were not diminutives. However, the children also used the "-ette" ending more often when the preceding sound was a /r/ (/vitaret/) than when it was and /f/ (/vitafet/), and this result is undoubtedly an effect of the relative frequency of different sounds that immediately precede the "-ette" ending. As it happens, more words in French end in "-rette" than in "-fette."

Pacton and Deacon argue that this result shows that the children make associations between features on the basis of frequencies and then use these associations to spell. So the children associated the "feature" "r" more strongly than the feature "f" with the feature of the "-ette" ending. They also claim that the fact that the children use the diminutive ending more with diminutive nouns than with other nouns shows that they associate the feature diminutive with the feature of the "-ette" ending. The first of these two claims seem plausible to us. The fact that children are more prepared to end use the diminutive ending when it is immediately preceded by a /r/ than by a /f/ sound is very probably the result of fairly low-level, specific associative learning. It is indeed quite plausible that form rules are learned in this way. However, it seems misleading to us also to describe the relatively common use of the diminutive ending with diminutive pseudowords as the association of two features. Diminutiveness is an abstract grammatical concept, not a feature of objects: not all small things are words in the diminutive (e.g. "a fly") and large objects can have a diminutive (a flatlet is certainly bigger than a fly). If children can recognize and know how to represent this concept with a particular spelling sequence, this is a clear indication that some children in the sample being studied had acquired an abstract spelling rule.

The fact that children in the Pacton et al. (2005) study and adults and children in the Kemp and Bryant (2003) study also applied a lower-level and far less abstract spelling strategy does not, as Pacton and Deacon suggest, detract from the undoubted evidence of knowledge of an abstract morphemic spelling rule that emerged in the second of these studies. It is quite feasible that people might know a rule, and yet fail sometimes to apply it. However, there is still a question to answer about this evidently common use of more than one spelling strategy by the sample of participants being studied. This question concerns individual differences. Did some of the participants in these studies only apply the appropriate morphemic spelling rule while others resorted just to a lower-level frequency-based spelling strategy? Or did most of the participants apply both these very different strategies during the task that they were given? Neither study gives us an answer to this crucial question, and it is difficult to see how either could, given the relatively small number of trials in each task.

Bryant and Mitchell's (2007) research on people's choice of spellings appropriate to the endings of one- or two-morpheme words contained tasks with a relatively large number of trials, and the results of these certainly suggested a sharply divided population. The division was between those who used morphemic spelling rules and those who did not, and it suggests that individual differences might account for the use of more than one spelling strategy by the participants in Pacton et al.'s and in Kemp and Bryant's studies. However, we need more evidence about, for example, the use of the French diminutive ending to be sure about this conclusion.

Nevertheless Bryant and Mitchell's results certainly suggest a rather more complicated answer than the positive answer that we have already given to our question about whether children acquire and use anything else than the basic letter–sound rules and word-specific knowledge when they learn how to read and spell. Now, we must conclude that some children and some adults depend far more on word-specific learning and far less on morphemic spelling rules than others. Some may by-pass these rules altogether, even though others learn them to a high degree of sophistication.

The positive side of this conclusion then raises another question. Given the pronounced lack of systematic teaching of morphemic spelling rules in schools in the countries where we have done our research, how is it that some people seem to know them quite well? Our hypothesis takes us back to word-specific knowledge, which we view not just as an alternative to learning about morphemic spelling rules, but also ironically as the only possible source that many children have to work out these rules. The results of Chliounaki and Bryant's (2007) study of Greek children's knowledge about how to spell inflections suggest that they first accumulate a body of knowledge about the spelling of the inflected endings of real words, and then use this knowledge to infer why, for example, some /ɔ/ endings are spelled as "-o" and others as "-ω." In our next section, we try to show how children are able to make such inferences.

Learning and Making Inferences from Experience

A written language is a cultural product, and written languages vary in many ways: in the types of marks that they use, the way these marks are connected to oral language, the functional units that connect written and oral language, and in form rules. It would be unreasonable to expect that the specific characteristics of an orthography could be pre-inscribed in the brain. However, we know that there are structures and processes in the brain that make it possible for people to invent and learn a written language, and that if there is damage to these, learning to read and spell may turn out to be too difficult or may have to follow an alternative path. We do not consider here the neuropsychological mechanisms that make learning possible: we focus only on how people learn from experience. We need experience with written English to learn to read and write in English just as we need experience with Chinese or Greek to learn to read and write in these languages. The question is not *whether* we learn from experience but *how* we learn from experience. For the purposes of this analysis, we will consider only the learner who has no inherent difficulty due to brain abnormalities or lack of sensory or linguistic experiences.

How can a learner process environmental input and stored knowledge so as to benefit from experiences with reading and writing in order to learn to read and spell? This question was posed in a more general way by Holland, Holyoak, Nisbett and Thagard (1986) whose endeavour was to understand the processes involved in induction. According to their definition, induction encompasses "all inferential processes that expand knowledge in the face of uncertainty." So if a child is shown a written word—let's say, his or her own name—and all that the child learns is to say his/her name when presented with this word or to reproduce its spelling when asked to write his/her name, there is no need to invoke the participation of induction processes. We only need to invoke induction processes when the learner goes beyond the particular information given, to use and expand knowledge in the face of uncertainty. This is undoubtedly the case of reading and spelling. Our claim was, from the first line in this book, that word reading and spelling are generative: we do not read and spell only the specific words that we encountered in the past but use past knowledge to read and spell novel words. How do learners organize their experience so that it becomes the basis for action—i.e. reading or spelling new and unfamiliar words?

Holland and colleagues (1986) suggest that the answer is in the induction of rules, which they consider the building blocks of knowledge. The most basic element of knowledge, they suggest, is a "condition-action *rule*, which has the form "IF such-and-such, THEN so-and-so," where the IF part is the condition and the THEN part is the action" (p.14; italics and capitals in the original). They argue that such condition-action rules are the most appropriate representations of knowledge in inductive systems for different reasons.

First, condition-action rules are clear about the procedures that must be carried out for action to take place. This idea can be applied to word spelling: learners would think of the word they want to spell, and test which conditions match this word—sequences of sounds, morphemes—in order to produce the spelling. Condition-action rules do not have to be explicitly formulated in order for action to take place. If you get to your front door and it is locked, you reach for your keys without having to say to yourself: If the door is locked, then I need to get my keys to open it. Condition-action rules can reach an automaticity that precludes the need for explicit formulation, even if you can become aware of the rule under special circumstances.

Second, rules can be applied in sequence or simultaneously, and this allows for the existence of conflicting rules as well as mutually reinforcing rules in the knowledge system of the same learner. When spelling the word "kissed," for example, learners might find that two sets of rules fit the spelling of the end sound, one based on phonograms (IF the sound is /t/, THEN use the letter "t") and one based on semiograms (IF the /t/ sound is at the end of a regular past verb, THEN use the ending "-ed"). These are conflicting rules but they can be part of the same knowledge system without resulting in an inability to act: the second rule would be used to generate the spelling because it provides a more specific match to the word. This is an important aspect of induction: specific matches are more useful and will be preferred to less specific ones.

Third, it is possible to add and modify rules without drastic consequences for the overall knowledge (i.e. without causing chaos and leading to a complete collapse in action). Learners might start learning to read and spell with a smaller set of rules than they end up with—indeed, it is almost certain that they do so, as no one could learn all the letters simultaneously; learning new letters and new rules should not lead the knowledge system into chaos.

Finally, there is support from research for the idea that people use rules, implicitly or explicitly, to guide their actions. In the case of spelling, the studies involving pseudowords reviewed in earlier chapters suggest that (at least some) people use rules in spelling and reading pseudowords. Sometimes people are even able to explain these rules explicitly.

A detail of terminology should be dealt with here. In Chapter 2, we referred to simple letter–sound correspondences as "basic rules" and to other rules, such as the use of digraphs and morphemes in spelling as "conditional rules." In the context of Holland et al.'s theory of induction in systems of knowledge, this distinction is treated as a matter of how specific the rules are. All spelling and reading rules are condition-action rules, but some are relatively general, such as the letter–sound correspondences, and others are relatively specific, such as the conditional rules involving digraphs and morphemes.

When more than one rule matches the environment, as in the case of spelling the final sound in /kist/, the different rules compete to generate the action. The outcome of this competition depends on four factors: match, strength, specificity, and support. As mentioned above, two rules match the IF part of the rule for spelling the end sound of /kist/: a phonological rule and a morphological rule. The morphological rule is more specific since it is about the ending of a past verb. It is supported by another morphological rule which matches another element in this word: the first portion of the word "kissed" provides a match to the meaning of the stem and thus strengthens the morphological rule about the use of the "-ed" ending. So, on the three conditions of match, specificity, and support, the morphological rule might "win" the right to produce the spelling. However, there is still a factor that Holland et al. call "strength," which refers to how well a rule has performed in the past. For children who have abundantly and successfully used letter–sound correspondences as a spelling rule, this rule may well win, even if the children have already inferred the "-ed" rule from their experience. If some children have not yet discovered the "ed" rule, then there is no competition, so that the letter–sound correspondence rules produce the spelling. Thus, in this theory there are two possible explanations for a child not giving a regular past verb the correct "-ed" ending,: the child may not have discovered the "-ed" rule yet but, alternatively, she may have discovered it but holds to it less strongly than the simpler and widely used letter–sound rule. Later, we shall discuss these two possible explanations in greater detail.

Condition-action rules, implicit or explicit, might be the building blocks of the learner's knowledge of word reading and spelling, but this is not sufficient to understand learning. We still need to know how rules are created and modified. This is where induction comes into the picture.

> Induction is not simply something the cognitive system does to occupy its idle moments, nor does it have the character of undirected inference making or random combination of ideas. Rather, induction is a problem-directed activity, executed in response to specific system objectives such as seeking plausible explanations for an unexpected outcome. In a rule based system there are only two fundamental types of inductive change: the refinement of existing rules and the generation of new ones. . . . [a] third task, the generation of larger knowledge structures, must be accomplished by a combination of rule generation and rule refinement, serving to cluster related rules together. In addition to these self-initiated activities, it is possible to insert new rules from the outside. In the case of organisms this is called education. (Holland et al., 1989, p. 68)

We think that this description is a good starting point to outline a framework that can be used to understand how children learn to read and spell words. Children are indeed trying to solve a problem when learning to be literate, and their efforts are oriented towards understanding how written language works. They often ask others to read and spell words for them, and instruction is likely to insert new rules into their knowledge system from the outside. They are likely to have to learn rules, refine existing ones and generate larger knowledge structures, by clustering together related rules, such as those for reading and spelling the same sorts of units. The analysis of how and when new rules are generated, refined or clustered into larger knowledge structures might indeed help us understand how children make progress in word reading and spelling.

We now attempt to translate this highly abstract description into a description of how children learn to read and spell. We will start with learning rules related to the representation of phonology, then turn to the representation of morphology, and conclude the section by considering word-specific learning.

Learning about the Representation of Sounds in English Orthography

When children are exposed to written English, they learn sooner or later that letter–sound correspondences can help them read and spell words that they have not encountered before. This is an important set of rules and children's spelling in the first year of learning undoubtedly reflects the use of these rules. If the children are taught to read, it is more likely (at least in English) that they will be taught about letters as units within words. Letters are units that maintain their identity and are used repeatedly, with much larger frequency than other chunks that could be treated as units within words, phonological or morphological. A learner who seeks to understand the role of letters is on the right track, and will be able to infer condition-action rules useful in reading and spelling. If children think of all letter–sound correspondences as a cluster of rules, we might say that they form a mental model (which is a higher knowledge-structure according to Holland et al., 1986) of English orthography as alphabetic.

However, English orthography involves other sorts of regularities—such as the use of other units besides single letters—and it would be advantageous if learners could infer these rules too. The difficulty in inferring other rules is that the representation of written words as single letter–sound correspondences is a strong set of rules, and there are many rules in this set which would support each other. Therefore, a theory of induction would predict that learners will infer simple letter–sound rules, and that they will have greater strength than other rules in the beginning of the learning process, even if the learner has inferred other rules. There is much evidence to support this prediction.

The analyses by Charles Read (1971) and Rebecca Treiman (1993) of children's spontaneous spelling, as well as our own analysis of children's written stories reported in Chapters 2 and 3, converge in showing that young learners have a strong preference for the use of a one-letter-one-sound rule in spelling. The work of Ehri and her colleagues (Ehri & Soffer, 1999; Ehri & Wilce, 1980) also shows that, when children are asked to show explicitly what sorts of segments in written words correspond to a single phoneme, young learners demonstrate a strong bias towards using a one-letter-one-sound rule. Children produce many spellings which can be interpreted by adult readers but which they most certainly have not learned before in the form of word-specific knowledge: just think of spellings such as "trict" for "tricked" and "killd" for "killed" (Figure 5.3) and "pepole" for "people" and "fritend" for "frightened" (Figure 5.2). However, even children in their first year of school seem to have inferred rules that include the use of two letters to represent a phoneme, particularly when the phoneme cannot be represented by a single letter—i.e. the cases that we called obligatory digraphs, such as "sh" and "th." In Chapter 2, we reported Treiman's study of children's spontaneous writing, which showed that these young learners were correct about 70% of the time when they needed to use a digraph to represent a consonant sound that could not be represented by a single letter. They were more often correct in the one-letter-one-sound use of consonants, but it still seems safe to conclude that they had inferred the rule that phonemes which cannot be represented by a single consonant must be represented by two letters. So, they have rules not only for one-letter-one-sound situations but also for grapheme–phoneme correspondences.

Can this be interpreted as a sign that young children learn a new type of idea about how spelling represents sounds—i.e. that they learn about conditional rules? The evidence that we presented in Chapter 2 leads us to think that this is not so. It is quite possible to add digraph rules to the set of phoneme-grapheme correspondences without inferring the existence of conditional rules. A stringent test of whether children have learned about the existence of conditional rules would be obtained by looking at doublets. A single "t" or the doublet "tt" are pronounced in the same way, but when a suffix is added to a stem, doubling the consonant has the effect of preserving the pronunciation of another letter, the short vowel that precedes it. Treiman (1993) observed a large discrepancy between the correct use of obligatory digraphs (70%) and the correct use of doublets (37%) in her analysis of spontaneous spellings. Results by both Cassar and Treiman (1997) and Davis (2005) show that there is a large discrepancy in the time when children master obligatory digraphs (which they conquer early on) and doublets (which they do not seem to master until they are about 11 years). Learning about obligatory digraphs, which have a function similar to that of single letters, may be a refinement of the one-letter-one-sound rule, whereas conditional rules may be an instance of learning a new type of rule.

The mastery of doublets is not accomplished suddenly: it takes place over time, and Davis' results indicate that it happens first in reading, and later on in spelling. Achieving a good use of these rules in reading seemed to be part of the process for achieving it in spelling. Throughout this book we often considered the possibility that the gradual mastery of conditional rules could be explained by word-specific learning (or the learning of specific grapheme–phoneme correspondences, in the case of the split digraph) and that the children might not have inferred any rules at all. There is, to our knowledge, no comprehensive research programme yet that allows us to say whether the gradual increase is due to isolated learning of words and some graphemes, or rule learning, or both. Word-specific learning must result in gradual learning, as performance will improve when new items are added to the archive of words that are known. If a conditional rule is inferred, it is likely that it will initially be weaker than grapheme–phoneme correspondence rules, which are successful and reinforce each other. Their gradual strengthening would result in gradual improvement in performance. The question is then whether there is evidence that conditional rules are ever learned; whether it doesn't all boil down to more concrete and specific learning of particular correspondences (at the word or at the rime level, for example).

We have provided two types of evidence for the learning of conditional rules that are involved in the representation of phonology in Chapters 2, 3 and 4. One is from the study of pseudowords. Even though the spelling of pseudowords could ultimately be accomplished by the use of more concrete analytical chunks in words, children succeed in reading and spelling pseudowords and also with doublets with infrequent split digraph rimes. The second type of evidence comes from the study that showed that children make a connection between two different split digraphs, "a-e" and "o-e"; they show transfer across the two digraphs if they learn these in sequence, rather than learning one of them and an unrelated spelling rule. This transfer could not happen if the children were using more concrete and specific learning whereas it is quite expected if the children use a rule like "IF there is an 'e' at the end of the word, THEN the vowel before it is long." This would be a synthesis of the two specific rules, connected into a more general framework of knowledge.

Finally, we considered the question of whether knowledge of grapheme–phoneme correspondences and word-specific knowledge gained in the early phases of learning is part of the process that leads to the inference of conditional rules. In Piagetian theory, which pioneered the idea of stages in cognitive development, the assumption that one form of knowledge was necessary, but not sufficient, for the construction of another was at the core of the definition of developmental stages. Under this assumption, the first form of knowledge must precede the second. This necessary order does not imply that the second form of knowledge replaces the first: they could either co-exist in the system or the second could replace the first. There is no reason to propose a replacement model in children's learning of rules in word reading and spelling: grapheme–phoneme correspondences can co-exist with conditional rules. Do grapheme–phoneme correspondences play a part in the inferential process that leads to the induction of conditional rules?

Holland et al. (1986) proposed that the need for induction of new rules arises from uncertainty and novelty. If a child is consistently using grapheme–phoneme correspondences in reading and spelling and receives feedback that indicates that this has not worked well, the child faces the need to solve a problem and to account for this mismatch between the known condition-action rules and the particular event. This feedback could come from the outside, when the child's decoding or spelling of a word is corrected by another person. Alternatively, it could come from the child's own actions, if the child realizes that the word that he has written does not exist or does not fit into a text. In Chapter 3, we said that in order to test children's use of the split digraph in word reading we chose words such as "hope," and "cape," which could be misread as "hop" and "cap" in order to prevent this self-correction; we did not include words such as "grape" which, if misread, would result in a non-word. Our previous work in Portuguese (Nunes, Roazzi, & Buarque, 2003) and also the work of others (Share, 1996, 1999) had clearly shown that children make such corrections, and can learn from them. It is quite reasonable to expect that children do not start just with a bias towards grapheme–phoneme correspondences, but that they simply have not inferred any conditional rules. As they acquire some word-specific knowledge, through tutoring by others or through self-teaching, they start to create a pool of words from which they can infer conditional rules. Self-correction would be more effective in reading than in spelling. In reading, children can become aware that they have just said something that is not a word or does not fit in the text, whereas, in spelling, this awareness would not arise without the participation of others. If all these assumptions were correct, one would predict that children first make progress in conditional rules in reading, and only later in spelling. This is what Davis and Bryant found. But the reader must not be too excited about the prediction we are making here, as we knew these results already. What is necessary to test these predictions is, for example, to carry out experimental studies where these predictions are put to a more precise test through interventions.

In summary, both with split digraphs and doublets, we found that there is evidence for word-specific knowledge as well as for rule learning. The flexibility of Holland et al.'s (1986) framework is that different, conflicting as well as mutually supporting rules can be part of the same knowledge system. Furthermore, it is possible to make some developmental predictions: in the case of phonological representation, conditional rules are hypothesized to be discovered when grapheme–phoneme rules prove insufficient. This sequence of learning is not a matter of age but a matter of how one set of rules gives origin to another. There is much evidence to support the idea of a sequence in learning—but more stringent tests of this sequence should be carried out in the future.

Learning about the Representation of Meaning in English Orthography

Our studies of how children spell the endings of regular past verbs have suggested some hypotheses about how children learn that the English orthography represents not only sounds but also meaning. Our hypotheses were quite simple: at first, children work with the mental model that orthography represents phonology; then they start to realize that some words that end in /t/ and /d/ are spelled with "ed" at the end. Their initial attempts to know when to use and when not to use the "ed" ending do not seem to be about function but about form: they know that "ed" is a possible form at the end of these words but they have not discovered the functional rule that indicates when it is right to use the "ed" ending, and when it is not. Learning form rules is an early

event; the evidence suggests that form rules can actually precede function rules (Lehtonen & Bryant, 2005). In the case of the "ed" ending,
they certainly seem to do so. To be sure, most children use the "ed"
ending more often correctly than incorrectly, but this could be entirely
due to word-specific learning.

Our hypothesis is that grapheme–phoneme correspondences participate in the process of induction of conditional rules of morphological
representation: children search for new rules because they become aware
of the existence of some forms that do not conform to the grapheme–
phoneme rules. This is, again, a developmental hypothesis, not connected to age but to processes. Some children will discover these rules
early on, others will do so much later. However, they are quite expert
at using grapheme–phoneme correspondences by the time that they discover these conditional morphological rules. So, children should make
few errors when the /t/ and /d/ end sounds of words are spelled phonetically before they notice that these rules do not suffice and then try to
solve this new problem. Some of the previous critics of theories of
developmental sequences in spelling were more concerned with the age
at which the children displayed the ability to use morphological strategy
than with the processes in development. Experience and learning, not
age, are the relevant processes. Other critics were concerned with proposing that children showed a homogenous performance, but as we
argued in Chapter 5 this is a misplaced emphasis: children's knowledge
of reading and spelling rules can include different types of rules, which
in some cases conflict with each other and in others reinforce each
other.

A much more important, and yet so far unanswered, question is
whether there is an order in the use of morphological rules: do children
first become aware of stems and then of affixes or are these morphological units two sides of the same coin? To put the question in stronger
terms: is it necessary for children to become aware of stems in order to
be able to think about affixes or does the stripping of affixes lead to the
awareness of stems? It is not difficult to imagine experimental studies
where children are helped to think more about the function of affixes or
about the conservation of stems and see how each of these interventions
affects children's learning of morphological rules. The work by Rosa
and Nunes (in press), cited in Chapter 5, which was about the effect of
priming stems, suggests that young learners do not take advantage of
the spelling of stems that are right in front of them when they spell a
derived word that contains a differently pronounced vowel. This lack
of disposition to use a stem to spell a derived word does suggest that

awareness of stems is not a very simple achievement, and that stripping affixes might indeed be the other side of the coin.

Finally, we raise the question whether it really is appropriate to use the terms "conditional representation of meaning" and "morphological rules," which imply that learners make a connection between the different instances of morphological rules. There is some correlational evidence that this is so: there are significant and specific correlations between children's conservation of the stem across words and their correct use of the "ed" ending in regular past verbs, even after the effect of their general verbal intelligence on both tasks has been partialled out (Nunes, Bryant, & Bindman, 2006). However, we think that more convincing evidence would come from a transfer study which showed that children benefit from learning two morphological rules in sequence, and thus would demonstrate that learners make a connection between these different types of rule and cluster them into a higher knowledge structure.

Acquiring Word-specific Knowledge

We have repeatedly used the idea that learners acquire word-specific knowledge. One reason for this is the unpredictability of some word spellings from any set of rules, grapheme–phoneme, or conditional rules. Words such as "sword" and distinctions between words such as that made between "meet" and "meat" are not explained by any set of rules. It is then necessary to invoke some cognitive process that can help us understand how this word-specific knowledge is acquired.

We think that the most helpful framework to understand word-specific knowledge comes from theories of memory—more specifically, Tulving's (2000) theory.

Tulving proposed that we have two types of memory system: episodic memory and semantic memory. *Episodic memory* is the memory of specific encounters with objects in the past. For example, one day Natalia's mother wrote her name in capital letters on a piece of paper and said: "Here, this is your name, this says Natalia."[1] Natalia copied the letters over and over on the same paper and after much practice she could reproduce the sequence of letters without having to look at the model. When shown *that* piece of paper and asked what was written on it, she could say with no difficulty that it was "Natalia." What did she

---

[1] This example is from a real event and it is used here only illustratively, not as sufficient evidence.

learn? Initially, she could only recognize her name on the same piece of paper but later on she could also recognize her name when it was written in capital letters on other paper by other people. At this point, we might say that she had acquired word-specific knowledge (though it was limited to capital letters).

What sort of knowledge is this? According to Tulving's theory, she had initially some *explicit knowledge* or memory of when and what her mother had written. But later she also developed some implicit knowledge, which was used in the recognition of this sequence of letters (or any sequence that seemed to her very much the same) as her name. *Implicit knowledge* is knowledge that we use without actually being aware that we are using this knowledge. So Natalia might not have thought any more in an explicit way about the day when her mother wrote her name but she still recognized some letters sequences as saying Natalia (although she saw the word "Natal"—the Portuguese word for Christmas—on a Christmas card and thought it was her name).

According to Tulving, when we recognize an object or a word, we are implicitly using memories (see Tulving, 2000, for a more detailed discussion) of previous encounters with objects or words that help us in this identification process. This is part of what he calls semantic memory, but the memories used in object recognition in semantic memory are not of specific encounters with the object because they can be used to identify a particular object that was never encountered before. If someone who lives in a culture where there is no writing came across a pen, they could not recognize it "as a pen," because they have no memories that are relevant to this. In contrast, those of us who have seen pens can recognize pens in different ways. I can recognize "my pen," with an explicit memory of what it looks like—"this is the pen that my husband gave me on my birthday." This recognition is based on explicit memories or explicit knowledge, specifically identified in time and space. But I can also recognize something that I see for the first time as "a pen," even though I never saw that particular pen before—or any other pink and golden pen like the one I just encountered for the first time. I may not make any explicit connection between this pen I'm looking at and other pens that I saw before. In this case, I am using implicit memory or knowledge to achieve object recognition.

If word-specific knowledge is like object recognition, it should be learned in the same way that we learn about objects. People should learn to recognize words as wholes, not as assembled from smaller parts. Fortunately, there is some evidence that word-specific knowledge is best acquired for words as wholes. Teachers have for some time insisted on the use of multi-sensory methods for teaching spelling, and sensibly enough these methods have been applied most to the teaching of words with unpredictable spellings rather than to teaching words that can be predicted from rules. We do not review this evidence here (for a review, see Bream, 2004) but the evidence seems to show that the use of multi-sensory approaches in learning these spelling is indeed more effective than using just vision. This would be in line with the idea that words are identified as wholes when word-specific knowledge is acquired: the total experience of the whole word, looking at it and saying it at the same time, is more effective than just looking at it.

A recent set of studies (Reitsma, 2007) confirmed these results in two ways. First, children learned the spelling of words that require word-specific knowledge better if they copied the word down than if they simply looked at it. This result was maintained even four weeks after teaching. Second, children learned the spelling of a word better if they copied the whole word rather than just filled in the unpredictable part or chose it from a set of alternatives on a computer screen. This second result, which as far as we know is an entirely novel one, is completely consistent with the notion that word-specific knowledge works like object recognition: it is the recognition and reproduction of a whole, not an assembling of its parts.

It should be noted that the vast majority of these studies, including those reported by Reitsma, is carried out with poor spellers. Any gener-alization to spellers who are not falling behind may be inappropriate, as poor speller may indeed rely more on whole words exactly because they have difficulty with mastering the different types of spelling rules. The replication of such studies with spellers whose performance is age-appropriate is therefore essential.

Although word-specific knowledge appears to be non-analytical, it does not seem to be non-generative. The results that we reviewed in Chapter 5 showed that children who have learned the specific spelling of an unpredictable word, such as "sword," are more likely to spell this stem consistently when it is part of a derived word that those children who generated the spelling of this same word phonologically. The chil-dren used their word-specific knowledge generatively, even though the knowledge of the stem might not be analysable. We also established, with Greek children at least, that they use their assembly of word-specific knowledge as a basis for inferring abstract morphemic spelling rules.

Finally, studies of acquired dyslexic patients—i.e. of people who, after some form of brain damage lost some of their reading ability—

suggest that the use of this process of word-specific knowledge in word reading does differ from the use of phonological rules in reading. Some patients, whose reading difficulty is termed "deep dyslexia," retain their ability to read frequent words that include such difficulties but find it impossible to read simple pseudowords that can be read by using letter–sound rules. So they retain their word-specific knowledge and lose their ability to use rules in reading. In contrast, other patients, whose difficulty is known as "surface dyslexia," can read regular words and pseudowords by using grapheme–phoneme rules, but fail to read even very frequent words that require word-specific knowledge, which they are likely to have encountered many times in their lives. These different patterns of performance do suggest that induction and use of rules, on the one hand, and word-specific knowledge, on the other, depend on different processes: the latter would not depend on the induction of rules but on the recognition of words as wholes. However, once you have acquired sufficient word-specific knowledge, you can use it to induce new spelling rules.

In the previous sections we considered the first two aspects of our triad in trying to understand how children learn to read and spell words. In this final section, we will turn to the learning environment.

The Context of Learning

One of the important sources of new rules for children's knowledge of word reading and spelling is education. There is much print in the environment in a modern society, but most children do not learn to read and write without instruction, simply by exposure to environmental print. However, it is likely that they can learn about form rules from environmental print, even if they learn relatively little about function rules of the orthography surrounding them.

The pioneering work of Emilia Ferreiro and her colleagues (Ferreiro & Teberosky, 1983), replicated and extended by others (e.g. Karmiloff-Smith, 1992; Tolchinsky, 1988; Tolchinsky-Landsmann & Levin, 1985), shows how much children learn about form rules before school. Many children are able to pick out letters from numbers, and accept letter-strings as something that can be read while rejecting sequences or numbers and mixtures of letters and numbers for the same purpose. They use quantitative criteria as well as qualitative criteria to decide whether something can be read or not: they think that a single letter or two will not suffice for reading and that there must be internal variation in the letter strings, because the same letter used repeatedly will not be good for reading. Children can be even more sophisticated than this in their use of form rules: Letohnen and Bryant (2005) found that Finnish children knew that words cannot start with doublets before they knew that doublets represent long (as opposed to short) sounds in Finnish, and Treiman and her colleagues found that children judged words that contained doublets that are not used in English were less word-like than those that contained doublets that do exist in English orthography. These form rules are probably learned without instruction, from induced environmental print, as they are not explicitly formulated by parents or teachers and seem to be used by pre-school children in making judgments about what is and what is not good for reading. This remarkable learning about form is not confined just to Western children or to readers of alphabetic orthographies; Chan and Nunes (1998) documented similar learning of form rules among young Chinese pre-readers.

Ferreiro and her colleagues observed that children from poor homes, where books and other printed materials are less common (see, for example, Neuman & Celano, 2001, for a description of the ecology of reading in lower-income homes), showed less knowledge of form rules. This result, which is certainly not surprising, shows the importance of the environment even in the absence of teaching.

Children's learning at home is not just about environmental print. Many parents start their children's literacy instruction before they go to school by teaching them about alphabetic letters. A survey of children's knowledge of letters when they entered kindergarten in the U.S. showed that about one in four already knew all the letters of the alphabet (Nord, Lennon, Liu, & Chandler, 1999). These children start school with a good knowledge of the visual units of analysis that they need to use when discovering letter–sound rules. Parents also play language games and sing songs with their children, which might prepare them for discovering some of the rules that they need to find out when they start to learn to read and spell. Bryant and his colleagues (Bryant, MacLean, & Bradley, 1990; Bryant, MacLean, Bradley, & Crossland, 1990; MacLean, Bryant, & Bradley, 1987) have shown that such games prepare children for learning about the phonological units that have to be connected to visual units, if the children are going to discover phoneme-grapheme correspondence rules.

Parents expose children to more than just letters: they also provide them with experiences that develop word-specific knowledge. One of the best predictors of children's literacy success is whether they can write their own name correctly at the start of school (Carraher & Rego, 1982).

Finally, parents also teach children about the forms of language used in writing (Snow, 1991; Teale & Sulzby, 1986), facilitating their understanding of the indirect connection between oral and written language, which operates through meanings encoded in syntax and morphology. Rego (1999) has argued that some pre-readers can anticipate some characteristics and meanings of texts through knowledge of the context in which they appear: they can distinguish among lists, story books, newspaper articles and personal letters from the way these are presented on the page, and this anticipation is hypothesized to facilitate later reading development.

The evidence seems to indicate unambiguously that much knowledge about reading starts to develop before school. In a recent analysis of this evidence, Sénéchal, LeFevre, Smith-Chant, & Colton (2001) suggested that we need a more systematic approach to the analysis of how these different types of input facilitate the induction of principles used in reading and spelling.

The effects of the home environment on children's reading and spelling progress are easier to document than those of school instruction, even though it is almost self-evident that the latter are more dramatic: most children only learn to read when they receive instruction in school. Why should it be more difficult to document the effects of school instruction than those of home instruction? The answer is probably in the statistical techniques that we use to analyse the effects of home and school on children's progress. There is large variation in the amount and type of instruction that children receive at home: it is this variation that allows the statistical techniques of correlation and regression to show that individual differences in children's progress correspond to these home variations. In contrast, although there is certainly variation across teachers and schools in the daily activities used in reading instruction, these differences are more difficult to measure and thus it is more difficult to show how they affect individual differences in children's progress. This is one reason why intervention studies are so important for establishing connections between systematic instruction provided to children and their progress in reading and spelling.

The previous chapters on intervention effects show that instruction does indeed have important consequences for children's success and also for how they organize their knowledge of word reading and spelling. Our intervention studies demonstrated that it is not easy for children to discover morphological conditional rules but that providing them with systematic experiences that help them induce the rule, and also supporting this experience with a discussion of how the rule works, are effective ways of introducing new condition-action rules into the children's learning system.

The results of these various interventions suggest that there are better and worse ways of providing children with this guided experience. Our experiments on the teaching of the split digraph "a" vs "a-e" and "o" versus "o-e" as well as the contrast between "k" and "ck" showed that creating uncertainty by mixing the trials in which the different spellings appear produced more successful learning. In the case of the "k" versus "ck" rule, the children who were able to acquire and explain the rule showed a radically different pattern of correct responses from that observed among the children who did not seem to have acquired this rule at a conscious level: the lowest scores of the children who were able to explain the rule was much higher than the scores for the children who could not explain the rule, and the distribution of the scores for the former group tended towards the maximum possible score.

The contrast between the modest success of McMillan's (1999) attempt to teach children about apostrophes with the considerable effects of our much shorter intervention is another indication that there are better and worse ways of teaching. We analysed in Chapter 5 several of the possible explanations for this difference. One of these could have been the design of the instruction. In McMillan's teaching programme, the children practised sentences with apostrophes and without apostrophes on different days, which means that they did not really have a problem to solve on any particular day: they did not face uncertainty which needed to be resolved by the induction of rules.

However, the differences between forms of teaching was consistently smaller than the difference between taught and untaught groups: even in those conditions of instruction where the children were provided with samples of experience that facilitated the induction of rules and were left to their own resources to discover these rules, performance was typically better than that of untaught groups. We conclude that education has a major role to play in helping children acquire conditional morphological rules. Because this learning shows such strong and specific connections with other forms of language learning, such as vocabulary development and second language learning, there is an urgent need for systematic instruction about morphological principles to be included in the school curriculum.

Conclusion

Our last step in this book was to provide a framework for understanding children's word reading and spelling. We argued that three elements are necessary in this framework:

1 a sound description of the object to be learned, which considers the different types of rules that describe the orthography;
2 an understanding of the building blocks that make up learners' cognitive systems, of how they develop and compete or support each other in producing competent reading and spelling, and of how they might be organized into larger knowledge structures;
3 an understanding of the context of learning, and in particular of instruction.

There is much evidence for the importance of all three elements, and this evidence is not only relevant to the study of reading and spelling. If we want to know how children learn a mathematical concept, we need to think about the concept itself, the learners' constraints and possibilities, and the experiences that the learner has had and can have that will promote concept learning. It is reassuring to think that this triad has wide applications.

We cannot find any previous attempt to consider the three elements together, and yet in our view they should lie at the heart of any theory about children's reading and spelling. So, we finish our book with a thought that is new in this domain and we hope that you will continue thinking about children's reading and spelling beyond the first steps.

References

Adams, M.J. (1990). *Beginning to read*. Boston: MIT Press.

Adams, M.J. & Huggins, A.W.F. (1985). The growth of children's sight vocabulary: A quick test with educational and theoretical implications. *Reading Research Quarterly, 20,* 262–81.

Adlof, S.M., Catts, H.W., & Little, T.D. (2006). Should the simple view of reading include a fluency component? *Reading and Writing: An Interdisciplinary Journal, 19,* 933–95.

Akita, K. & Hatano, G. (1999). Learning to read and write in Japanese. In M. Harris & G. Hatano (Eds.), *Learning to read and write: A cross-linguistic perspective* (pp. 214–34). Cambridge: Cambridge University Press.

Alegria, J. & Mousty, P. (1997). Lexical spelling processes in reading disabled French-speaking children. In C.A. Perfetti, L. Rieben & M. Fayol (Eds.), *Learning to spell: Research, theory, and practice across languages* (pp. 115–28). Mahwah, NJ: Lawrence Erlbaum.

Alexander, A.W., Andersen, H.G., Heilman, P.C., Voeller, K.K.S., & Torgesen, J.K. (1991). Phonological awareness training and remediation of analytic decoding deficits in a group of severe dyslexics. *Annals of Dyslexia, 41,* 193–206.

Anglin, J.M. (1993). Vocabulary development: A morphological analysis. *Monographs of the Society for Research in Child Development,* Serial no. 238, 58.

Arnback, E. & Elbro, C. (2000). The effects of morphological awareness training on the reading and spelling of young dyslexics. *Scandinavian Journal of Educational Research, 44,* 229–51.

Berko, J. (1958). The child's learning of English morphology. *Word, 14,* 150–77.

Berninger, V.W. (1989). Orchestration of multiple codes in developing readers: An alternative model of lexical access. *International Journal of Neuroscience, 48,* 85–104.

Berninger, V.W., Abbott, R., Billingsley, F., & Nagy, W. (2001). Processes underlying timing and fluency: Efficiency, automaticity, coordination and morphological awareness. In M. Wolf (Ed.), *Dyslexia, fluency and the brain* (pp. 383–414). Baltimore, MD: York Press.

Berninger, V.W., Chen, A.C.N., & Abbott, R.D. (1988). A test of the multiple connections model of reading acquisition. *International Journal of Neuroscience*, 42, 283–95.

Berninger, V.W., Vermeulen, K., Abbott, R.D., McCutchen, D., Cotton, S., Cude, J. et al. (2003). Comparison of three approaches to supplementary reading instruction for low-achieving second-grade readers. *Language, Speech, and Hearing Services in Schools 34*, 101–16.

Bindman, M. (2004). Grammatical awareness across languages and the role of social context: Evidence from English and Hebrew. In T. Nunes & P. Bryant (Eds.), *Handbook of children's literacy* (pp. 691–710). Dordrecht: Kluwer Academic Publishers.

Blachman, B.A., Tangel, D.M., Ball, E.W., Black, R., & McGraw, C.K. (1999). Developing phonological awareness and word recognition skills: A two-year intervention with low income, inner-city children. *Reading and Writing: An Interdisciplinary Journal*, 11, 239–73.

Bloomfield, L. (1933). *Language*. New York: Holt, Rinehart and Winston.

Bradley, L. & Bryant, P.E. (1978). Difficulties in the auditory organization as a possible cause of reading backwardness. *Nature*, 271, 746–7.

Bradley, L. & Bryant, P.E. (1983). Categorising sounds and learning to read: A causal connection. *Nature*, 301, 419–521.

Bream, V. (2004). The effectiveness of multi-sensory methods with older poor spellers. Department of Psychology, University of Bristol, Bristol.

Brown, R. (1957). Linguistic determinism and the part of speech. *Journal of Abnormal and Social Psychology*, 55, 1–5.

Bryant, P. & Bradley, L. (1980). Why children sometimes write words which they do not read. In U. Frith (Ed.), *Cognitive processes in spelling* (pp. 355–70). London: Academic Press.

Bryant, P. & Bradley, L. (1985). *Children's reading problems*. Oxford: Blackwell.

Bryant, P., Devine, M., Ledward, A., & Nunes, T. (1997). Spelling with apostrophes and understanding possession. *British Journal of Educational Psychology*, 67, 93–112.

Bryant, P., MacLean, M., & Bradley, L. (1990). Rhyme, language, and children's reading. *Applied Psycholinguistics*, 11, 237–52.

Bryant, P.E., MacLean, M., Bradley, L.L., & Crossland, J. (1990). Rhyme, alliteration, phoneme detection and learning to read. *Developmental Psychology*, 26, 429–38.

Bryant, P. & Mitchell, P. (2007). There are different ways of spelling "education": morphemic knowledge versus word specific learning. Paper presented at the Annual Conference of the Society for the Scientific Understanding of Reading (SSSR), Prague, July.

Bryant, P., Nunes, T., & Aidinis, A. (1999). Different morphemes, same spelling problems: cross-linguistic developmental studies. In M. Harris & G. Hatano (Eds.), *Learning to read and write: A cross-linguistic perspective* (pp. 134–56). Cambridge: Cambridge University Press.

Bryant, P., Nunes, T., & Bindman, M. (1998). Awareness of language in children who have reading difficulties: Historical comparisons in a longitudinal study. *Journal of Child Psychology and Psychiatry*, *39*, 501–10.

Burani, C., Salmaso, D., & Caramazza, A. (1984). Morphological structure and lexical access. *Visible Language*, *18*, 342–52.

Butterworth, B. (1983). Lexical representation. In B. Butterworth (Ed.), *Language production*, Vol. 2: *Development, writing and other language processes* (pp. 257–94). London: Academic Press.

Byrne, B. (1998). *The foundation of literacy: the child's acquisition of the alphabetic principle*. Hove: The Psychology Press.

Byrne, B. & Fielding-Barnsley, R. (1993). Evaluation of a programme to teach phonemic awareness to young children: a 1-year follow-up. *Journal of Educational Psychology*, *85*, 104–11.

Campbell, R. (1983). Writing non-words to dictations. *Brain and Language*, *19*, 153–78.

Campbell, R. (1985). When children write nonwords to dictation. *Journal of Experimental Child Psychology*, *40*, 133–51.

Caramazza, A., Laudana, A., & Romani, C. (1988). Lexical access and inflectional morphology. *Cognition*, *28*, 297–332.

Caramazza, A., Miceli, G., Silveri, M.C., & Laudanna, A. (1985). Reading mechanisms and the organization of the lexicon: Evidence from acquired dyslexia. *Cognitive Neuropsychology*, *2*, 81–114.

Carlisle, J. (1987). The use of morphological knowledge in spelling derived forms by learning-disabled and normal students. *Annals of Dyslexia*, *37*, 90–108.

Carlisle, J. (1988). Knowledge of derivational morphology and spelling ability in fourth, sixth and eighth graders. *Applied Psycholinguistics*, *9*, 247–66.

Carlisle, J.F. (1995). Morphological awareness and early reading achievement. In L.B. Feldman (Ed.), *Morphological aspects of language processing* (pp. 189–210). Hillsdale, NJ: Lawrence Erlbaum.

Carlisle, J.F. (2000). Awareness of the structure and meaning of morphologically complex words: impact on reading. *Reading and Writing*, *12*, 169–90.

Carlisle, J.F. & Stone, C.A. (2003). The effects of morphological structure on children's reading of derived words in English. In *Reading complex words: Cross-language studies* (pp. 27–52). New York: Kluwer Academic/Plenum Publishers.

Carlisle, J.F. & Stone, C.A. (2005). Exploring the role of morphemes in word reading. *Reading Research Quarterly*, *40*, 428–49.

Carney, E. (1994). *A survey of English spelling*. London: Routledge.

Carraher, T.N. & Rego, L.B. (1982). Understanding the alphabetic system. In D.R. Rogers and J.A. Sloboda (Eds.), *The acquisition of symbolic skills*. New York: Plenum Press.

Casalis, S. & Louis-Alexandre, M.F. (2000). Morphological analysis, phonological analysis and learning to read French: A longitudinal study *Reading and Writing*, *12*, 303–35.

Cassar, M. & Treiman, R. (1997). The beginnings of orthographic knowledge: Children's knowledge of double letters in words. *Journal of Educational Psychology*, 89(4), 631–44.

Castro, A., Nunes, T., & Strecht-Ribeiro, O. (2004). Relação entre consciência gramatical na linguagem materna e progresso na aprendizagem de uma língua estrangeira. *Da Investigação às práticas. Estudos de Natureza Educacional*, 5, 51–66.

Chan, L. & Nunes, T. (1998). Children's understanding of the formal and functional characteristics of written Chinese. *Applied Psycholinguistics*, 19, 115–31.

Chialant, D. & Caramazza, A. (1995). Where is morphology and how is it processed? The case of written word recognition. In L.B. Feldman (Ed.), *Morphological aspects of language processing* (pp. 55–76). Hillsdale, NJ: Lawrence Erlbaum Associates.

Children's Printed Word Database: http://www.essex.ac.uk/psychology/cpwd/.

Chliounaki, K. & Bryant, P. (2007). How children learn about morphological spelling rules. *Child Development*, 78, 1360–73.

Chomsky, N. (1965). *Aspects of the theory of syntax*. Cambridge, MA: MIT Press.

Chomsky, N. (1975). *Reflections on language*. New York: Pantheon Books.

Claiborne, R. (1989). *The roots of English*. Boston: Houghton Mifflin.

Colchester, E. (2006). Do children use rule-based or frequency-based knowledge when spelling? Unpublished Diploma dissertation. Oxford Brookes University.

Collins, L. (2002). The roles of L1 influence and lexical aspect in the acquisition of temporal morphology. *Language and Learning*, 52(1), 43–94.

Coltheart, M., Rastle, K., Perry, C., Langdon, R., & Ziegler, J. (2001). DRC: A dual route cascaded model of visual word recognition and reading aloud. *Psychological Review*, 108, 204–56.

Cossu, G. (1999). The acquisition of Italian orthography. In M. Harris & G. Hatano (Eds.), *Learning to read and write: A cross-linguistic perspective* (pp. 10–33). Cambridge: Cambridge University Press.

Coyne, M.D., Kame'enui, E.J., Simmons, D.C., & Harn, B.A. (2004). Beginning reading intervention as inoculation or insulin: first-grade reading performance of strong responders to kindergarten intervention. *Journal of Learning Disabilities*, 37, 90–104.

Cummins, J. (1979). Linguistic interdependence and the educational development of bilingual children. *Review of Educational Research*, 49(2), 222–51.

da Fontoura, H.A. & Siegel, L. (1995). Reading, syntactic and working memory skills of bilingual Portuguese-Canadian children. *Reading and Writing: An Interdisciplinary Journal*, 7, 139–53.

Davis, C. (2005). The development of orthographic understanding in school-children. Unpublished DPhil thesis, University of Oxford.

Davis, C. & Bryant, P. (2006). Causal connections in the acquisition of an orthographic rule: A test of Uta Frith's developmental hypothesis. *Journal of Child Psychology and Psychiatry*, 47, 849–56.

Dawson, J. (2005). Do undergraduates use rule-base or frequency-based knowledge when spelling? Unpublished BA dissertation. Oxford Brookes University.

Deacon, S.H. & Kirby, J.R. (2004). Morphological awareness: just "more phonological"? The roles of morphological and phonological awareness in reading development. *Applied Psycholinguistics, 25*, 223–38.

Deacon, S.H., Wade-Woolley, L., & Kirby, J. (2007). Crossover: The role of morphological awareness in French immersion children's reading. *Developmental Psychology, 43*, 732–46.

Defior, S. (2004). Phonological awareness and learning to read: A cross-linguistic perspective. In T. Nunes & P. Bryant (Eds.), *Handbook of children's literacy* (pp. 631–50). Dordrecht, the Netherlands: Kluwer.

Defior, S., Alegria, J., Titos, R., & Martos, F. (2008). Using morphology when spelling in a shallow orthographic system: The case of Spanish. *Cognitive Development, 23*, 204–15.

DeKeyser, R.M. (2005). What makes learning second language grammar difficult? A review of issues *Language Learning, 55*, 1–25.

Denton, C.A., Fletcher, J.M., Anthony, J.L., & Francis, D.J. (2006). An evaluation of intensive intervention for students with persistent reading difficulties. *Journal of Learning Disabilities, 39*, 447–66.

Derwing, B.L., Smith, M.L., & Wiebe, G.E. (1995). On the role of spelling in morpheme recognition: Experimental studies with children and adults. In L.B. Feldman (Ed.), *Morphological aspects of language processing* (pp. 3–28). Hillsdale, NJ: Lawrence Erlbaum.

Diringer, D. (1968). *The alphabet: A key to the history of mankind.* New York: Funk and Wagnalls.

Droop, M. & Verhoeven, L. (1998). Reading comprehension problems in second language learners. In P. Reitsma & L. Verhoeven (Eds.), *Problems and interventions in literacy development* (pp. 193–208). Dordrecht, the Netherlands: Kluwer.

Egan, J. & Pring, L. (2004). The processing of inflectional morphology: A comparison of children with and without dyslexia. *Reading and Writing: An Interdisciplinary Journal, 17*, 567–91.

Ehri, L.C. (2005). Learning to read words: theory, findings, and issues. *Scientific Studies of Reading, 9*, 167–88.

Ehri, L.C., Nunes, S.R., Stahl, S.A., & Willows, D.M. (2001a). Systematic phonics instruction helps students learn to read: evidence from the National Reading Panel's meta-analysis. *Review of Educational Research, 71*, 393–447.

Ehri, L.C., Nunes, S.R., Willows, D.M., Schuster, B.V., Yaghoub-Zadeh, Z., & Shanahan, T. (2001b). Phonemic awareness instruction helps children learn to read: evidence from the National Reading Panel's meta-analysis. *Reading Research Quarterly, 36*, 250–87.

Ehri, L.C. & Soffer, A.G. (1999). Graphophonemic awareness: Development in elementary students. *Scientific Studies of Reading, 3*(1), 1–30.

Ehri, L.C. & Wilce, L.S. (1980). The influence of orthography on readers' conceptualisation of the phonemic structure of words. *Applied Psycholinguistics*, *1*, 371–85.

Ellis, N.C. (2006). Selective attention and transfer phenomena in L2 acquisition: contingency, cue competition, salience, interference, overshadowing, blocking, and perceptual learning. *Applied Linguistics*, *27*, 164–94.

Fayol, M., Thénevin, M.-G., Jarousse, J.-P., & Totereau, C. (1999). From learning to teaching to learn: French written morphology. In T. Nunes (Ed.), *Learning to read: An integrated view from research and practice* (pp. 43–64). Dordrecht, The Netherlands: Kluwer.

Ferreiro, E. & Teberosky, A. (1983). *Literacy before schooling*. Exeter, NH: Heinemann Educational Books.

Fletcher, J.M., Francis, D.J., Rourke, B.P., Shaywitz, S.E., & Shaywitz, B.A. (1992). The validity of discrepancy-based definitions of reading disabilities. *Journal of Learning Disabilities*, *25*, 555–61.

Fletcher, J.M., Morris, R., Lyon, G.R., Stuebing, K.K., Shaywitz, S., Shankweiler, D.P., Katz, L., & Shaywitz, B.A. (1997). Subtypes of dyslexia: An old problem revisited. In B. Blackman (Ed.), *Foundations of reading acquisition and dyslexia* (pp. 95–114). Mahwah, NJ: Lawrence Erlbaum.

Fletcher-Flinn, C., Shankweiler, D., & Frost, S.J. (2004). Coordination of reading and spelling in early literacy development: An examination of the discrepancy hypothesis. *Reading and Writing: An Interdisciplinary Journal*, *17*, 617–44.

Foorman, B.R. (2003). *Preventing and remediating reading difficulties: Bringing science to scale*. Baltimore, MD: York Press.

Foorman, B.R., Francis, D.J., Fletcher, J.M., Schatsschneider, C., & Mehta, P. (1998). The role of instruction in learning to read: preventing reading failure in at-risk children. *Journal of Educational Psychology*, *90*, 37–55.

Foorman, B.R., Francis, D.J., Shaywitz, S.E., Shaywitz, B.A., & Fletcher, J.M. (1997). The case for early reading intervention. In B.A. Blackman (Ed.), *Foundations of reading acquisition and dyslexia* (pp. 243–64). Mahwah, NJ: Lawrence Erlbaum.

Foorman, B.R., Seals, L.M., Anthony, J., & Pollard-Durodala, S. (2003). A vocabulary enrichment program for third and fourth grade African-American students: Description, implementation, and impact. In B.R. Foorman (Ed.), *Preventing and remediating reading difficulties: Bringing science to scale* (pp. 419–41). Baltimore, MD: York Press.

Fowler, A.E. & Liberman, I.Y. (1995). The role of phonology and orthography in morphological awareness. In L.B. Feldman (Ed.), *Morphological aspects of language processing* (pp. 157–88). Hillsdale, NJ: Lawrence Erlbaum.

Frith, U. (1985). Beneath the surface of developmental dyslexia. In K.E. Patterson, J.C. Marshall & M. Coltheart (Eds.), *Surface dyslexia: Neuropsychological and cognitive studies of phonological reading* (pp. 301–30). Hillsdale, NJ: Lawrence Erlbaum.

Gathercole, S.E., Service, E., Hitch, G.J., Adams, A.M., & Martin, A.J. (1999). Phonological short-term memory and vocabulary development: Further evidence on the nature of the relationship. *Applied Cognitive Psychology, 13,* 65–77.

Gathercole, S.E., Service, E., Hitch, G.J., & Martin, A.J. (1997). Phonological short-term memory and new word learning in children. *Developmental Psychology, 33,* 966–79.

Gathercole, S.E., Willis, C.S., Emslie, H., & Baddeley, A.D. (1992). Phonological memory and vocabulary development during the early school years: A longitudinal study. *Developmental Psychology, 28,* 887–98.

Gelb, I.J. (1963). *A study of writing.* Chicago: University of Chicago Press.

Geva, E. (1995). Orthographic and cognitive processes in learning to read English and Hebrew. In I. Taylor & D.R. Olson (Eds.), *Scripts and literacy* (pp. 81–114). Dordrecht: The Netherlands: Kluwer.

Geva, E. & Siegel, L. (2000). Orthographic and cognitive factors in the concurrent development of basic reading skills in two languages. *Reading and Writing: An Interdisciplinary Journal, 12,* 1–31.

Geva, E. & Zadeh, Z.Y. (2006). Reading efficiency in native English-speaking and English-as-a-second-language children: the role of oral proficiency and underlying cognitive-linguistic processes. *Scientific Studies of Reading, 10,* 31–57.

Gleitman, L.R. (1990). The structural sources of verb meaning. *Language Acquisition, 1*(3), 3–55.

Gleitman, L.R. & Gleitman, H. (1992). "A picture is worth a thousand words, but that's the problem", *Current Directions in Psychological Science, 1,* 31–5.

Goodman, K.S. (1969). Analysis of oral reading miscues: applied psycholinguistics. *Reading Research Quarterly, 5,* 9–30.

Goodman, K.S. (1982). Orthography in a theory of reading instruction. In F.V. Gollasch (Ed.), *Language and literacy: The selected writing of Kenneth S. Goodman* (Vol. II, pp. 87–98). London: Routledge and Kegan Paul.

Goodman, N. (1976). *Languages of art.* Indianapolis: Hackett.

Graves, M.F. (1986). Vocabulary learning and instruction. In E.Z. Rothkopf (Ed.), *Review of research in education* (Vol. 13, pp. 49–89). Washington, DC: American Educational Research Association.

Green, L., McCutchen, D., Schwiebert, C., Quinlan, T., Eva-Wood, A., & Juelis, J. (2003). Morphological development in children's writing. *Journal of Educational Psychology, 95,* 752–61.

Grigorenko, E.L. (2001). Developmental dyslexia: An update on genes, brains, and environments. *Journal of Child Psychology and Psychiatry, 42,* 91–126.

Grigorenko, E.L. & Kornilova, T.V. (1997). The resolution of the nature–nurture controversy by Russian psychology: Culturally biased or culturally specific? In R.J. Sternberg & E. Grigorenko (Eds.), *Intelligence, heredity, and environment* (pp. 339–93). New York: Cambridge University Press.

Grigorenko, E.L., Wood, F.B., Meyer, M.S., Hart, L.A., Speed, W.C., Shuster, A., & Pauls, D.L. (1997). Susceptibility loci for distinct components of developmental dyslexia on chromosomes 6 and 15. *American Journal of Human Genetics*, 60, 27–39.

Guthrie, J.T. (1973). Reading comprehension and syntactic responses in good and poor readers. *Journal of Educational Psychology*, 65, 294–99.

Hagtvet, B.E. (2003). Listening comprehension and reading comprehension in poor decoders: Evidence for the importance of syntactic and semantic skills as well as phonological skills. *Reading and Writing: An Interdisciplinary Journal*, 16, 505–39.

Harris, R. (1995). *Signs of writing*. London: Routledge and Kegan Paul.

Hatcher, P.J. (2000). Reading intervention need not be negligible: Response to Cossu (1999). *Reading and Writing: An Interdisciplinary Journal* 13, 349–55.

Hatcher, P.J. & Hulme, C. (1999). Phonemes, rhymes, and intelligence as predictors of children's responsiveness to remedial reading instruction: Evidence from a longitudinal study. *Journal of Experimental Child Psychology*, 72, 130–53.

Hatcher, P., Hulme, C., & Ellis, A.W. (1994). Ameliorating early reading failure by integrating the teaching of reading and phonological skills: the phonological linkage hypothesis. *Child Development*, 65, 41–57.

Henderson, A.J. & Shores, R.E. (1982). How learning disabled students' failure to attend to suffixes affects their oral reading performance. *Journal of Learning Disabilities*, 15, 178–82.

Henderson, E. (1990). *Teaching Spelling* (2nd ed.). Dallas, TX: Houghton Mifflin.

Henry, M.K. (1989). Decoding instruction based on word structure and origin. In P.G. Aaron & R.M. Joshi (Eds.), *Reading and writing disorders in different orthographic systems* (pp. 25–49). Dordrecht: Kluwer Academic Publishers.

Hohnen, B. & Stevenson, J. (1995). Genetic effects in orthographic ability: A second look. *Behaviour Genetics Association Meeting: Abstracts*, 271.

Holland, J.H., Holyoak, K.J., Nisbett, R.E., & Thagard, P.R. (1986). *Induction: Processes of inference, learning and discovery*. Cambridge, MA: MIT Press.

Hoover, W.A. & Gough, P.B. (1990). The simple view of reading. *Reading and Writing: An Interdisciplinary Journal*, 2, 127–60.

Howard, D. & Best, W. (1996). Developmental phonological dyslexia: Real word reading can be completely normal. *Cognitive Neuropsychology*, 13, 887–934.

Isaacs, S.S. (1930). *Intellectual growth in young children*. London: Routledge and Kegan Paul.

Jaffré, J.P. (1997). From writing to orthography: The functions and limits of the notion of system. In C.A. Perfetti, L. Rieben, & M. Fayol (Eds.), *Learning to spell. Research, theory, and practice across languages* (pp. 3–20). Mahwah, NJ: Lawrence Erlbaum.

Jarmulowicz, L., Hay, S.E., Taran, V.L., & Ethington, C.A. (2008). Fitting derivational morphophonology into a developmental model of reading. *Reading and Writing: An Interdisciplinary Journal*, in press.

Jenkins, J.R., Matlock, B., & Slocum, T.A. (1989). Two approaches to vocabulary instruction: The teaching of individual word meanings and practice in deriving word meaning from context. *Reading Research Quarterly, 24*, 215–35.

Job, R., Peressotti, F., & Cusinato, A. (1998). Lexical effects in naming pseudowords in shallow orthographies: Further empirical data. *Journal of Experimental Psychology: Human Perception and Performance, 24*, 622–30.

Johnston, R.S., Rugg, M.D., & Scott, T. (1988). Pseudohomophone effects in 8 and 11 year olds good and poor readers. *Journal of Research in Reading, 11*(2), 110–32.

Johnston, R.S. & Watson, J.E. (2005). A seven year study of the effects of synthetic phonics teaching on reading and spelling attainment. In Scottish Education Executive Department (Ed.), Analysis and Communication Department, Edinburgh: Scottish Executive Education Department.

Karmiloff-Smith, A. (1992). *Beyond modularity: a developmental perspective on cognitive science*. Cambridge, MA: MIT Press.

Kavanagh, J. & Mattingly, I.G. (1972). *Language by eye and by ear*. Cambridge, MA: MIT Press.

Kemp, N. & Bryant, P. (2003). Do beez buzz? Rule-based and frequency-based knoweldge in learning to spell plural -s. *Child Development, 74*, 63–74.

Kibel, M. & Miles, T.R. (1994). Phonological errors in the spelling of taught dyslexic children. In C. Hulme & M. Snowling (Eds.), *Reading development and dyslexia* (pp. 105–27). London: Whurr.

Largy, P. (2001). La revision des accords nominal et verbal chez l'enfant. *L'Année Psychologique, 101*, 221–45.

Largy, P., Dédéyan, A., & Hupet, M. (2004). Orthographic revision: A developmental study of how revisers check verbal agreements in written French. *British Journal of Educational Psychology, 74*, 533–50.

Largy, P., Fayol, M., & Leclaire, P. (1996). The homophone effect in written French: The case of noun-verb inflection errors. *Language and Cognitive Processes, 11*, 217–55.

Lehtonen, A. & Bryant, P. (2005). Doublet challenge: Form comes before function in children's understanding of their orthography. *Developmental Science, 8*(3), 211–17.

Leong, C.K. (1989). The effects of morphological structure on reading proficiency: A developmental study. *Reading and Writing: An Interdisciplinary Journal, 1*, 357–79.

Leong, C.K. (1991). Modelling reading as a cognitive and linguistic skill. In R.F. Mulcahy, R.H. Short, & J. Andrews (Eds.), *Enhancing learning and thinking* (pp. 161–73). New York: Praeger.

Leong, C.K. (1992). Cognitive componential modelling of reading in ten- to twelve-year-old readers. *Reading and Writing: An Interdisciplinary Journal, 4*, 327–64.

Leong, C.K. (2000). Rapid processing of base and derived forms of words and grades 4, 5 and 6 children's spelling. *Reading and Writing: An Interdisciplinary Journal, 12*, 277–302.

Leong, C.K. & Parkinson, M.E. (1995). Processing English morphological structure by poor readers. In C.K. Leong & R.M. Joshi (Eds.), *Developmental and acquired dyslexia* (pp. 237–59). Dordrecht: Kluwer Academic Publishers.

Levin, I., Ravid, D., & Rapaport, S. (1999). Developing morphological awareness and learning to write: A two-way street. In T. Nunes (Ed.), *Learning to read: An integrated view from research and practice* (pp. 77–104). Dordrecht: Kluwer.

Lovett, M.W., Borden, S.L., DeLuca, T., Lacarenza, L., Benson, N.J., & Brackstone, D. (1994). Treating the core deficits of developmental dyslexia: evidence of transfer of learning after phonologically- and strategy-based reading programmes. *Developmental Psychology, 30*, 805–22.

Lovett, M.W., Ransby, M.J., & Barron, R.W. (1988). Treatment, subtype and word-type effects in dyslexic children's response to remediation. *Brain, 34*, 328–49.

Lovett, M.W., Ransby, M.J., Hardwick, N., Johns, M.S., & Donaldson, S.A. (1989). Can dyslexia be treated? Treatment specific and generalised treatment effects in dyslexic children's response to remediation. *Brain, 37*, 90–121.

Lovett, M.W., Warren-Chaplin, P.M., Ransby, M.J., & Borden, S.L. (1990). Training the word recognition skills of dyslexic children: treatment and transfer effects. *Journal of Educational Psychology, 82*, 769–80.

Lundberg, I. (1999). Learning to read in Scandinavia. In M. Harris & G. Hatano (Eds.), *Learning to read and write: A cross-linguistic perspective* (pp. 157–72). Cambridge: Cambridge University Press.

Lyster, S. (2002). The effects of morphological versus phonological awareness training in kindergarten on reading development. *Reading and Writing, 15*, 295–316.

Mackey, A. (2006). Feedback, noticing and instructed second language learning. *Applied Linguistics, 27*, 405–30.

MacLean, M., Bryant, P.E., & Bradley, L. (1987). Rhymes, nursery rhymes and reading in early childhood. *Merrill-Palmer Quarterly, 33*, 255–82.

Mahony, D.L. (1994). Using sensitivity to word structure to explain variance in high school and college level reading ability. *Reading and Writing: An Interdisciplinary Journal, 6*, 19–44.

Mahony, D., Singson, M., & Mann, V. (2000). Reading ability and sensitivity to morphological relations. *Reading and Writing, 12*, 191–218.

Manis, F., Seidenberg, M., Doi, L., McBride-Chang, C., & Peterson, A. (1996). On the basis of two subtypes of developmental dyslexia. *Cognition, 58*, 157–95.

Mann, V.A. (1986). Phonological awareness: the role of reading experience. *Cognition, 24*, 65–92.

Marsh, G., Desberg, P., & Cooper, J. (1977). Developmental strategies in reading. *Journal of Reading Behavior, 9,* 391–4.

Marsh, G., Friedman, M.P., Welch, V., & Desberg, P. (1980). The development of strategies in spelling. In U. Frith (Ed.), *Cognitive processes in spelling* (pp. 339–53). London: Academic Press.

Mattingly, I.G. (1972). Reading, the linguistic process, and linguistic awareness. In J. Kavanagh & I.G. Mattingly (Eds.), *Language by eye and by ear.* Cambridge, MA: MIT Press.

McBride-Chang, C., Wagner, R.K., Muse, A., Chow, B.W.Y., & Shu, H. (2005). The role of morphological awareness in children's vocabulary acquisition in English. *Applied Psycholinguistics, 26,* 415–35.

McMillan, A. (1999). Words, letters and smurphs: Apostrophes and their uses. In T. Nunes (Ed.), *Learning to read: An integrated view from research and practice* (pp. 369–91). Dordrecht: Kluwer.

Miskin, R. (2004). *Read write Inc. Teacher's handbook.* Ruth Miskin Literacy.

Mitchell, P. (2004). Do adults rely on rules to inflect plural nouns and singular verbs? Unpublished MSc dissertation, University of Oxford.

Mody, M. (2003). Phonological basis in reading disability: A review and analysis of the evidence. *Reading and Writing: An Interdisciplinary Journal, 16,* 21–39.

Montessori, M. ([1918] 1991). *The advanced Montessori method: Scientific pedagogy as applied to the education of children from seven to eleven years.* Oxford: Clio.

Morton, J. (1979). Word recognition. In J. Morton and J.C. Marshall (eds), *Psycholinguistics 2: Structures and processes* (pp. 107–56). Cambridge, MA: MIT Press.

Murrell, G. & Morton, J. (1974). Word recognition and morphemic structure. *Journal of Experimental Psychology, 102,* 963–8.

Nagy, W.E. & Anderson, R.C. (1984). How many words are there in printed school English? *Reading Research Quarterly, 19,* 304–30.

Nagy, W.E., Berninger, V.W., & Abbott, R.D. (2006). Contributions of morphology beyond phonology to reading outcomes of upper-elementary and middle-school students. *Journal of Educational Psychology, 98,* 134–47.

Nagy, W.E., Herman, P.A., & Anderson, R.C. (1985). Learning words from context. *Reading Research Quarterly, 20,* 233–53.

Naigles, L. (1990). Children use syntax to learn verb meanings. *Journal of Child Language, 17*(2), 357–74.

Nation, K. & Snowling, M.J. (1998). Individual differences in contextual facilitation: evidence from dyslexia and poor reading comprehension. *Child Development, 69,* 996–1011.

National Reading Panel (2000). *Teaching children to read: An evidence-base of the scientific research literature on reading and its implications for reading instruction.* Bethesda, MD: National Institutes of Health.

Neuman, S.B. & Celano, D. (2001). Access to print in low-income and middle-income communities: An ecological study of four neighborhoods. *Reading Research Quarterly, 36,* 8–26.

Nord, C.W., Lennon, J., Liu, B., & Chandler, K. (1999). *Home literacy activities and signs of children's emerging literacy: 1993 and 1999.* Washington, DC: US Department of Education.

Notenboom, A. & Reitsma, P. (2007). Spelling Dutch doublets: Children's learning of a phonological and morphological spelling rule. *Scientific Studies of Reading, 11,* 133–50.

Nunes, T. & Aidinis, A. (1999). A closer look at the spelling of children with reading problems. In T. Nunes (Ed.), *Learning to read: An integrated view from research and practice* (pp. 155–71). Dordrecht: Kluwer.

Nunes, T. & Bryant, P. (2006). *Improving literacy through teaching morphemes.* London: Routledge.

Nunes, T., Bryant, P., & Bindman, M. (1997a). Morphological spelling strategies: developmental stages and processes. *Developmental Psychology, 33,* 637–49.

Nunes, T., Bryant, P., & Bindman, M. (1997b). Learning to spell regular and irregular verbs. *Reading and Writing, 9,* 427–49.

Nunes, T., Bryant, P., & Bindman, M. (2006). The effects of learning to spell on children's awareness of morphology. *Reading and Writing: An Interdisciplinary Journal, 19,* 767–87.

Nunes, T., Bryant, P., & Olsson, J. (2003). Learning morphological rules and phonological spelling rules. *Scientific Studies of Reading, 7,* 289–307.

Nunes, T., Roazzi, A., & Buarque, L.L. (2003). Learning to mark stress in written Portuguese. *Faits de Langues, 22,* 99–108.

Nunes Carraher, T. (1985). Explorações sobre o desenvolvimento da competência em ortografia em português (Exploring the development of spelling competency in Portuguese). *Psicologia, Teoria e Pesquisa, 1,* 269–85.

O'Connor, J.D. (1982). *Phonetics.* Harmondsworth: Penguin Books.

Olofsson, A. & Lundberg, L. (1985). Evaluation of long-term effects of phonemic awareness training in kindergarten. *Scandinavian Journal of Psychology, 26,* 21–34.

Olson, D.R. (1994). *The world on paper.* Cambridge: Cambridge University Press.

Olson, D.R. (1996). Towards a psychology of literacy: on the relations between speech and writing. *Cognition, 60,* 83–104.

Olson, R., Wise, B., Conners, F., Rack, J., & Fulker, D. (1989). Specific deficits in component reading and language skills: Genetic and environmental influences. *Journal of Learning Disabilities, 22,* 339–49.

Olson, R.K., Wise, B., Johnson, M., & Ring, J. (1997). The etiology and remediation of phonologically based word recognition and spelling disabilities: Are phonological deficits the "Hole" story? In B. Blackman (Ed.), *Foundations of reading acquisition and dyslexia* (pp. 305–26). Mahwah, NJ: Lawrence Erlbaum.

Otaiba, S.A. & Fuchs, D. (2006). Who are the young children for whom best practices in reading are ineffective? An experimental and longitudinal study. *Journal of Learning Disabilities, 39,* 414–31.

Paap, K.R. & Noel, R.W. (1991). Dual-route models of print to sound: Still a good horse race. *Psychological Bulletin*, *53*, 13–24.

Pacton, S. (2004). Children's use of syntactic information in spelling. Paper presented at the Society for the Scientific Study of Reading, 27–30 June, Amsterdam.

Pacton, S. & Deacon, H. (2008). Implicit and explicit learning in children's use of morphology in spelling: A review of evidence from French and English. *Cognitive Development*, *23*, 339–59.

Pacton, S., Fayol, M., & Perruchet, P. (2005). Children's implicit learning of graphotactic and morphological regularities. *Child Development*, *76*, 324–39.

Patrick, M. (2006). Frequency effects in split-digraph development: implicit learning or conditional spelling rule. University of Oxford, Oxford.

Patterson, K.E., Marshall, J.C., & Coltheart, M. (1985). *Surface dyslexia: Neuropsychological and cognitive studies of phonological reading*. London: Erlbaum.

Payre-Ficout, C. & Chevrot, J.P. (2004). La forme contre l'usage. Étude exploratoire de l'acquisition du prétérit anglais par des apprenants français. *Revue de Linguistique et de Didactique des Langues*, *30*, 101–15.

Pennington, B.F. (1999). Toward an integrated understanding of dyslexia: Genetic, neurological, and cognitive mechanisms. *Development and psychopathology*, *11*, 629–54.

Pennington, B.F., Gilger, L.W., Pauls, D., Smith, S.A., Smith, S., & DeFries, J.C. (1991). Evidence for a major gene transmission of developmental dyslexia. *Journal of the American Medical Association*, *266*, 1527–34.

Piaget, J. (1954). *The construction of reality in the child*. London: Routledge and Kegan Paul.

Ravid, D. (2001). Learning to spell in Hebrew: Phonological and morphological factors. *Reading and Writing: An Interdisciplinary Journal*, *14*, 459–85.

Ravid, D. & Schiff, R. (2006). Roots and patterns in Hebrew language development: evidence from written morphological analogies. *Reading and Writing: An Interdisciplinary Journal*, *19*, 789–18.

Read, C. (1971). Pre-school children's knowledge of English phonology. *Harvard Educational Review*, *41*, 1–34.

Read, C. (1986). *Children's creative spelling*. London: Routledge and Kegan Paul.

Read, C., Zhang, Y., Nie, H., & Ding, B. (1986). The ability to manipulate speech sounds depends on knowing alphabetic spelling. *Cognition*, *24*, 31–44.

Rego, L.L.B. (1999). Phonological awareness, syntactic awareness and learning to read and spell in Brazilian Portuguese. In M. Harris & G. Hatano (Eds.), *Learning to read and write: A cross-linguistic perspective* (pp. 71–88). Cambridge: Cambridge University Press.

Rego, L.L.B. & Bryant, P.E. (1993). The connection between phonological, syntactic and semantic skills and children's reading and spelling. *European Journal of Psychology of Education*, *8*, 235–46.

Reichle, E.D. & Perfetti, C.A. (2003). Morphology in word identification: a word-experience model that accounts for the morpheme frequency effects. *Scientific Studies of Reading*, 7, 219–37.

Reitsma, P. (2007). Scientific studies of spelling. Paper presented at the Society for the Scientific Study of Reading, Prague.

Rispens, J.E., McBride-Chang, C., & Reitsma, P. (2007). Morphological awareness and early and advanced word recognition and spelling in Dutch. *Reading and Writing*, in press.

Rosa, J. (2004). Morphological awareness and the spelling of homophone forms in European Portuguese. *Revue de Linguistique et de Didactique des Langues*, 30, 133–46.

Rosa, J. & Nunes, T. (2008). Morphological priming effects on children's spelling. *Reading and Writing: An Interdisciplinary Journal*, in press.

Sadoski, M. & Paivio, A. (2007). Toward a unified theory of reading. *Scientific Studies of Reading*, 11(4): 337–57.

Sampson, G. (1985). *Writing systems*. Stanford, CA: Stanford University Press.

Saussure, F. de ([1916] 1983). *Course in general linguistics*. London: Duckworth.

Schatz, E.K. & Baldwin, R.S. (1986). Context clues are unreliable predictors of word meanings. *Reading Research Quarterly*, 21, 439–53.

Schlagal, R. (1992). Patterns of orthographic development into the intermediate grades. In S. Tempelton & D.R. Bear (Eds.), *Development of orthographic knowledge and the foundations of literacy: A memorial Festschrift for Edmund H. Henderson* (pp. 31–52). Hillsdale, NJ: Lawrence Erlbaum.

Schonell, F. & Goodacre, E. (1971). *The psychology and teaching of reading*. London and Edinburgh: Oliver and Boyd.

Schonell, F.J. & Schonell, F.E. (1950). *Diagnostic and attainment testing: including a manual of tests, their nature, use, recording, and interpretation*. Edinburgh: Oliver and Boyd.

Schreuder, R. & Baayan, R.H. (1995). Modeling morphological processing. In L.B. Feldman (Ed.), *Morphological aspects of language processing* (pp. 131–54). Hillsdale, NJ: Erlbaum.

Scribner, S. & Cole, M. (1981). *The psychology of literacy*. Cambridge, MA: Harvard University Press.

Sénéchal, M. (2000). Morphological effects in children's spelling of French words. *Canadian Journal of Experimental Psychology*, 54, 76–85.

Sénéchal, M., Basque, M. T., & Leclaire, T. (2006). Morphological knowledge as revealed in children's spelling accuracy and reports of spelling strategies. *Journal of Experimental Child Psychology*, 95, 231–54.

Sénéchal, M., LeFevre, J.A., Smith-Chant, B.L., & Colton, K.V. (2001). On refining theoretical models of emergent literacy: The role of empirical evidence. *Journal of School Psychology*, 39, 439–60.

Shankweiler, D., Crain, S., Katz, L., Fowler, A.E., Liberman, A.M., Brady, S.A., Thornton, R., et al. (1995). Cognitive profiles of reading-disabled children:

Comparison of language skills in phonology, morphology, and syntax. *Psychological Science, 6*, 149–56.

Share, D. (1996). Phonological recoding and self-teaching: sine qua non of reading acquisition. *Cognition, 55*, 151–218.

Share, D. (1999). Phonological recoding and orthographic learning: a direct test of the self-teaching hypothesis. *Journal of Experimental Child Psychology, 72*, 95–129.

Siegel, L. (2004). Bilingualism and reading. In T. Nunes & P. Bryant (Eds.), *Handbook of children's literacy* (pp. 690–773). Dordrecht: Kluwer Academic Publishers.

Siertsema, B. (1965). *A study of glossematics* (2nd ed.). The Hague: Nijhoff.

Simos, P., Fletcher, G., Foorman, J.M., Francis, B.R., Castillo, D.J., Davis, E.M., et al. (2002). Brain activation profiles during the early stages of reading acquisition. *Journal of Child Neurology, 17*, 159–63.

Singson, M., Mahony, M., & Mann, V. (2000). The relation between reading ability and morphological skills: Evidence from derivational suffixes. *Reading and Writing: An Interdisciplinary Journal, 12*, 219–52.

Snow, C. (1991). The theoretical basis for relationships between language and literacy in development. *Journal of Research in Childhood Education, 6*, 5–10.

Snowling, M.J. (1980). The development of grapheme–phoneme correspondence in normal and dyslexic readers. *Journal of Experimental Child Psychology, 29*, 294–305.

Snowling, M.J., Goulandris, N., & Defty, N. (1996). A longitudinal study of reading development in dyslexic children. *Journal of Educational Psychology, 88*, 653–69.

Stanovich, K.E. (1980). Toward an interactive-compensatory model of individual differences in the development of reading fluency. *Reading Research Quarterly, 16*, 32–71.

Stanovich, K.E., Cunningham, A.E., & Cramer, B. (1984). Assessing phonological awareness in kindergarten children: Issues of task comparability. *Journal of Experimental Child Psychology, 38*, 175–90.

Stanovich, K., Cunningham, A.E., & West, R.F. (1998). Literacy experiences and the shaping of cognition. In S.G. Paris & H.M. Wellman (Eds.), *Global prospects for education: Development, culture and schooling* (pp. 253–90). Washington, DC: American Psychological Association.

Stanovich, K.E., Siegel, L.S., Gottardo, A., Chiappe, P., & Sidhu, R. (1997). Subtypes of developmental dyslexia: Differences in phonological and orthographic coding. In B. Blackman (Ed.), *Foundations of Reading Acquisition and Dyslexia* (pp. 115–42). Mahwah, NJ: Lawrence Erlbaum.

Stanovich, K. & West, R. (1983). On priming by a sentence context. *Journal of Experimental Psychology: General, 112*, 1–36.

Taft, M. (1985). The decoding of words in lexical access: A review of the morphographic approach. In D. Besner, T.G. Waller, & G.E. Mackinnon

(Eds.), *Reading research: Advances in theory and practice* (Vol. 5, pp. 83–123). New York: Academic Press.

Taft, M. (1988). A morphological-decomposition model of lexical representation. *Linguistics, 26*, 657–68.

Taft, M. (2003). Morphological representation as a correlation between form and meaning. In E.G.H. Assink & D. Sandra (Eds.), *Reading complex words: Cross-language studies* (pp. 113–37). New York: Kluwer Academic.

Taft, M. & Zhu, X. (1995). The representation of found morphemes in the lexicon: A Chinese study. In L.B. Feldman (Ed.), *Morphological aspects of language processing* (pp. 293–316). Hillsdale, NJ: Erlbaum.

Teale, W.H. & Sulzby, E. (1986). *Emergent literacy: Writing and reading*. Norwood, NJ: Ablex.

The National Literacy Strategy (1998). *Module 2. Word level work: Teachers' note. Unit 2. Phonics*. London: Department for Education and Employment.

Tijms, J., Hoeks, J.J.W.M., Paulussen-Hoogeboom, M.C., & Smolenaars, A.J. (2003). Long-term effects of a psycholinguistic treatment for dyslexia. *Journal of Research in Reading, 26*, 121–40.

Tolchinsky, L. (1988). Form and meaning in the development of writing. *European Journal of Psychology of Education, 3*, 385–98.

Tolchinsky, L. (2003). *The cradle of culture and what children know about writing and numbers before being taught*. Mahwah, NJ: Lawrence Erlbaum.

Tolchinsky-Landsmann, L. & Levin, I. (1985). Writing in preschoolers: An age related analysis. *Applied psycholinguistics, 6*, 319–39.

Torgerson, C., Brooks, G., & Hall, J. (2006). *A systematic review of the research literature on the use of phonics in the teaching of reading and spelling*. London: Department for Education and Skills Research Report no: RB711.

Torgesen, J.K. (1999). Phonologically based reading disabilities: A coherent theory of one kind of learning disability. In R.J. Sternberg & L. Spear-Swerling (Eds.), *Perspective on learning disabilities* (pp. 106–35). Boulder, CO: Westview Press.

Torgesen, J.K. (2000). Individual differences in response to early interventions in reading: The lingering problem of treatment resisters. *Learning Disabilities Research & Practice, 15*, 55–64.

Torgesen, J.K. (2004). Lessons learned from research on interventions for students who have difficulty learning to read. In P. McCardle & V. Chhabra (Eds.), *The voice of evidence in reading research* (pp. 355–82). Baltimore, MD: Brookes.

Torgesen, J.K. (2005). Recent discoveries on remedial interventions for children with dyslexia. In M.J. Snowling & C. Hulme (Eds.), *The science of reading: A handbook* (pp. 521–37). Oxford: Blackwell.

Torgesen, J.K., Rashotte, C.A., & Alexander, A.W. (2001). Principles of fluency instruction in reading: Relationships with established empirical outcomes. In M. Wolf (Ed.), *Dyslexia, fluency, and the brain* (pp. 333–56). Timonium, MD: York Press.

Torgesen, J.K. & Wagner, R.K. (1992). Language abilities, reading acquisition and developmental dyslexia. *Journal of Learning Disabilities*, 25, 577–81.

Totereau, C., Barrouillet, P., & Fayol, M. (1998). Overgeneralisation of number inflections in the learning of written French: The case of noun and verb. *British Journal of Developmental Psychology*, 16, 447–64

Totereau, C., Thénevin, M.-G., & Fayol, M. (1997). The development of the understanding of number morphology in written French. In C.A. Perfetii, L. Rieben & M. Fayol (Eds.), *Learning to spell: Research, theory and practice across languages* (pp. 97–114). Mahwah, NJ: Lawrence Erlbaum.

Treiman, R. (1993). *Beginning to spell: A study of first-grade children*. New York: Oxford University Press.

Treiman, R. & Baron, J. (1983). Phonemic-analysis training helps children benefit from spelling-sound rules. *Memory and Cognition*, 11, 382–9.

Treiman, R. & Cassar, M. (1997). Spelling acquisition in English. In C.A. Perfetti, L. Rieben, & M. Fayol (Eds.), *Learning to spell: Research, theory, and practice across languages* (pp. 61–80). Mahwah, NJ: Lawrence Erlbaum.

Treiman, R., Cassar, M., & Zukowski, A. (1994). What types of linguistic information do children use in spelling? The case of flaps. *Child Development*, 65, 1318–37.

Tsesmeli, S.N. & Seymour, P.H.K. (2006). Derivational morphology and spelling in dyslexia. *Reading and Writing. An Interdisciplinary Journal*, 19, 587–625.

Tulving, E. (1972). Episodic and semantic memory. In E. Tulving & W. Donaldson (Eds.), *Organization of memory* (pp. 381–403). New York: Academic Press.

Tulving, E. (2000). Concepts of memory. In E. Tulving & F.I.M. Craik (Eds.), *The Oxford handbook of memory* (pp. 33–44). Oxford: Oxford University Press.

Tunmer, W. (1989). The role of language-related factors in reading disability. In D. Shankweiler & I.Y. Liberman (Eds.), *Phonology and reading disability* (pp. 91–132). Ann Arbor, MI: The University of Michigan Press.

Tunmer, W.E. (2008). Recent developments in reading intervention research: Introduction to the special issue. *Reading and Writing: An Interdisciplinary Journal*, in press.

Tunmer, W.E. & Bowey, J. (1984). Metalinguistic awareness and reading acquisition. In W.E. Tunmer, C. Pratt, & M.L. Herriman (Eds.), *Metalinguisitc awareness in children: Theory, research and implications*. Berlin: Springer-Verlag.

Tunmer, W.E., Herriman, M.L., & Nesdale, A.R. (1988). Metalinguistic abilities and beginning reading. *Reading Research Quarterly*, 23, 134–58.

Tunmer, W.E. & Nesdale, A.R. (1985). Phonemic segmentation skill and beginning reading. *Journal of Educational Psychology*, 77, 417–27.

Uldall, H.J. (1944). Speech and writing. *Acta Linguistica*, 4, 11–6.

Vachek, J. (1973). *Written language: general problems and problems of English*. The Hague: Mouton.

Varnhagen, C.K., McCallum, M., & Burstow, M. (1997). Is children's spelling naturally stage-like? *Reading and Writing: An Interdisciplinary Journal, 9,* 451–81.

Vellutino, F.R., Scanlon, D.M., & Sipay, E.R. (1997). Toward distinguishing between cognitive and experiential deficits as primary sources of difficulty in learning to read: The importance of early intervention in diagnosing specific reading disability. In B. Blackman (Ed.), *Foundations of reading acquisition and dyslexia* (pp. 347–80). Mahwah, NJ: Lawrence Erlbaum.

Vellutino, F.R., Scanlon, D.M., Small, S., & Fanuele, D.P. (2006). Response to intervention as a vehicle for distinguishing between children with and without reading disabilities: Evidence for the role of kindergarten and first-grade interventions. *Journal of Learning Disabilities, 38,* 157–69.

Venezky, R.L. (1999). *The American way of spelling: The structure and origins of American English orthography.* New York: The Guilford Press.

Verhoeven, L. & Perfetti, C.A. (2003). The role of morphology in learning to read. *Scientific Studies of Reading, 7,* 209–18.

Vygotsky, L. (1986). *Thought and language.* Cambridge, MA: MIT Press.

Wagner, R.K., Torgesen, J.K., & Rashotte, C.A. (1994). Development of reading-related phonological processing abilities: New evidence of bidirectional causality from a latent variable longitudinal study. *Developmental Psychology, 30,* 73–87.

Walker, J. & Hauerwas, L.B. (2006). Development of phonological, morphological, and orthographic knowledge in young spellers: The case of inflected verbs. *Reading and Writing: An Interdisciplinary Journal, 19,* 819–43.

Watson, J.E. & Johnston, R.S. (1998). Accelerating reading attainment: the effectiveness of synthetic phonics. In Scottish E.E.R. Unit (Ed.), The Scottish Office Education and Industry Department.

White, T.G., Power, M.A., & White, S. (1989). Morphological analysis: implications for teaching and understanding vocabulary growth. *Reading Research Quarterly, 24,* 283–304.

Wysocki, K. & Jenkins, J.R. (1987). Deriving word meaning through morphological generalization. *Reading Research Quarterly, 22,* 66–81.

Author Index